THE SON OF LEICESTER

THE STORY OF
SIR ROBERT DUDLEY

*Titular Earl of Warwick, Earl of Leicester,
and Duke of Northumberland*

Only surviving issue
of
Queen Elizabeth's Favourite,
THE EARL OF LEICESTER

by

ARTHUR GOULD LEE

LONDON
VICTOR GOLLANCZ LTD
1964

MADE AND PRINTED IN GREAT BRITAIN BY
THE GARDEN CITY PRESS LIMITED
LETCHWORTH, HERTFORDSHIRE

CONTENTS

NOTE

The frontispiece and jacket illustration are from
the miniature painted *c.*1595 by Nicholas Hilliard.
Drawn by G. P. Harding, F.S.A., engraved by
J. Brown, it was first published in 1884.

PREFACE

Sir Robert Dudley would undoubtedly have played an out-standing role in his country's affairs had Fate been a little kinder. He had aristocratic blood, for he was second cousin to Queen Elizabeth. He had courage, enterprise, a handsome presence, an engaging person-ality, and a brilliant, original mind. But he had one formidable handi-cap. He was, according to his father, Elizabeth's magnificent Favourite, the Earl of Leicester, "his base sonne and the badge of his synne".

When, after Leicester's death, young Dudley learned that his parents had been validly wed, he tried to prove his legitimacy. It was his head-long reaction to the unworthy suppression of his claim, through the actions of King James and the Star Chamber, that led to the rest of his adventurous life being spent in active and distinguished exile at the Court of the Medici in Florence.

Some of the more colourful episodes in his career have been related in various contexts, among them his kissing of Mistress Cavendish in the regal presence, or his forestalling Raleigh in entering the River Orinoco, or his proposals to King James for a military dictatorship, or his draining of the marshes of Pisa, or his wife's remarkable account of the last hours of Queen Elizabeth. But the whole detailed story has not been told before.

This first full portrayal is a synthesis of all traceable information about Dudley, from sources that range from volumes dealing speci-fically with selected aspects of his life to a profusion of isolated items lying in a wide range of books and documents. The chief of these sources are named in the Bibliography. Many of the scattered items used have not hitherto been identified as belonging to Dudley's history.

Because so many minor sources have been drawn upon, and because the book is addressed not to the historian or scholar but to the general reader, the narrative has not been impeded with footnotes and refer-ences. These can be assessed from the Bibliography. There is, however, an Appendix of Notes and References, in which sources are named for statements of particular significance.

The use of quotations from contemporary writings raised the problem of whether or not to retain the quaint original spelling. But because Elizabethan writers spelt according to their phonetic notions, or even according to whim, the spelling of any given word may vary not only from person to person, but within an individual's single missive. In short quotes, this haphazard orthography can be entertaining, but in lengthier doses it becomes wearisome. Except for a few expressive examples, spelling has therefore been modernised, though the phraseology has usually been retained. This treatment places such quotations in reasonable harmony with translations of extracts from Italian documents.

Dates are given according to the Gregorian Calendar, which though not adopted in England until long after the period of Dudley's lifetime was then in general use on the Continent.

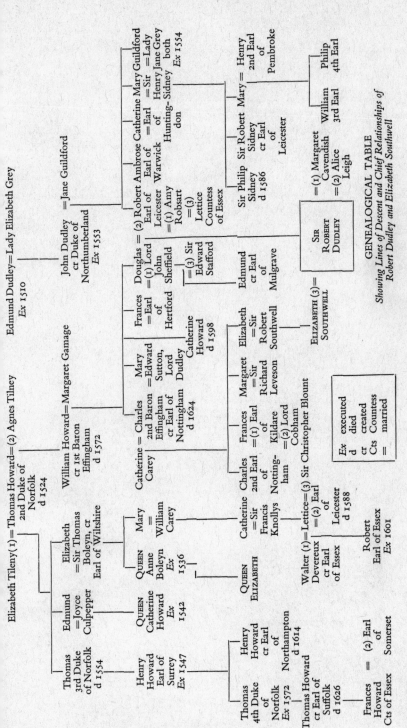

GENEALOGICAL TABLE

*Showing Lines of Descent and Chief Relationships of
Robert Dudley and Elizabeth Southwell*

© Arthur Gould Lee, 1964

THE SON OF LEICESTER

CHAPTER I

"HOW DOTH MY LADY AND MY BOY?"

IT HAS NEVER been clearly established when and where Queen Elizabeth's splendid Favourite, Robert Dudley, Earl of Leicester, became the lover of Her Majesty's kinswoman, the young and dazzlingly beautiful Douglas, wife of Lord John Sheffield of Butterwick in Lincolnshire. Nor is it even known when their paths first crossed.

He may have encountered her in London, during Lord Sheffield's periodical appearances at Court with his lady. Chance may have brought them together in some provincial place during the Queen's Progresses. They may have met on the occasion of the Queen's visit to Oxford University in September, 1566, when Sheffield was one of the several "nobles and persons of quality" created Master of Arts in honour of the royal presence. His wife would perhaps have accompanied him to Oxford, and might there have won Leicester's interest, for he was in attendance on the Queen, both as Master of the Horse, her inseparable escort, and as Chancellor of the University.

According to an account which, in a later generation, was put out by Gervase Holles, the antiquarian, their first meeting took place during Queen Elizabeth's Progress to Lincolnshire, in the same year as the trip to Oxford. This version, which until Holles reduced it to writing, had been repeated only as a below-stairs family skeleton, told how the Queen set up her Court for some days at Belvoir Castle as guest of the Earl of Rutland. "Thither the principal persons of Lincolnshire repaired to see their Queen and do their duty", states Holles, "amongst others the Lord Sheffield and the fair young lady of his, who shone like a star in the Court, both for her beauty and the richness of her apparel. Leicester, seeing her and being much taken with her perfections, paid court to her, and used all the art, in which he was master enough, to debauch her. To be short, he found her an easy purchase, and he had the unlawful fruition of her bed and body."

The seventeen-year-old Douglas, it was alleged, putting aside her husband and her infant son, Edmund, and even her blood and estate, for she was a Howard of Effingham, a cousin of two former Queens, Catherine Howard and Anne Boleyn, and so half-cousin to Elizabeth herself, recklessly surrendered everything to her passion.

According to Holles, Lord Sheffield began to suspect her, and being "a gentleman of spirit", cut short her opportunities of meeting the handsome Favourite. Soon afterwards, she carelessly let fall a letter, which her husband's sister, Eleanor, who had married into the Holles family, picked up and handed to her brother. In it, Leicester wrote that he "had not been unmindful in removing that obstacle which hindered the full fruit of their contentments; he had endeavoured by one expedient already, which had failed, but he would lay another which he doubted not would hit more sure".

Says Holles, Lord Sheffield "that night parted beds, and the next day houses, meditating in what way he might have just and honourable revenge. Having resolved, he posts up to London to effect it". But very soon he mysteriously died, upon which Eleanor and the Holles family concluded that Leicester had moved first, and contrived to have his rival poisoned.

Even if it were true that Leicester and Douglas were already lovers, for him, wanting no more than a safely married woman as a mistress, to have murdered her husband would have been a pointless folly. But it was in the way of the times to attribute any sudden death not due to an obvious cause to the machinations of a poisoner. Had poisoning been suspected of the head of so prominent a family as the Sheffields, a post-mortem would certainly have been held, and of this there is no record. But the accusation, not only that Leicester was the murderer but that he and Douglas "plotted to make away with Lord Sheffield", though only whispered then, remained alive within the Holles family, from which it was not to emerge in detail for public edification until nearly a century later.

Though characteristic of the indiscretions of more than a sprinkling of Elizabethan high society, this sordid story, which was told to Gervase Holles by the aged crone who had been gentlewoman to Eleanor Holles, his aunt, must be regarded as an old wives' tale. The picture of Douglas's calculated wickedness is entirely out of keeping with the irresolute character she was soon to display. More, there is no record of the Queen ever visiting Belvoir Castle, and at the time she was supposed to have been entertained there by the Earl of Rutland, he was a boy of only fourteen, a Ward of Court, and living not with his recently widowed mother at Belvoir, but in London, with Sir William Cecil.

But even had there been some occasion during the Queen's Progresses at this period for Douglas and Leicester to meet, the hour would have been a dangerous one for him to risk a love affair, however fugitive, for he had only recently emerged, and precariously at that, from the aftermath of a similar transgression.

From the beginning of her reign, Elizabeth had openly shown, often to the scandal and alarm of her Court, that Dudley, her Sweet Robin, whom she had known since childhood, was dearer to her than any other man. There was scarcely a soul in England, or in the Courts of Europe, who did not believe that they were lovers, and that they had been so since the anxious days when, both barely out of their 'teens, they were held by Queen Mary in the Tower of London, waiting day by day for the summons to the block.

Since her accession, for nearly seven years, Elizabeth and he had lived in constant intimacy, with his chambers adjacent to hers in every residence, and his fine person always within call and at her capricious disposal. In return for his devotion, she had heaped upon him a succession of riches and preferments, culminating only the previous year in the Earldom of Leicester, and the gift of the regal castle and estate of Kenilworth. And with this, the dominant role he held against every rival had seemed beyond dispute.

But towards the end of August, 1565, Elizabeth suddenly displayed a decided coolness, which everyone at Court observed and wondered at. "The Queen's Majesty", wrote Cecil, her Secretary of State, to the Ambassador in Paris, "is fallen into some disfavour with my lord of Leicester, and he therewith much dismayed. You know how busy men in Court will be to descant hereupon." They descanted the more because for the first time she smiled upon another man, a gentleman of the Privy Chamber, Thomas Heneage, presentable enough but hardly of sufficient distinction and charm to account for Elizabeth's surprise attentions.

Leicester's ire at this intrusion into his privileged domain was the warmer because Heneage, one of his own protégés, lost no time in putting on patronising airs. Finding that his attempts to break down the Queen's ill-humour were futile, he consulted her trusted courtier and his own close friend, Sir Nicholas Throckmorton, whose advice was to "make love to another lady, and discover how the Queen's Majesty takes it".

The regard which Leicester held for Elizabeth, buttressed by his real devotion to her as his Queen, had held him faithful to a degree that was unusual in times when manners and morals were lax, and nowhere more than at Court. Not that her womanly attractions were so strong as to rule out chance of competition. Surrounded as he was by delectable young Maids of Honour, with little to fill their idle hours except thoughts of dalliance, and by the older more sophisticated Ladies of the Bedchamber, not always averse to a stolen amour, he would have needed superhuman will to resist all temptation. But if he ever succumbed, he kept his philanderings supremely well hidden, for neither Elizabeth's alert eye nor the equally vigilant watch of his many ill-wishers at Court had ever raised a specific word of slander against him.

But now the notion of provoking his royal mistress's jealousy by paying open attention to a rival was one that suited his resentful mood. For this experiment, he chose a Lady of the Privy Chamber, a married noblewoman whom he reckoned, possibly because of some earlier understanding that had existed between them when she had been a Maid of Honour, would neither rebuff him nor fear Elizabeth's reaction. This was the spirited, captivating Lady Letitia Knollys, wife of Walter Devereux, Viscount Hereford, and a close blood relation of the Queen, for her grandmother Mary was Anne Boleyn's younger sister. By this same link, Lettice, as she was familiarly known, was also a kinswoman of Douglas Sheffield.

Leicester could have picked on no one more certain to excite Elizabeth's wrath, for Lettice was not only her junior by seven years, but much more feminine, indeed voluptuous, in her allure. The Queen had perhaps suspected something previously, for in contrast with her normally obstructive attitude over losing her Maids of Honour by marriage, she had readily agreed to Lettice's espousal and departure from Court five years before. How far the new wooing progressed nobody could say, though this lustily blooded age had no time for half-measures, and neither Lettice nor Leicester was of the stuff to deal in mere romantic gestures.

But their liaision ended abruptly when news of it reached Elizabeth. Alternating between bouts of tears and bursts of wrath, she sent Lettice packing from Court, and subjected the Favourite, then and for months afterwards, to bitter scoldings and reproaches, accompanied by public warnings that "she could lower him just as easily as she had raised him".

Rendering these humiliations the more unpalatable to Leicester was the realisation that his strategem had failed, for the Queen continued to admit Heneage to increasingly familiar favour. But towards the Favourite, her acerbity so sharpened as the weeks passed that his enemies began to look hopefully to the prospect of his downfall. Very much disgruntled, he withdrew from Court with the announcement, as was the usual resort in such predicaments, that he was sick, and divided his time between his Leicester House by the Thames and his Castle at Kenilworth. He knew he was treading on slippery ground that might lead to ruin, but he knew also the depths of her affection for him, and that she would not be able to bear him out of her sight for long. His judgement was sure, and gradually he began to be received again into favour.

That a few months after this episode, he would hazard his fate for a casual adventure with a young girl is highly unlikely, for the background of death by summary execution in his family had at least taught him not to step too far. It is certainly possible that the affair with Douglas Sheffield began before her husband died in December, 1568, but such evidence as exists suggests that it started afterwards, probably when she came to Court as a widow to serve in the Privy Chamber. This evidence lies in an undated letter of Leicester's, not addressed to Douglas by name, but clearly meant for no one else, in which he writes of "after your widowhood began, upon the first occasion of my coming to you".[1]

The earliest written linking of their two names did not appear until 1573, by which date she had been installed for some time as a Lady of the Bedchamber. At Court also was her nineteen-year-old sister, Frances. In a letter sent in May by a young Court gossip, Lord Gilbert Talbot, to his father, the Earl of Shrewsbury, there is mention of how "my lord of Leicester is very much with Her Majesty, and she shows the same great affection to him that she was wont; of late he hath endeavoured to please her more than heretofore. There are two sisters now in the Court that are very far in love with him, as they have been long; my lady Sheffield and Frances Howard; they of like striving who shall love him are at great war together, and the Queen thinketh not well of them, and not the better of him; by this means, there are spies over him".

If Frances did not know the truth, and was not in league with her sister to help distract attention from the real situation, then Douglas Sheffield and Leicester had indeed carried on their intrigue discreetly. For though Talbot, by his "as they have been long", shows himself to be aware of some minor romance, he could hardly have known of any story of Leicester poisoning Lord Sheffield, and still less could he have

---

[1] See item 1, Appendix III, *Notes and References*.

known that in this very month of May, my lady Sheffield had become the Countess of Leicester.

One of the few people who had learned earlier of their association was Douglas's kinsman, Thomas, the fourth Duke of Norfolk, and head of the Howard family, who, jealous of the honour of his House, had urged the two to legalise their union. All that came of this intervention was a secret contract of marriage, pledged between them in 1571, at one of the mansions in Cannon Row, Westminster, which they sometimes visited as a trysting place.

But when in 1572, the Duke was beheaded for treasonable plottings in the cause of Mary, Queen of Scots, and the pressure of his influence vanished, Leicester did nothing to redeem his promise, not even when, as rumour later declared, Douglas found herself with child. The story went that the birth was kept a profound secret, for she retired to Dudley Castle in Staffordshire, home of her younger sister, Mary, who barely a couple of years before had married Edward Sutton, Lord Dudley, a kinsman of Leicester. Her child dying a few hours after birth, she was quickly hurried back to Court before the Queen's suspicions were aroused by her absence.

Whether all this were true or not, such happenings were far from rare among the amorous ladies and gentlemen of the Court of the Virgin Queen, for scarcely a season passed without some lively indecorum, such as mysterious pregnancies among the young Maids of Honour or unblushing adulteries between their married elders. But Douglas's reputed lapse was so well hidden, and her meetings with Leicester so circumspectly pursued, that never a word reached the Queen of her Sweet Robin's deep involvement.

Yet successful secrecy was not everything to Douglas, for though, as Leicester inferred in the undated letter, she may have initially accepted the role of mistress, she could not rest content indefinitely with "the subjection you are in to all reports to the touch of your good name and fame", as her lover's letter put it. Was she not a Howard, cousin to the Throne, and widow of a baron of long lineage? She loved Leicester perhaps too well, and not wisely, for she was not a wise woman, but unlike some of the lighter ladies of the Court, there was no other man in her heart. With him, she wanted nothing less than marriage, and because this was the very boon that Leicester could not extend to her, the course of their love began to run unsmoothly.

For him, the one man who had always enjoyed Elizabeth's intimate favours, to seek diversion in the arms of another woman would surely provoke her jealous displeasure, but to flaunt his faithlessness openly by marriage would wound her pride and goad her to frantic rages, in which she might inflict irretrievable punishment. Of this he could be sure from the violence of her reactions against even the ordinary run of courtiers and Maids who were sufficiently rash to wed without the consent she so reluctantly gave. For such Contempt of Court there followed, for the man, imprisonment in Marshalsea or Fleet or some other prison, or even maybe in the Tower, while for the woman came revilings and beatings from the Queen herself, such as that frenzied pummelling which broke the erring Mary Scudamore's fingers.

Not without reason did Leicester write in the undated letter that Douglas must not expect him "to proceed to some further degree than is possible for me without mine utter overthrow". This enforced abstinence from marriage, he pointed out, "forceth me thus to be the cause almost of the ruin of mine own house; for there is no likelihood that any of our bodies will have heirs; my brother (*Ambrose, Earl of Warwick*) you see long married, and not like to have children, it resteth so now in myself; and yet, as I have told you ere now, if I should marry, I am sure never to have favour of them that I would rather never have wife than lose; yet there is nothing in the world next that favour that I would not give to be in hope of leaving some children behind me, being now the last of our house".

The letter rings true, yet behind the fear of losing the Queen's favour and the conflicting longing for an heir, lay another even more potent reason against being fettered by marriage. Ever since Elizabeth's accession, he had hoped and planned, as the man she loved, to become her husband, and so the Prince or even King of England. There had been times when she would have wed him willingly, but the project had been too hotly opposed by her most powerful nobles, and by trusted officials, such as William Cecil. Twice he had come near to achieving his aim, in 1559 and 1566, but each time circumstances had thwarted him. When other suitors, foreign princes, had sought her hand in vain, her dallyings had confirmed him in the view he once confided to the French Ambassador, "that she would never want to marry anyone, but if she did, it would be himself".

Though the project had receded in recent years, he, who knew her changeable mind and fickle nature better than any other man, still had hope. Everyone urged her to marry and bear an heir to secure the succession, even though she had now turned forty. And her closest advisers did not show such hostility towards him as in the past. His chance might yet come, as indeed it had all but come in the previous year, 1572, when she was recovering from a serious illness, during which he and Cecil, now Lord Burghley, had sat by her bed for two days and nights. She had fallen into a most tender fondness for him, which, before he could profit from it, had unfortunately been dissipated by urgent State perplexities.

And so, determined never to marry Douglas, he tried in the undated letter to persuade her either to accept the situation or to reconsider one of the several offers of marriage she had received and rejected. "It is not my part to bid you to take them", he wrote cautiously, "so it is not mine honesty to bid you refuse them." But there is no evidence that Douglas ever saw his letter, or even that it was actually sent to her. That it has survived suggests the opposite, for had she read it, and especially the promptings to marry somebody else, she would certainly have torn it to shreds.

The affair continued, but against a background of resistance to her entreaties to fulfil the vows he had made at Westminster. For her, there was nothing better to wish for than her personal happiness; for him, so deeply involved with the Queen and in pragmatic undertakings, private happiness could hold only secondary consequence. Thus it was that arguments and estrangements alternated with reconciliations and renewed chapters of their passion.

It was perhaps during one of these susceptible moments of high emotion that his resolution began at last to falter. Perhaps she declared the expectation of a child, though if she did, her hopes, or her fears, were unfounded at this stage. But the possibility of a boy, who would be the longed-for heir to carry on the name of Dudley, weighed heavily, for if the child were born a bastard, he would be legally under Douglas's complete control. Leicester was driven to find a solution that would satisfy her, that would give him legal possession of the boy, but that would leave him uncommitted should things go wrong.

Whether or not this was his reason, despite all the arguments he had produced against marriage, as well as those he had kept to himself, he finally gave way, though clearly with inward reservations dictated by his subtle temporising character.

Throughout the years that had elapsed since he had waited in the Tower for the dread journey to the headsman's axe that had ended the lives of his grandfather, his father and his brother, he head learned the prudent course of seemingly bending before the strong wind. He had kept Elizabeth's love and trust largely because of his uncomplaining submission to her exacting will, just as he had held his place among her jealous, intriguing courtiers and officials by his calculated pliability and manoeuvre.

And now he resorted to similar guile to put an end to Douglas's importunities. For though he consented to a ceremony of marriage, he meant it to be one whose legality could, if need arose, be disputed. He insisted therefore on one vital stipulation, that the wedding must take place in secret, and must remain secret. He declared again "if the Queen should know of it, I were undone and disgraced and cast out of favour for ever". He made her vow never to reveal the marriage until he gave leave, and Douglas agreed the less reluctantly because she well knew that around the throne, because of Elizabeth's dislike of others enjoying the states of matrimony and parentage that she would not, or could not, herself enjoy, such secret unions were not uncommon.

On a night in May, 1573, they were wed in her private chamber in a house at Esher, in Surrey. She was given away by Edward Horsey, the Captain of the Isle of Wight, and a crony of Leicester's. The minister was unknown to her, but he produced a licence or dispensation from his bishop. The witnesses included a kinsman, Robert Sheffield, and his wife, and Leicester's Italian doctor, Guilio Borgherini. The other witnesses were Douglas's personal servants, including her gentleman usher, Henry Frodsham, and her gentlewoman, Frodsham's relation, Magdalen Frodsham. The matter of secrecy scarcely counted with these lowly people, for none would have the ear of any member of the Court circle.

In front of these witnesses, Leicester took Douglas to be his wife, and vowed to have no other wife than her. He presented her with a ring, set with five pointed diamonds centred on a table diamond, which he had been given by the lately deceased Earl of Pembroke, father-in-law of his niece, Mary Sidney, on condition that "he should bestow it on no other woman but the one he made his wife".

The detailed circumstances of this wedding are significant because they were not only to be ventilated in two notable legal actions more than two centuries apart, but also to give rise to consequences that were to bedevil the life of the child of the union. For whatever chicaneries may have been in Leicester's wary mind, no doubt whatever lay in Douglas's that she was now the Countess of Leicester, even though the fact must be hidden from the world, at least until the Queen died.

Fully alive to the dangers her husband would face in the event of discovery, she loyally kept her secret. She was happy in her stolen meetings with him, and happier still when, as they entered into 1574, she could announce that she hoped for a child. On August 7th, at Shene House by Richmond, she was delivered of son, in a room called the Duke's Chamber.

Leicester was not with her, for he was in attendance on the Queen in her Progress to Bristol and the West. Except for the servants, her only companions were Doctor Guilio and her intimate friend, Mrs. Avice Erisa, who had been with her for the past fortnight for the lying-in. One of the household, William Clewer, rode hard with the news to Bristol, returning in time to act at the baptism as proxy for Sir Henry Lee, the Queen's Champion, and Leicester's close friend since boyhood. The other godparents were Leicester's brother, Ambrose, whose proxy was Doctor Guilio, and a distant but understanding kinswoman, Lady Margaret Dacre of the South, represented by Mrs. Erisa.

With Clewer came a letter from Leicester, in which he "thanked God for the birth of their son, who might be the comfort and staff of their old age", and subscribed himself, "Your loving husband, Rob. Leicester".

About a month after the birth, Mrs. Erisa set out for her home in Cornwall. On the way, at Salisbury, she met Leicester, still in attendance on the Queen, and told him, in answer to his "How doth my lady and my boy?", that both were well.

So confident now was Douglas of her position as a married woman that "she had herself served in her bedchamber as a countess", but Leicester, on his return, fearing that reports on this indulgence must reach the Queen, ordered it to stop. So trivial a matter did not disturb Douglas unduly, for she was a simple-natured woman, with no suspicion of the design that absorbed him at this time. For in spite of his being now a husband and father, he had still not lost sight of his life's aim, to share the throne with Elizabeth. Once more the situation was moving in his favour, because the prospect of any foreign alliance had become increasingly distasteful to parliament and people, and to most sections of the nobility.

Could he but induce her to declare herself willing to marry him, the hour might not yet be too late. And already in his pertinacious mind a notion was revolving to prepare for her, at his castle at Kenilworth, an entertainment of such unprecedented magnificence that none, not even Elizabeth, could deny him the princely stature that fitted him to be her husband.

And should all this fail, and his high aspirations come to nothing once more, then at least he had now the infant Robert, whom in the course of time he might openly acknowledge as heir to the titles and domains of the earldoms of Warwick and Leicester, and for whom, perhaps, within a few years, there might unfold some as yet undreamt-of path to even higher estate.

CHAPTER II

"HIS BASE SONNE AND THE BADGE
OF HIS SYNNE"

IN SPITE OF Leicester's insistence on secrecy, he could hardly have expected to keep his marriage completely hidden, for apart from his own kin and close friends there were his wife's relations, including young Frances, who would not have gone in ignorance of the situation. Yet no report of it ever reached the Queen. No doubt those of his enemies who were in the secret would have been happy to injure him by enlightening her, but they well realised that such revelations could be dangerous, for her immediate fiery outburst was likely to be inflicted as much on the informant as on the offender.

During the months that followed the birth of his son, like himself familiarly called Robin, Leicester, whenever he could briefly elude Elizabeth's possessive demands, contrived to indulge in his furtive existence, visiting wife and child at Esher and other homes, and perhaps sometimes at his Leicester House in the Strand, opposite St. Clement's Dane. With all this, he was able, with ingenuous lack of scruple, to press on with his scheme to dazzle the Queen into matrimony by his forthcoming display of "princely pleasures" at Kenilworth.

Already he had spent much money in improving the two-centuries-old castle, and encompassing it with parks and woodlands. Now, in 1575, at a total cost of over £60,000, he enlarged the building with a spacious new wing and gatehouse[2] to accommodate his honoured guest and her Court and attendants, sustained by "400 inferior servants", and furnished the whole with extravagant richness. For he was determined that his hospitality should be without parallel within memory.

For nineteen days, at a cost of over a thousand pounds a day, a cavalcade of entertainments went on before the enchanted Queen and a gay company, of "31 barons and the Ladies of the Court", as well as handpicked gentry from a hundred miles around. Every hour of the hot July days was filled with pageantry and amusement, with ingenious spectacle and surprise, with morris dancing and fireworks and rustic frolics, with tilting at the quintain and mock fights, with hunting, bear baiting and cockfighting, and with play acting, mummery and masquerades, culminating in a sumptuous water-pageant of the Lady of the Lake. This succession of carefully staged events was leavened with Lucullian feastings, including an "Ambrosial Banket", the grandest of the reign, at which a hundred and sixty of the quality sat at table with their Queen and her host.

Among the guests who thronged the Castle and its grounds during these many festivities was Douglas, in attendance on the Queen, but rightfully the chatelaine of the whole proud edifice, yet unable to proclaim it, or even to show outwardly that her place was different from that of any of the other fine ladies who graced the revels with their good looks and elaborate attire.

Such discontent as she might have felt would have been a hundred-fold deeper had she possessed an inkling of her husband's ultimate purpose in staging this dazzling display. Even more acute would have been her disquiet had she known that Fate had taken a fresh hand in her affairs by producing a rival before whom her claims on Leicester were soon to be put aside.

For from her home at Chartley Castle in Staffordshire came Lettice Knollys, now the Countess of Essex, her husband having been created an earl in the previous year. But she was alone, for he was in Ireland, attempting as Earl Marshal to bring order and security to an isle that struggled only to be an outpost of Roman Catholic Spain. When she and Leicester met once more at Kenilworth, the flame kindled in their earlier relations broke out afresh, and with far greater ardour. Lettice was ten years older than Douglas, and not more beautiful, but her spell was stronger and more sensual, and Leicester fell completely under it.[3]

The Kenilworth Pleasures over, the Queen, accompanied by Leicester, rode to other country houses in the Midlands, including Dudley Castle, where Douglas's sister, Mary, was hostess, and Chartley Castle, where Lettice had the, to her, dubious honour of entertaining her royal cousin and her immense suite. It was doubtless here, with Douglas possibly out of the way, and with more privacy than was possible at crowded Kenilworth, that Leicester and Lettice, though still with extraordinary circumspection, confirmed the reawakening of their mutual passion.

The stolen affair that followed after the return to London was quickened when Leicester realised that his Kenilworth bid for the

Queen's hand had come to nothing. But he was obliged to move most adroitly, not only because of the trouble from her that would attend discovery, or of the reaction he could expect from Douglas, but because of the jealousy of the Earl of Essex.

And from this last direction embarrassment did come, for Essex had been deeply suspicious over his wife's flirtation with the Favourite ten years before, and particularly over the later arrival of a son, Robert, who could have been Leicester's, and for whom, perhaps in consequence, he held, according to Sir Henry Wotton,[4] "a very cold conceit", giving his affection to his second son, Walter. Now, in November, hearing rumours of Lettice's frailties, the Earl hastened to England, and declared his intention of staying there for good.

For a time, Leicester's ardour was held in check. Whether Lettice or he instigated the next step is a matter for speculation, but early in the next year he was, by reason of his authority as one of the most influential members of the Privy Council, pressing that Essex should be sent back to Ireland to complete his mission. Despite the Earl's protests, he was ordered to go, and in August set out for Dublin, fiercely resentful at his shabby treatment. Within a few days he fell ill, with severe abdominal pains and died in September, at the age of thirty-six, after vowing that he had been poisoned.

A post-mortem was held, and death declared due to dysentery, following the drinking of impure water. But the official responsible for conducting the inquiry, the Lord Deputy of Ireland, was Sir Henry Sidney, who although a man of the highest integrity, was the husband of Leicester's sister, Mary, a circumstance that seemed to confirm the generally held belief that the Favourite had arranged for Essex to be poisoned in order to possess his wife.

That this could be true is scarcely credible, for there was little point in Leicester running so great a risk when with Essex in Ireland he might have continued his affair with Lettice without either complication or responsibility. Now he would fall into difficulties, as he must have well realised. Fortunately for him, one of the few people in England who remained unaware of the suspicions against him was the Queen. Similar ignorance would hardly have been shared by Douglas, yet he still continued to visit her, and to take an ever-growing interest in young Robin. For in his agile mind yet another scheme was simmering, which might demand before long that he openly proclaim the boy as his lawful son.

In the course of three generations, the fatal mirage of the House of

Dudley had been to see one of their line sharing the throne of England. The first advance, which Henry VIII abruptly ended with execution, was made by Leicester's grandfather, Edmund Dudley. His son, John Dudley, Duke of Northumberland, attempting to install Lady Jane Grey, child wife of his youngest son, Guildford, as Queen in place of Princess Mary, paid for failure with his head, and those of his two hapless puppets. His remaining sons, Leicester among them, were also sentenced to death, to be reprieved only after long harrowing delay. In spite of these grim deterrents, Leicester had pursued the same mirage for most of his adult life in his consuming desire to marry Queen Elizabeth. As a hostile contemporary wrote, "The disposition of this man is bent wholly to a sceptre".

And now, when his chances of achieving this high ambition were growing more distant, though still not beyond all hope, he perceived another route for his house to reach the throne. He had a son who would be marriageable in a little over a decade. The Queen was mortal, she seemed not strong in health, and one day she must die and be succeeded by someone of the blood. Until recently, the next in line were James the Sixth, King of the Scots, his mother, Mary, Queen of Scots, and his father's brother, Charles Stuart, Earl of Lennox. But Lennox, to Queen Elizabeth's deep displeasure, had a few years previously contracted a secret marriage with Elizabeth Cavendish, who shortly bore him a daughter, Arabella. With the death of Lennox at the end of 1576, this infant, Mary's niece and James's first cousin, became third claimant to the succession. And she was of an age with Leicester's son.

In the summer of 1577, Leicester went to take the waters at Buxton spa, then in favour among the more rheumy members of the aristocracy. Twelve miles away was Chatsworth, where the Queen of Scots was lodged in honourable captivity in the charge of his boyhood friend, George Talbot, Earl of Shrewsbury, whose acquisitive, ambitious wife was the redoubtable Lady Elizabeth Hardwick. And Bess of Hardwick was the mother by one of her three previous unions of Elizabeth Cavendish, and so the grandmother of the Lady Arabella Stuart.

In spite of her grasping nature, the Countess Bess was a woman whom Leicester had earlier found he could talk to. He met her on the way to Buxton, and it was then or soon afterwards that they came to a secret understanding that her Arabella and his Robert should be contracted in marriage. When the hour came, he would throw his all-powerful influence into ensuring that James of Scotland and his mother were barred the succession, and Arabella named instead.

Unfortunately for these stratagems, he did not sufficiently allow for the seductive charms of the Countess of Essex, nor for her long-sighted hopes. For not far away from Buxton lay her home, Chartley. In the resumption of their passionate intrigue, Leicester allowed himself to be deflected from all his grand aims for young Robert. The enchantment which the provocative Lettice cast over him strengthened with every meeting, until at last she prevailed on him to break his links with his wife. So deep was his infatuation that he agreed to stop living with Douglas, and soon he ceased to visit her at all. Then, as the estrangement worsened, he avoided even meeting her, except for a single prearranged encounter in the Close Arbour of the Queen's Garden at Greenwich.

Here, according to her statement made long afterwards, he told her, in the presence of his friends, Sir John Hubard and George Digby, that their romance was over. He offered her seven hundred pounds a year to forget their past relationship and "disavow the marriage", and when she angrily refused, he too became angry, and swore that "he would never come at her again", nor give her another penny. She left them, indignant, mortified, and baffled as to what course to follow.

It is understandable why she could not raise the courage to announce her marriage openly. Leicester told her that the careful secrecy of their wedding made it possible for him to disclaim it. There was no one she could petition to challenge so impregnable an opponent. It was no help to be a cousin of the Queen, especially if younger and prettier, and especially over an affair with the cherished Favourite. Her father, Lord William Howard of Effingham, was dead these four years, and his successor, her brother, Charles, would know that if by his intervention the Queen disgraced her Favourite, she would always hold it against him afterwards. Above all, Douglas was not a woman of ruthless, or even determined character. And so it was that she weakly surrendered to the situation, possibly with the temporising hope that it might yet turn in her favour.

But Leicester, committing himself more and more deeply, entered into a secret betrothal with Lettice at his Castle of Kenilworth, where she was living with him. Some time later she was discreetly installed at the White House at Wanstead, the manor and estate he had recently acquired in the Essex countryside, six miles to the north-east of London.

He was not long permitted to enjoy his love on such easy terms, for he had allowed himself to slide, or perhaps be steered, into a position from which he now found it impossible to withdraw, as he had done so brusquely with Douglas. For Lettice was with child, and her father, Sir Francis Knollys, close kinsman and trusted servant of the Queen, had no intention of seeing his daughter treated in the same way as Douglas. Either in ignorance of the Esher wedding, or convinced that it could be ignored, he insisted on a formal and binding ceremony of marriage, and such was his unassailable standing with Elizabeth that Leicester, though refusing to allow any public acknowledgement, had no option but to agree.

In what certainly in effect, was a shotgun wedding, he and Lettice, now seven months pregnant, were wed at Wanstead in September, 1578, in the presence of his brother, Ambrose, his brother-in-law, Lord North, the bride's father, and some others. There was little that was secret about this ceremony, it was merely not public. Everyone knew of it save the Queen, for none had the hardihood to tell her.

That Leicester had repudiated his union with Douglas and gone through a formal ceremony with another woman was no proof that the first marriage was null. Such brazen matrimonial duplicity was not then uncommon among the higher levels of the aristocracy, whose annals were freely leavened with deserted wives and bigamous espousals. For bigamy was no temporal crime, punishable in common law, but subject only to action in the ecclesiastical courts. Because at this time nothing was done to control and register the proper solemnisation of marriages,[5] a secret wedding could easily be disavowed if the priest, real or pretended, and witnesses, disappeared or gave false testimony. The only certain seal on a marriage was for it to be held in public, and so known to all.

It was because of this situation that Douglas, with nothing of Lettice's scheming and tenacious character to impel her to resistance, submitted to the final loss of her good name, by which her son was labelled as a bastard. It was this last consequence that proved the strength of the pressure brought on Leicester to give legality to his union with Lettice. Not only had he exposed himself to the Queen's unbridled anger when the news reached her, but he had rendered illegitimate the son on whom he had placed such high hopes, of whom he was greatly fond, and whom, within the affection of his family circle, he had so far treated almost as his lawful son and heir.

Any expectation he might have had of a son from Lettice was in vain, for no baby was born that lived. On account of this, he showed that he did not want to lose Douglas's boy, the only child of his loins. Soon after the Wanstead marriage, he sent Douglas an offer of a thousand pounds to surrender Robert to Horsey, now Sir Edward, who would bring him up in the Isle of Wight, of which he was still Captain. This offer she roundly refused, and it is possible that for once she was bold enough to promise trouble, for as she afterwards declared, she was next subjected to threats.

Her defiance quickly deflated, she became a frightened woman, suspecting that Leicester had designs on her life. By now she had come to understand well his smooth lack of scruple. She knew of the still persisting rumours that, years before, after trying to poison his young first wife, Amy Robsart, he had had her murdered because, while she was still alive, he could never marry Queen Elizabeth. She may have heard that he was believed to have arranged the death of her first husband, and would certainly have been told that he was probably the poisoner of the Earl of Essex. And when, as she afterwards testified, she found that her hair and nails were falling out, she was sure that he was secretly having her poisoned too.

Driven by this fear, she not only agreed to give up the boy, but, convinced that her life was in hazard so long as she was a threat to the legality of Lettice's marriage, and believing that this marriage had released her from her own vows, she decided herself to wed. In November, 1579, she married Edward Stafford of Grafton, whose mother, Lady Dorothy, was Mistress of the Robe to the Queen.

Meanwhile, no one had yet dared to tell Elizabeth of Leicester's marriage. But there had recently come to London a Monsieur Jean de Simier, envoy of the latest suitor for the royal hand, Francis, Duke of Alençon. Like most of the members of the Privy Council, Leicester was now opposed not only to a French marriage but to any marriage at all, for the presence of a consort prince or king might well see the end of their favoured status. When, presently, an attempt was made to kill the too-persuasive Simier, he chiefly suspected Leicester, and in revenge, while the Court was at Greenwich, revealed to the Queen the secret of the marriage.

Elizabeth received the news with paroxysms of frantic rage, at one moment in floods of tears as if utterly heartbroken, the next cursing and raving and threatening vengeance for this double treachery by her trusted Robin and her own cousin, the she-wolf. In her passion, she would have sent him to the Tower, but his magnanimous enemy, the Earl of Sussex, fearing the public scandal that would follow, persuaded her to be content with confining him in the Miraflore Tower in Greenwich Park.

At this critical hour, someone had the intrepidity to tell her of Leicester's previous union with Douglas. Her anger reinforced, she sent for Edward Stafford, whom she thought much of and had recently knighted. According to a statement which he afterwards made, she pressed him "to importune his wife whether there had been a contract between her and the Earl of Leicester, which if it were, then she would have him make good her honour with a marriage, or rot in the Tower".

Stafford questioned Douglas, who "answered with great vows, grief and passion that she had trusted the said Earl too much to have anything to show to constrain him to marry her". Persisting, Elizabeth sent for her too, but "the like she said to the Queen, and the like to the Earl of Sussex: and that she had told Stafford the truth before she married him".

The Queen would not have needed legal proof, but would have acted on Douglas's mere testimony, for apart from punishing Leicester by forcing him into a marriage he did not want, nothing could have consoled her more than to humiliate Lettice by proclaiming her marriage void. But, understandably, Douglas did not respond. What would she gain now from her rival's discomfiture, or, except for legalising her son, from a loveless forced union? What good would come to her or the boy by having Leicester disgraced and deprived of his estates? The harm was done, the broken pitcher could not now be mended. And why should she destroy her new marriage, and hurt the man who had given her security and happiness, above all now that his child was on the way?

The storm eventually subsided. Some years later, in 1583, the Queen appointed Stafford as her ambassador to the King of France. Douglas, accompanied by her first son, Lord Edmund Sheffield, joined her husband in Paris, where she built up a fresh existence with this kind and able man, with whom she was to live in affectionate harmony with their two sons, and through whom she was later to recover her previous standing with the Queen. But toward Lettice, Elizabeth was to remain implacable, though not to her family, for her sister, her brother, her two daughters, and her two sons, were all to bask in the royal favour.

As for Leicester, Elizabeth soon forgave him, and allowed him to return to his former place and influence. For whatever the intimacies they had enjoyed as lovers in their younger days, they had now reached the stage, like a long-married couple, where, though still united by the links of early passions, they could shut their eyes to the lesser affections that had since entered each other's lives. This could explain why, before long, with his Countess now openly mistress of Leicester House, Leicester had no compunction in bringing to Court his seventeen-year-old stepson, Robert, Earl of Essex, to counter the too great esteem which his former protégé, Sir Walter Raleigh, had recently won from the Queen.

Douglas's boy, Robin, who was about five years of age when she surrendered his custody, lived under the care of his father's kinsman, John Dudley, in his manor house at Stoke Newington. Here Leicester sometimes visited him, for it was recorded later by a servant that he did "very often times discover his love and care he had of his son, and the desire he had to have him receive good usage and education". In spite of his marital involvements, and although he sometimes styled the boy "his base sonne and the badge of his synne", he clearly intended that Robin should be the eventual heir to part of his estate, and still the potential husband for the Lady Arabella Stuart.

But at the end of 1579, the youngster's great expectations were dissipated at a blow, for Lettice gave birth to a son. This other Robert, and Robin, now became his father's hope and pride, the veritably legal heir he yearned for. And because Lettice was one degree nearer to the Queen than even James of Scotland, the boy would make a better match for Arabella than Douglas's son. The girl lost her mother in 1582. Soon after, Leicester renewed his understanding with the Countess of Shrewsbury, and the two children, the girl aged eight and the boy two, were formally betrothed. In March, 1584, Mary Queen of Scots, who had now reached terms of hostility with the unsympathetic Bess, wrote to the French ambassador, Castelnau de Mauvissière, "I would wish you to mention privately to the Queen that nothing has alienated the Countess of Shrewsbury from me but the vain hope which she has conceived of settling the Crown of England on the head of her little girl, Arabella, and this by means of marrying her to a son of the Earl of Leicester. These children are also educated in this idea, and their portraits have been sent to each other."

The message was never passed to the Queen, which was fortunate for Leicester, though he was still taking great risks, for his dangerous design was known to others, especially the Catholic exiles in Paris, headed by Charles Paget, who were in touch with the Queen of Scots.

Another scheme of Leicester's, to marry Lettice's daughter Dorothy to the young King of the Scots did come to Elizabeth's ear, and although Leicester escaped trouble, she is said to have furiously declared that if Lettice persisted in this impudent idea, she would "proclaim her over all Christendom as a whore, even now cuckolding her husband". The situation was saved by Dorothy eloping with Sir Thomas Perrot, but the Queen's anger gave good indication of how she would have reacted to knowledge of the plan for Arabella.

Apart from the dubious promise of his father's high aims, young Robert, Lord of Denbigh, could look forward to an illustrious future, for he would in the course of time not only inherit the dignities and possessions of Leicester and Warwick, but perhaps win back the Dukedom of Northumberland forfeited by his grandfather. He was quick and intelligent, and soon, by virtue of his high birth, was appointed page to the Queen. Yet in spite of the care and affection lavished upon him, the Noble Impe, as his parents came to call him, was both frail in body and delicate in health.

Although now relegated to the shade, the other Robert was by no means neglected. That he did not live with his father's family, as often occurred in these tolerant times with even incontestably illegitimate children, was probably due more to his stepmother's jealous objections than his father's indifference. By 1583, Leicester had sent him to be educated by a tutor at the village of Offington, near Worthing in Sussex, where he may have come occasionally under the eye of his uncle Ambrose, who owned a seat, Warwick House, in the district.

Then in the summer of 1584, his prospects were once more suddenly transformed, for the Noble Impe fell ill at Wanstead, and lacking the stamina of a normally robust child, died within a few days. Leicester was sorely shaken at this cruel blow to his burning ambition, an ambition that he indicated equivocally in the inscription on the boy's tomb in the Beauchamp Chapel,[6] telling of "a child of great parentage but far greater hope"—the hope of regality that had also come to an end.

His loss drew to him much sympathy, from Queen Elizabeth, from his friends and even from his opponents. But his resilient nature would not allow him to nurse disappointment too long. Before many months had passed, he had put his misfortune aside, and was turning his gaze once more towards his other son.

CHAPTER III

BRAVE HORIZONS

As HE WAS to show plainly later, Leicester now returned to his design to make Robert Dudley his principal heir, and despite the bar sinister, to prepare him for high station. For the next four years, Robert stayed with the tutor at Offington, and no record exists of any other schooling until he went to Oxford in 1587. Judged by the scope of the learning which he afterwards displayed, the education he received both from the unknown tutor and at university was of a remarkably high order.

Little is known of his life during the years prior to Oxford. Leicester provided him with a lackey, one Owen Jones, and visited them occasionally until he embarked for the Low Countries as Governor-General at the end of 1585. He was still not able to draw the boy into homely contact with his stepsons, Robert and Walter Essex, but young Dudley was now old enough to be alive to the paternal domestic background, and so could understand why he was not wanted. He was content to be fascinated by his father's personality, by the famous charm, and the good-natured disposition that was extended to every member of the Dudley family. But the father he knew was not the elegant, handsome cavalier who had won the heart of the young Elizabeth, but a man beginning to age a little, with florid face, greying hair and beard, and a portly middle-aged spread, though still erect and distinguished in his bejewelled velvet doublet, with his black bonnet and its white plume tilted as rakishly as ever.

The boy heard occasionally from his mother, still in Paris. If he ever saw her on her infrequent visits to England he would have found not the soft prettiness of her earlier years but a woman matured by bitter experience, dignified, aristocratic, the ambassador's wife, a role which contemporary writers declare her to have filled with honour. She had found maturity too in the upbringing of the children she had borne to Stafford, as well as of Edmund Sheffield, now reaching early manhood, and engaging already in the privileged existence which his birth and wealth conferred on him.

But Robert never knew any home and normal family background, other than that provided by the anonymous tutor. Nowhere in the writings of his later life does he refer to this period except to mention briefly that he "had from his youth a natural sympathy for the sea". His rustic condition at Offington, with its easy access to the coastal fishing villages, may explain this early bent for what was later to become a dominating devotion.

Leicester entered him at Christchurch, Oxford, at the beginning of 1587, where he was described in the register as "an earl's son", and placed him under the care of Thomas Chaloner, a tutor of outstanding worth and sagacity. Though only twenty-six years of age, he had travelled widely in Europe, especially in Italy, and his accomplished stimulating character, as subsequent events were to prove, exercised a lasting influence on Robert's outlook and personality. He not only led the boy's interests towards his own, which lay in the field of mathematics and natural science, particularly in application to maritime problems, but inspired him with the questing urge for experience and adventure that was in the true spirit of Queen Elizabeth's reign.

Chaloner was probably instrumental too in retrieving Robert from the harmful effects of an extraordinarily malevolent attack launched against his father, in which he himself, his mother, and most of his father's friends were involved. In 1584, there had been printed in English at Antwerp a two-hundred page book with the title "Copy of a Letter Written by a Master of Art of Cambridge to his Friends in London . . . about the Present State and Some Proceedings of the Earl of Leicester and some Friends in England". Inspired by hatred of Leicester because of his active Protestant and Puritan associations, it was written, some said, by Robert Parsons, a prominent Jesuit in exile, or as others, including Sir Francis Walsingham, thought, by agents of the Queen of Scots living in Paris as pensioners of the King of Spain.

This volume, which subsequently became known as *Leycester's Commonwealth*, contained every derogatory accusation that an envenomed ingenuity could devise. The author, who showed so detailed an acquaintance with confidential Court affairs that people said only Lord Burghley himself could have been the source, had collected every tit-bit of gossip and scandal that had circulated round

Leicester since his youth, and by a skilful and readable blending of truth, rumour, lies and sheer invention, produced an arraignment so apparently authentic that almost everyone accepted it as true.

In its vivid pages, Leicester was depicted as an inhuman monster who shrank from no infamy to achieve his political and private ends. The charges that he had prevented the Queen's marriage by his "preoccupation with Her Majesty's person", and that through his influence over her, he held the reins of government, were the mildest of his supposed enormities. He was accused, in astonishing detail, of treason, rebellion, treachery, adultery and murder. His special crime was to practise the Italian art of poisoning upon anyone who stood in his way, and even on those who had merely offended him.

Among the many victims of his lethal habits, said the book, were the Cardinal de Chatillon, for knowing too many of his secrets, the King of Sweden for aiming to marry Queen Elizabeth, the Earl of Sussex for being his rival and enemy, Sir Nicholas Throckmorton, one of his closest friends and supporters, for some bibulous affront, and for no reason but sheer devilry, Arabella Stuart's grandmother, the Countess of Lennox, who died the day after he had dined at her mansion in Hackney. Also included was the attempt on the life of Simier.

Virulent attention was directed towards the deaths of others more closely linked with Leicester's personal life. He was taxed flatly with contriving the murder of Amy Robsart, at Cumnor, to be free to marry the Queen, and because many people already believed this, the other accusations seemed the more credible.

"His Lordship", the book declared, "hath a special fortune, that when he desireth any woman's favour, then what person so ever standeth in his way hath the luck to die quickly for the finishing of his desire. . . . Thus when he fell in love with the Lady Sheffield . . . then also had he the same fortune to have her husband die quickly . . . of an artificial catarrh that stopped his breath. The like good chance had he in the death of my Lord of Essex, and that at a time most fortunate for his purpose."

The book revealed the marriage contract made with Douglas, and also the subsequent birth of two children, "one a boy, Robin Sheffield, now living, the other a daughter born, as is known, at Dudley Castle". Leicester, it continued, was content to assign her a thousand pounds in money together with other paltry considerations—"the pittifullest abused that ever was poor Lady".

Written when the Impe was alive, also his cousin, Sir Philip Sidney, soon to die in battle but at that time Leicester's next heir, the book said of the union with Lettice, "Whether the marriage be good or no I leave to be tried hereafter between my young Lord of Denbigh and Master Philip Sidney, whom the same most concerneth: for my Lord was contracted to another Lady before, that yet liveth, and consummated the same by generation of children".

Leicester was charged not only with entering into a bigamous marriage with the Countess of Essex, but of having had a child by her while her husband was in Ireland, and another, made away with by abortion, just prior to Essex's return. But what the book called "the intolerable licentiousness of Leicester's carnality" was not confined to these two ladies, for "he hath descended to seek pasture among the waiting gentlewomen of Her Majesty's Great Chamber", and indeed, he pursued "whatever female doth please his eye—the keeping of the mother with two or three of her daughters at once or successively".

His chief agent in the poisonings, as well as in the abortions on Lettice and others, was stated to be Doctor Giulio. That the doctor enjoyed high repute at Court, where as physician to several prominent people, including Sir Christopher Hatton, he was known to the Queen, counted for little with the book's readers. The Doctor was a follower of Leicester's, he came from Italy, where as was well known, poisoning was the custom, and in any case, everyone was well aware that Leicester was a murderer. This view was held even by his supposed victims, two of whom, Essex and Sussex, declared on their death-beds that he was responsible.

So great was the impression made by this authentic corroboration, as it seemed, of all the past rumours of his evil-doings that even so staid a Court official as Sir Robert Naunton could write in his *Fragmenta Regalia*, a collection of pen-pictures of his contemporaries, that Leicester "was too well seen in the aphorisms and principles of Niccolo, the Florentine, and in the reaches of Caesar Borgia". Against such a background, general credence was given to the book's accusations not only in England but on the Continent, where versions existed in French and Latin, and where further editions were printed in later years.

But Leicester had his vindicators, chief among them the Queen, who in June, 1585, proclaimed that "Her Highness knoweth to assured certainty the books and libels against the said Earl to be most malicious,

false and scandalous, and such as none but an incarnate devil himself
could dream to be true". By an Order in Council she proscribed the
book, ordered the seizure of every copy, and placed a ban on its future
entry into England. A similar course was taken also by King James
of Scotland, who suppressed the book by proclamation from
Holyrood.

Another vigorous advocate was Leicester's nephew, Sir Philip
Sidney, held everywhere in the highest regard for his knightly qualities,
who in a spirited *Discourse in Defence*, wrote of "one of the most
scurrilous libels which the religious dissensions of the times has produced . . . everything raked together which the tongue of scandal has
uttered to the disparagement of the exalted statesman". Scornfully
repudiating "such a bundle of railings as if it came from the mouth of
some half-drunk scold in a tavern", Sidney declared "my chiefest
honour is to be a Dudley".

This *Defence* was not published until later, but even had it been
issued at once, it could not have neutralised the effect of a book which
showed such inside knowledge, was written with such apparent
authority, and contained so much that was nearly accurate, that few of
its readers troubled to examine where truth ended and falsehood
began.

Leicester himself did nothing to refute the long list of defamations,
which, like Walsingham, he believed the Queen of Scots had instigated, even though they consolidated the obloquy in which he was
generally held through most of his lifetime. Partly because of this, the
picture painted in *Leycester's Commonwealth* has ever since provided
writers with a ready-made view of his character. Even had he perpetrated the misdeeds imputed to him, they would have been in tune with
the harsh, unscrupulous temper of the times, but there is no confirmation that he did. There was none among his many enemies who could
ferret out the flimsiest evidence of his supposed enormities, not even a
confessing accomplice to incriminate him. More, in nearly four
centuries of exhaustive research, no vestige of proof has ever been
unearthed to show that he was guilty of any of the crimes attributed to
him.

In spite of the seizures and suppressions that followed the Order in
Council, many volumes were kept hidden, and from these, hundreds
of copies were made in manuscript, which circulated secretly throughout the country, and particularly in the universities. We can presume

with certainty that one of these copies was read by Robert Dudley during his time at Oxford. Its impact on the mind and spirit of a boy of barely fourteen could only have been deeply harmful.

Until then, he could have known but little of the way his mother had been treated, and had proudly regarded his father as one of the most illustrious and honourable men in England. Now came this apparently well-informed denunciation of a systematic traitor, murderer and adulterer. The whole sinister story, with all its squalid trimmings, yet with sufficient of the facts already known to him to render the rest plausible, was put crudely not only before him but before everybody in his little world. Not even the Queen's repudiation nor his cousin Philip Sidney's *Defence*, could have lessened the bewilderment and shame that must at first have filled his boyish soul.

In modern times, so profound a shock would be expected to implant some emotional twist into his character that would affect his later life, and this it may well have done. Not least would be the doubts put into his mind as to whether he were really only a natural son, a condition he would until now have accepted without reflection as of no great significance.

He may have learned too of the outcome of the book's publication in France, where his unhappy mother, the ambassador's wife, with her humiliating past cruelly exposed, and her present marriage and children deemed unlawful, was in despair. As her husband wrote to Sir Francis Walsingham, she was "prostrate with melancholy and near to losing her mind", for though her part was of "an honourable intent and a weak woman deceived", for which responsibility lay "between God and my lord of Leicester's conscience", yet the Court circles in Paris in which she moved could not fail to put the worst construction on the book's revelations.

It was fortunate that young Robert had at his side at this critical time a man of such understanding and good sense as Thomas Chaloner, for above anyone else would he, with the influence he had soon acquired over the lonely, sensitive and gifted boy, have been able to neutralise the potentially warping poison of the *Commonwealth* revelations.

Through Chaloner's eyes, the youngster would be led to see his father not in the common view as a relentless schemer and criminal but, with due allowance for Leicester being the tutor's employer, as one of the country's distinguished leaders, a patron of the arts, of commerce and exploration, and of the true Protestant religion. No longer merely the Favourite, he was an able statesman, seeking always the best interests of his Queen and of England, and in conjunction with Burghley and Walsingham, dominating the affairs of State.

True, he had maintained his place at Court, not only in his private relations with the volatile Queen, but in the high role he occupied in her Councils, against a succession of rivals such as Hatton, Heneage and Raleigh, chiefly by manoeuvrings that drove his baffled opponents to distrust him, and accuse him of bad faith. But in the shifting quicksands of Court intrigue, these were the means of self-preservation, common to all, and no man could be blamed for using them. And such circumventions were worlds apart from murder and all the other misdeeds which the *Commonwealth* had laid at his door.

Would their wise Queen, Chaloner might have asked the boy, have allowed a villain such as the book portrayed to retain her trust, to serve her not only as Master of the Horse and Lord Steward of the Household but as a chief minister in her Privy Council? Would she have chosen him to go to the Low Countries as her Lieutenant-General to aid the Dutch in their struggle against the might of Spain? Certainly, her army had not always done too well there, and many good men had lost their lives, brave Philip Sidney among them, but Leicester, as everyone of judgement knew, had done his best under immense difficulties. And on his return to England, had he not at once been accorded the full esteem of his Queen and colleagues, so that not a voice had been raised against his becoming "Captain-General of the Queen's armies and companies in England"?

By such talk, Chaloner would succeed not only in dispersing the clouds gathered by the *Commonwealth*, but in instilling his charge with a renewed pride in his blood and heritage. What boy, bastard or not, could fail to react to the challenge of the current achievements of his various relations, and their share in the momentous events that had lately overtaken their country?

For it was now the summer of 1588, a year of destiny for England. Robert had matriculated in May, and with much of his routine studying behind him, could turn his eyes to the exciting happenings of the hour, the hour when Philip of Spain, persisting in his life's aspiration to conquer Elizabeth's realm, had sent his armada of a hundred and fifty galleons to beat down the English fleet, and carry the Duke of Parma's army from France to the heretic shore.

At sea, the English fleet awaited them. On land, troops and volunteers and musters assembled in the south, some in London to guard the Queen's person, others on the coast, and the main body in Essex to defend London from the east. It was Leicester, appointed by Elizabeth as her Captain-General to defend the approach up the Thames, who through July and August had vigorously organised, armed and trained some 23,000 men under his direct control.

Responding ardently to this example, Robert contrived to get a message to his father, asking that he might volunteer in the service of his Queen. Soon, escorted by Chaloner, he was riding eagerly to the great camp pitched around a low hill at Tilbury, by the Thames. There, Leicester, approving of his spirit, commissioned him, according to his own later statement, as colonel of a regiment of foot, with whom he took up his post under the guidance of an older officer. That a youth should hold such rank was not out of the ordinary, for in these times, most boys were adult at fifteen, often married and carrying man's burdens. And as Robert was soon to show, he was made of manly metal.

The danger-laden weeks passed in unfamiliar training and trench digging. Meanwhile, stirring deeds had taken place at sea, for between Plymouth and the South Foreland, the Armada galleons had been harried and fought by the faster-sailing ships of Howard and Drake, and driven to seek refuge in the Calais Roads. From there they were dislodged by fire-ships and forced into the open, only to meet the fierce attacks of the Queen's Navy, and to turn off northwards. But Parma and his troops still waited at Calais, and the Armada could still return south. Peril was not yet gone, and at Tilbury, the army waited alert for the expected invasion.

It was in these several sea battle that leading roles had been played by some of Robert's blood and other relations. His mother's brother, Lord Charles Howard of Effingham, now Lord High Admiral of England, was commanding the fleet that held the Armada at bay, while his company of captains included, among such men of prowess as Drake, Frobisher, Hawkins, Grenville and Cavendish, Robert's half-brother, Lord Edmund Sheffield, his distant cousin, Lord Thomas Howard, and the husbands of his cousins Elizabeth and Margaret Howard, Sir Robert Southwell and Sir Richard Leveson.

And now, at Leicester's prompting, the Queen came to Tilbury to review and hearten her troops, for that very morning had come the rumour that Parma was moving. As she approached the assembled ranks, cannons sounded, drums rolled and fifes sang shrilly. Bareheaded, wearing a corselet of gleaming silver, and mounted on a white gelding, she rode among her soldiery, the embodiment of princely authority. Later, she took her stand for the review, then rode before the ranks, with the pikes and lances and colours lowered as she passed.

With what pride would not the boy have watched her, his own second cousin by his mother's blood, with his splendidly accoutred father, the Captain-General, unhelmeted too, riding at her side, and his elegant cousin and stepbrother, the young Earl of Essex, now Master of the Horse, at the other. With what unspoken resolutions must not this spectacle have inspired, that he too would one day try to match his sire's distinction and renown.

Now the Queen made her stirring speech, which resounded through England then, and has resounded in English ears ever since. "Let tyrants fear!", she cried, "I know I have the body of a weak and feeble woman, but I have the heart and stomach of a king, and of a King of England too, and think foul scorn that Parma of Spain or any Prince of Europe should invade the borders of my Realm: to which, rather than any dishonour shall grow by me, I myself will take up arms, I myself will be your General". But then, indicating Leicester by her side, and passing him her baton of command, she continued, "My Lord General shall be in my stead, than whom never Prince commanded a more noble or worthy subject".

The thousands of troops responded with great, heartful cheers, the standards dipped, the clarion trumpets rang, and she rode away. While she was taking refreshment in Leicester's pavilion, despatches arrived to tell her that Parma was poised ready to use the spring tides to make the crossing. Not until later did the thrilling news arrive that Charles Howard and his captains had chased the Armada into the North Sea, where fierce gales had taken up the task of scattering and destroying the hapless galleons.

The danger over, the camp at Tilbury was quickly broken and the army disbanded. What then happened to Robert is not on record. He may have spoken briefly to his father, probably rode through London and saw something of the jubilations of victory. So far as is known, he still had no home to go to, and may well have returned to Oxford. If he did, he could have seen his father again when he passed through the city at the end of the month.

For Leicester was ill, and in no mood to take part with the Queen in the Thanksgiving at St. Paul's, nor in any of the other celebrations. There was a further reason for his absence. So delighted was Elizabeth with the role that he, and she, had played in the defence of her realm, that, overcome by her old familiar fondness, she proposed to create for him the office of Lord Lieutenant of England and Ireland. The patent was actually made out, but before she could sign it, the earnest protests of Burghley and other councillors at investing a subject with such unprecedented powers induced her to abandon the project.

Disgruntled at this rebuff as well as sick with fever, Leicester declined to stay at Court, and set out to take the Buxton waters, travelling by way of Oxford and Kenilworth. He spent a night with Lord and Lady Norris at Rycote, near Thame, where Elizabeth and he had spent some of their happiest times together when they were young and in the full flower of their love. From here, on August 30th, he sent her a letter, in which, after expressing the hope "to find a perfect cure in the bath", he affirmed his unchanging loyalty "from your old lodging at Rycote this Thursday morning, ready to take on my journey".

Who could tell, as he added this remembrance of their early affections, what thoughts had been inspired by Rycote, this place which, though he had seldom stood so high in Elizabeth's regard as now, could only remind him that he had failed in his life's ambition to marry her. He had failed, yet perhaps the way was nearly clear for his blood to attain the throne when the time should come for her to die. For in February of the previous year, Mary, Queen of Scots had at last paid the penalty for her ceaseless intriguings, and with her execution at Fotheringay, Arabella Stuart had become second in succession. Not long before, he had re-established his agreement with the Countess of Shrewsbury, and the contract of marriage between his son and the girl would soon be carried through.

To fit the boy for this future, Leicester had already decided, he should receive the bulk of his fortune, less a sufficiency for Lettice and her family. Lettice, the woman for whom he had bastardised this son, and about whom disturbing suspicions had arisen during recent months, doubts about her fidelity which he would not openly contemplate.

Next day, passing through Oxford to one of his several estates, Cornbury, close by a favourite hunting ground, Wychwood Forest, he could have spoken a while to Robert of the great future he might enjoy should he show the spirit and ability of his line. We may picture the youngster watching his still superb father ride north, with his escort and retainers wearing the badge of the bear and raguled staff, the emblem of the Dudleys that Robert himself might not claim.

Already the gates of manhood were opening to him, and before long this fine, all-powerful father of his would take him to London, to the Queen and her Court, and one day introduce him to a place in the affairs of State, or to some adventure of which the commission at Tilbury had been so stirring a foretaste.

But Robert's dreams did not last long. Soon he was to have his second lesson that in this life, nothing can be taken for granted. Within a few days his great hopes were dashed to the ground, for on September 4th came the shattering news that his father had died suddenly at Cornbury.

CHAPTER IV

HEIR TO KENILWORTH

"THE QUEEN IS sorry for his death, but no other person in the country", wrote the Spanish ambassador to King Philip. "She was so grieved that for some days she shut herself in her chamber alone, and refused to speak to anyone, until the Treasurer and other councillors had the door broken open."

The loss of Leicester filled Elizabeth with a desolating sadness she had never known before. He had been the man of her life, and no one else was to take his place in her inmost heart. When her own time came, there was found, in the pearl-crusted bedside casket in which she kept her dearest personal treasures, the letter he had written from Rycote. On it, below his signature, she had written, "His last letter". Not "Robin's last letter", but *his*, for to Elizabeth there was only one *him*.

But the hurt to her affection, sincere and sharp as it was, did not smother the hard-headed, unsentimental business woman in her. Leicester, because of the tremendous borrowings he had made to carry out his duties in her service in the Netherlands and at Tilbury, was in debt to her Treasury to the tune of £70,000, and her immediate grief once over, she caused certain of his estates to be sequestered to the Crown, and ordered his belongings to be sold at auction.

She took this churlish action for two reasons, the first because, as Sir William Camden candidly wrote, "However gentle the Queen might show herself in some respects, yet she did rarely remit what was owing to her Treasury", the second because she wished to ensure that the "she-wolf", Lettice Knollys, did not benefit a penny more than was legally avoidable from Leicester's death. Only after she had learned how he had disposed of his estate did she relax her grip of the properties, but not of the £20,000 raised by the sale of effects.

Leicester's not very lengthy will, considering the extent of his possessions, which he had prepared in his own hand only the year before at Middleburg in the Netherlands, reveals a character entirely

different from the concocted scoundrel of *Leycester's Commonwealth*.
Written not in the prolix and flowery style then in fashion, but in clear,
unaffected language, it shows him to be at heart a well-intentioned man,
trying to meet scrupulously every claim upon him, though obviously
the only two people who counted in his life after the Queen were his
wife and his son.

First, to Queen Elizabeth, he left a pendant of diamonds and
emeralds, strung on "a rope of fair white pearls to the number of six
hundred". He made small bequests to members of his family, including
his stepson, Robert, and his nephew, Robert, Philip Sidney's younger
brother, whom he had knighted in the Flanders campaign. He left
legacies to several friends, and to retainers and servants. He set aside
funds for charities, among them the hospital[7] he had founded at
Warwick for twelve old soldiers, "hurt in the wars", and endowed a
scholarship at University College, Oxford. He also ordered that lands
at Warrington in Lancashire be sold to pay off his heavy debts, among
them £16,000 "due to the merchants of London upon mortgage of the
Lordships of Denbigh and others".

The rest of his estate he divided between his "most dear, well-
beloved wife" and his "base sonne". To Lettice, beside the jointure she
already possessed, went the manor of Wanstead and the leases of
Drayton Basset and other residences and lands. To Robert went the
greater part of his possessions after the life enjoyment of his brother,
Ambrose, including Kenilworth Castle and its wide demesne, the lordships of Denbigh and Chirk and of several smaller manors. To Robert
also, after Lettice's life enjoyment, went his mansion Leicester House,
and other properties, and some manors and lands to be held by Lettice
until he reached the age of twenty. If he were to die without issue
before the age of twenty, almost everything went to Robert Sidney
and Robert Essex.

With such well-born men as Sidney and Essex as potential heirs to the
bulk of his estate, it is significant that Leicester should make his
illegitimate son the chief beneficiary, for the bastard children of the
highly placed, other than regal, were usually left no more than a
perfunctory allowance. The conclusion is inescapable that he was
making generous if tardy reparation for depriving the boy, because of
the passion for Lettice, of the legitimacy that was rightly his. And now,
although he treated Robert as equitably as though lawfully born, he
referred to him throughout the will as his base son, a course to which,
in a document which others might have to see while he was alive, there

was no alternative unless he were to renounce Lettice and admit bigamy.

The will had been left in the safe-keeping of a trusted cleric, who now handed it to Lettice, as executrix. She lost no time in establishing her rights. Within a few days of her husband's passing, she took out letters of administration.

The suddenness of Leicester's death, and the fact that he had written to Burghley from the little hamlet of Maidenhead to say he would be returning shortly, produced the usual crop of rumours that he had been murdered, and some said by his wife, who "had ratsbane put in his porridge at Cornbury". Indeed, one of the Gentlemen of his Chamber "testified that he had seen the Lady Lettice give the fatal cup to the Earl". There is no other evidence that she was even with him, but the rumours that he had been poisoned were so strong and widespread that the Privy Council was forced to hold an enquiry. It was decided that he had died of natural causes, probably a fever picked up in the Tilbury marshes. This finding had the advantage of elevating his death to the dignity of a casualty of the war against Spain.

But the rumours persisted, for she had, it was said, for some time been indulging in an affair with his Gentleman of the Horse, the twenty-three year old Sir Christopher Blount, whom Leicester had himself knighted after the young soldier lost a hand fighting in the Netherlands war. This intrigue was the cuckolding of which Queen Elizabeth had so contemptuously spoken. Rumour even declared, as Camden recorded, that Leicester was suspicious, that there had been quarrels between him and her, and that he had tried to have Blount made away with in Holland, but the would-be assassin had blundered. More, that since then, and since the making of the will, Leicester's misgivings had been confirmed, but that Lettice had struck before he could act against her.

Men of honour and sense dismissed these slanders, especially those who knew that Leicester was a sick man, until they were seemingly confirmed less than a year later, when she and Blount, nearly a quarter of a century her junior, were married.

Through Leicester's will there runs a strange undertone of disquiet in his repeated appeals to his wife's affection, as if there were a nagging doubt in his mind, though at the time he wrote he may have been moved only by a vague distrust. His reference to "having always found her a faithful, loving and very obedient wife", his appeal to Lord Howard of Effingham to "help, assist and comfort my dear and poor disconsolate wife", could mean that he was trying to convince himself that all was well.

The truth lay in Leicester receiving a taste of his own medicine: he loved her too much, and she did not love him enough. Her speedy marriage to Blount at least proved that, as did her subsequent conduct towards her stepson when she realised how much more than herself he had gained from his father's death.

When the Queen found how Leicester had disposed of his properties, though she distrained some of the more lucrative lordships, such as Denbigh and Chirk, she released Kenilworth and most of the other lands bestowed directly and indirectly on Robert, and concentrated her venom upon Lettice's share of the estate, even to taking a writ of extent for £300 a year against the jointure. In return, Lettice refused to pay out the legacy of £200 to the Warwick Hospital, and the grants to other charities. Her financial position was not improved by her extravagant new husband, on whom she doted, and who periodically sold fine pieces of her jewellery, as well as the leases and lordships of some of her possessions.

But Robert, despite the loss of Denbigh and other estates, could expect to be rich. Certainly, he had only an allowance while his uncle Ambrose lived, but in the will Leicester had written, "I do desire my good lord and brother, the lands aforesaid coming to his hands, that it will please him to give reasonable stipend to the boy when comes to more years for his maintenance". As Ambrose was of good and amiable nature, the young heir could have had nothing to complain of. But just over a year later, Ambrose died at his Bedford House in the Strand, and Robert, at the age of fifteen, entered into possession of his grand heritage.

In his will, Leicester had named his wife as executrix, but fortunately for Robert he added a codicil appointing as "overseers", Ambrose, Charles Howard and the Lord Chancellor, Christopher Hatton, latterly his most trusted friend. It was as well that the boy had such powerful patrons to watch his interests, for in March, 1590, the Lady Lettice, particularly resentful at not having been bequeathed Kenilworth, the richest prize in the Leicester dominion, took possession of it by force. But her trespass was reported to London by Robert's uncle, the Earl of Huntingdon. In mid-April, an Order of the Privy Council came to Sir Fulke Greville, Sir John Harington, Sir Thomas Lucy, Thomas Leigh and other Justices of the Peace of Warwickshire, regarding "the forcible entry made by servants of Sir Christopher Blount in the behalf of the Countess of Leicester, upon the Castle of Kenilworth, being then in the sole and quiet possession of Mr. Robert Dudley".

The Order required them to aid the Sheriff of the County "to preserve peace and quiet and the young gentleman's rights", and this they did speedily, for another Privy Council message a fortnight later ordered that "the persons committed to the gaol at Gloucester should now be released under bond to answer for the disorders by them committed".

Shortly afterwards, pursuing now her rights, Lettice and Blount engaged in a bill of revivor against Thomas Dudley, Leicester's factor and distant kinsman, "to recover the capital messuage called Leycester House, with tenement, shops and houses appertaining thereto, situate in the parish of St. Clement, without Temple Bar". The will had given her only a life possession, but she immediately renamed it Essex House. From now on, she and Blount lived mostly at Drayton Basset, where they were far from the Queen's enmity, while Essex House and Wanstead were used by her sons and daughters.

How and where Robert lived immediately after his father's death is not written. He may have stayed for a while at Warwick Castle with the hospitable Ambrose and his young wife, Ann Russell, or perhaps he still continued his studies with Chaloner. But after Ambrose's death, he began to reside at Kenilworth, and would certainly have taken Chaloner there with him.

In 1591, Hatton died, leaving only Lord Charles Howard to safeguard Robert's interests. That there is no record of his ever being a Ward of Court, or Ward of any individual nobleman or Court official, is not easy to understand, for such wardships were legally essential, and there must have been many, from Burghley downwards, who would have been happy to have had charge of the affairs of so well-shod a youngster. Later, there were indications that the needy Lord Henry Howard, younger brother of the executed Duke of Norfolk, and Dudley's second cousin by blood, may have undertaken this role.

In 1590 Douglas Stafford had returned from Paris with her husband, his term as ambassador having expired, and Robert's relations with her entered on a new phase. She became a Lady of the Bedchamber, and her son, in spite of his youth, quickly found a place at Court. Compared with the advancement he would have enjoyed under his father's wing, his status was modest, for he was given no special preferment. His hidden role as intended husband for the Lady Arabella Stuart had vanished, as was confirmed in a letter sent in 1589 by Charles Paget, who was not only a Catholic plotter in exile, but also a spy for Walsingham. He asked one of his agents in London to discover "what Arabella and her favourers adhere to, and how they mean to bestow her in marriage, seeing that Leicester's intention to match his bastard son with her is by his death made frustrate".

Because Leicester had few close friends among those of his contemporaries who had survived him, and none among the younger generation, there was no one person to whom his son could turn with the assurance of a kindly guidance and affection, a condition that may well have quickened the development of his character, but at the same time towards an assertive spirit of independence. But the Dudleys were a clannish family, and he drew some measure of support from most of them, while his link with the Howards, and through them with the Queen, enabled him to move in elevated circles everywhere.

That he had been born out of wedlock was no embarrassment socially. This was a time when it was blood that counted, and illegitimacy, though a handicap in some important aspects of law, counted far less than the handicap of lowly birth. Thus he was in regular attendance at Court, and Elizabeth, because he was his father's son, and a prepossessing youngster at that, regarded him not without approval, though in that domain, no one at Court could now rival his step-brother, the handsome Earl of Essex.

At first, as was perhaps natural in a stripling not yet seventeen, but eager to taste life, he engaged in flirtations with the "Maydens of Honor", who gave love and laughter to the everyday run of the Court. The earliest attachment of which there is written mention was with the recently arrived Frances Vavasour of Coppenthorpe, of whom the Queen's Vice-Chamberlain wrote, "Our new Maid, Mistress Vavasour, flourisheth like the lily and the rose". It was her sister Anne who, nearly ten years earlier, had been unexpectedly delivered of a child in the Maiden's Chamber, and sent next day to the Tower, together with her lover, the young Earl of Oxford. But she had eventually been forgiven, and was back at Court, irrepressibly tarnishing her reputation even further.

Whether Frances was as free with her favours as her sister is not told, but although she was a year or so older than Robert, they arrived at a swift understanding, and early in 1591 entered into a formal contract of marriage. It is likely that the Queen's permission was petitioned, and that she gave her grudging consent, but on condition that they waited until Robert was older. This supposition would explain the extreme ire which she displayed when, in September that same year, she learned that Frances had secretly married Sir Thomas Shirley, one of the renowned three brothers. Perhaps Frances and Robert had quarrelled, or perhaps she had surrendered to the more experienced lover. The result was that she was banished from Court in disgrace, and her husband, though son of one of the Queen's trusted ministers, was sent to the Marshalsea prison, where he stayed until the following spring.

The second mention of Robert's early romances at Court was in October, 1591, when as Dugdale briefly recorded, "Mr. Dudley is forbidden the Court for kissing Mistress Cavendish in the Presence, being his wife, as is said". From this it seems that his break with Frances had hardly wrecked his life, for he had lost no time in marrying another Maid of Honour: more, he had light-heartedly sealed his compact by kissing his new wife in front of the Queen, and of all places, in her Audience Chamber. That his punishment, compared with Shirley's, should be merely temporary banishment from Court indicates an indulgent attitude from Elizabeth, and events were to prove that while he never came within range of the grace extended to established favourites, he could rely on her interest and patronage.

That he was the husband of a Cavendish was less an indication of an appropriate marriage than a pointer that already he had been drawn by the glamour of the sea. For his wife, Margaret, was a young cousin of the renowned Captain Thomas Cavendish, the second Englishman to circumnavigate the globe, and Dudley's interest in her may well have been attendant on his acquaintance with that valiant sailor, who in matching Drake's achievement a couple of years before had seized and looted a score of Spanish and Portuguese vessels, and arrived home with a shipload of rich spoil.

The contact with the thirty-year-old explorer, made some months prior to the kissing episode, rekindled in Dudley all the longings for the sea that had held him since childhood. Always there had been the example of his own fighting kinsmen to inspire him, and the no less daring exploits of such captains as Drake, Frobisher and Hawkins, to whom the exploration of faraway lands was as stirring an adventure as the capture of a well-laden prize. But now there was Cavendish, also of this famous band, and at the zenith of his fame, to fire his imagination in person with audacious plans to return to the Philippines, and from there to open trading relations with Japan and China.

This friendship had developed quickly into active co-operation, for so intense was Dudley's interest in the other's ambitious design that he offered to find and equip the vessels for a new expedition, one of which, the 400-ton *Leicester*, had belonged to his father nine years before. In this enterprise "for the South Seas, the Philippines and the coast of China", Cavendish joined forces with John Davis, the famed navigator and inventor of the quadrant, whose ultimate aim was to resume his previous efforts to find the North West Passage. When in August, 1591, the little fleet of "three tall ships and two barkes" set out from Plymouth, Dudley watched them leave with envy and disappointment, for he had tried to join them, only to meet with the Queen's firm embargo.

During Cavendish's absence, he resolved to prepare himself for the time when he too would be allowed to go to sea, for the gesture he had made of financing a maritime venture, and so following the example of his father and uncle, and indeed of the Queen herself, did little to satisfy his urge to emulate the deeds of the great sea captains. It was not difficult to sustain these heady dreams, for the smell of the sea was there even in London. He had only to go down to the Thames, where in the four-mile stretch between London Bridge and Blackwall, there were always two or three hundred vessels lying, most at their buoys, but some just about to move on the tide.

Watching them, the day would seem nearer when he too would set out in a strong galleon, newly painted in red and green and blue, with sails unfurling and pennants flying, and with guns all mounted for a privateering venture to the Spanish Main, to seize rich carracks, discover new lands, even maybe find El Dorado, the constant lure for every adventuring seaman.

But he did more than dream. With prodigious thoroughness, he set about to learn the business of the sea. Long afterwards, recalling these days, he wrote of himself, "He determined at any cost to enter the marine army, on which at that time the reputation and greatness of England depended. He had also a desire to discover new countries. Therefore, from the age of seventeen, he gave himself to the study of navigation, and of marine discipline and war. In fact, he wanted to blend the naval command together with military emprise by land, in India and other parts, to which navigation should take him."

For such advanced projects to be in the mind of a youngster of seventeen was unusual but not unlikely, for in his learning and his urge to add to it, Dudley was something of a prodigy, certainly in comparison with the average high-born youth of his day. And during this period, he so devoted himself to the study of seamanship that there is no more mention of any activities at Court. Yet he did not unduly neglect the wider interests that were adjunct to his age and background. His Kenilworth and other country estates absorbed some portion of his time, though it was London, the only place where he could expand his maritime knowledge, that saw him most often.

His wife, Margaret, preferred this, for her Court and family interests lay mainly in the capital, her father being Richard Cavendish, the author, of Hornsey, an uncle of the absent Thomas. Her sister, another Douglas, was the wife of Richard Hakluyt, the cleric and writer, who for five years had been chaplain to Dudley's stepfather, Sir Edward, during his tour as ambassador in Paris.

Dudley also found time to assume, to a modest extent, the role which his father and uncle Ambrose had played before him, of patron of poetry and drama, for in 1593 a volume of lyrics, *The Shepherd's Garland*, was dedicated to him by its author, Michael Drayton, the poet and playwright. The theatre, too, would certainly have drawn him often enough, as it did every young man of quality, and he would, as a matter of course, have taken part in the several other forms of amusement open to the young bucks of town, such as the bear-baiting and cockfighting in the Paris Garden.

But to his serious nature, passionately intent on ships and the sea, such things were little more than frivolous distractions. And this he realised the more when, at the beginning of 1593, came news that showed how fortunate he had been not to sail with Cavendish. For dire ill-fortune had attended both his and Davis's voyagings. Although both very experienced seamen, they had not been sufficiently alert to watch for swindling by the chandlers, with the result that the vessels and their crews were blighted by decayed sails and cordage, mouldy victuals and similar vital defects.

After trying to round the stormy Straits of Magellan, the two groups of ships became separated, and each suffered severe hardships from violent tempests, and in costly fights with the Portuguese and Indians, before they were able to struggle back to England. Their privations, added to the usual wastage from disease, took heavy toll of the crews and officers, among them Cavendish himself, who died at sea from typhus.

It was Dudley who, as executor, took out letters of administration for the Cavendish estate. A Privy Council warrant of March, 1593, addressed to the Mayor of Portsmouth, where the ships had docked, required him "to cause the galleon *Leicester* and the *Roebuck*, with their lading, to be delivered to Mr. Dudley".

A young man of softer fibre might have been deterred by the disastrous outcome of this venture, over both the fate of Cavendish and the loss of a great amount of money. But to Dudley, the setback acted as a challenge, spurring him not only to renewed effort, but to a great resolve—the decision to build his own fleet and himself lead it to distant seas and strange horizons.

CHAPTER V

"TO SEEK NEW WORLDS . . ."

EVEN IN ELIZABETHAN times, when youth discovered manhood early, for a youngster of nineteen to build his own fleet in order to roam the world was rare, if not unique. But Dudley himself was rare, if not unique. Untrammelled by parental control, his ardent character had become impulsive, determined and supremely self-confident, but these qualities were tempered by an alert enquiring mind, a readiness and aptitude to learn, and a capacity for work and action.

Product of a vital, restless age, he showed already that he was conscious of its achievements and its possibilities. He knew he lived in a time of great men, and was resolved to be one of them. Perhaps it was his bastard birth that spurred him to prove his mettle, but just as probably it was his eager, adventuring spirit. Possibly something told him that this heroic age could not last for ever, for he seemed to be in a hurry to challenge it while the opportunity was there.

He undertook his tremendous enterprise entirely on his own authority, and without any notable help from any of his elders. If ever he received advice from his renowned kinsmen, the Howards of the Armada, he never afterwards put the discussions on record. The one man who might have acted as his mentor, because his own heart was with the sea, Thomas Chaloner, recently knighted while with the English army in France, was not in London, for he had been sent by Cecil to the Court of King James VI of Scotland, and there he stayed.

Dudley's ambition was unbounded, for he decided to have ships built to his own ideas, and to teach himself everything he needed to know in order to equip them, to keep them seaworthy, to engage in battle, and above all to navigate them across the oceans. In his choice of men to train and help him, he showed extraordinary sagacity, for they were among the pick of the experts of the time. As he wrote long afterwards, he "built and manned ships-of-war, in which he sought to place the best pilots that were to be found, and in whose great knowledge and experience he trusted implicitly. One, the famous Abraham

Kendal, might be called his master, from him he learned enough navigation for an admiral".

For instruction in shipbuilding, he went to Matthew Baker, Master of the Shipwrights' Company, and most noted shipwright of the day, under whom he worked for some time in the busy shipyards at Deptford. The Lord Admiral was a patron of Baker's, and took such interest in the theory of his designs for fighting vessels that he was often at the shipwright's modest house at Deptford, where Dudley also came. For the building of his principal ship, his "admiral", he chose the less occupied shipyards at Southampton, and here, spurred on by his enthusiasm and his consuming urge to get to sea, his helpers and workmen were inspired to complete the work in record time.

Then came the business of fitting out the vessels in proper style for a protracted voyage. That he was able, out of his own resources, to bear the entire cost of the expedition was sufficient evidence of his notable wealth. In addition to building or buying the ships, he had to find cash for "sail, canvas, flags, cordage, ensigns, and all manner of sea-stores", and for "great anchors, masts, yards, pinnaces, longboats", for cannon and culverin and muskets and "every manner of powder, shot, matches and suchlike". He had to buy merchandise for traffic with the natives of the lands he meant to visit. He had to pay for his crews, including soldiers, to be recruited or taken by press-gangs, for their safe conduct to the vessels, for their sea wages, and for their discharge money. He had to provide for their victuals, salted beef and fish, biscuits and flour and other storable foods, as well as beer over several months, and with the lesson of the faulty provisioning of the Cavendish voyage to reflect upon, he made sure that everything he bought was in good condition.

By the middle of 1594, he had the ships and their captains and officers all but ready. Above everything he had full confidence in his capacity to accept risk and responsibility, and to make a name for himself. His aim was to go far afield, to round the Straits of Magellan and steer for the fabulous Indies, and then to circumnavigate the globe. Preparations for so long and hazardous a voyage were far advanced, when everything had to come to a halt, for he had reckoned without the Queen. Although he now had the backing of his powerful uncle, Lord Charles Howard, and the direct approach to Elizabeth through his mother and his aunt, Catherine Howard, lifelong Lady of the Bed-chamber, and although he had the money to smooth the passage of a maritime commission past the hunchback new Secretary, Sir Robert Cecil, his lack of years told against him.

"Being", he wrote afterwards, "by special command contradicted of Her Majesty", he had to abandon his plan. But, "although Queen Elizabeth would not allow such a mere youth to break his maiden lance in an emprise requiring so much knowledge of the world, and in which many veteran captains had fared so ill, and lost both men and ships, she contented him by allowing him to make a voyage".

Elsewhere he continued, "I could not be suffered to hazard more of her Majesty's subjects upon so uncertain a ground as my desire, which made me by constraint (great charges already by me defrayed) to prepare another course, to the West Indies, without hope to do anything worth note".

The less dangerous commission that he did receive, by which the Queen permitted her trusty and well-beloved Robert Dudley to voyage oversea, but not to trespass in the lands of any other Christian Prince, was to the West Indies and Guiana. Though disappointed at the denial of his circumnavigation project, he accepted the alternative with good grace, especially as he knew that Sir Walter Raleigh was preparing an expedition for the same area, to explore Guiana and the River Orinoco.

Dudley contemplated some link-up with Raleigh, and it is possible that the Queen, conscious of the youngster's untried powers, intended this. The two fleets were fitted out at about the same time, and Dudley's was assembled in good order at Southampton by September, 1594. But Raleigh met with last minute difficulties. Ships were late for the rendezvous at Plymouth, there were arguments among the captains, the winds were unfavourable, and to cap all, he became involved in a lawsuit.

In contrast, Dudley's venture was either luckier or better organised. Certainly, he was fortunate in being served by so capable a group of officers, but it was a considerable achievement for a leader of such youth and inexperience to assemble a group of men, who in the test of action were all to prove of the first class. Even the crews, who usually consisted of brawling ruffians and fleeing criminals, he was to find well behaved, and responsive to his immature, but, as was to be shown, inspiring personality.

Chief among the officers were the ship's master, Captain Benjamin Wood, whose long acquaintance with the sea included an unsuccessful essay at encircling the globe, and a voyage to the West Indies in command of four ships owned by Lord Thomas Howard, by whom he had been recommended to his young relation. In charge of the soldiery required over and above the crew to man the ordnance and board enemy ships, was Captain Thomas Jobson, another well-seasoned sailor, who had served under Drake. Jobson, whose mother was half-sister to Dudley's grandfather, John, Duke of Northumberland, and whom Dudley addressed as cousin, was much older than his kinsman, and by virtue of his relationship and competence was, as the expedition's "Lieutenant-General", the younger man's mentor in matters of command throughout the voyage.

Second to Jobson was Captain Tom Wyatt, "commanding the main battle of pyke", through whose aptitude for writing, a full and vivid record of the voyage was kept. Two other accounts were written, one by Dudley himself, and one by his navigator, the Abraham Kendal already mentioned, whom Wyatt described as "excelling all others in his profession as a rare scholar, a most seldom thing in a mariner". Kendal's version is mainly a ruttier, a factual route or record of courses, fixes and other plotting data, while Dudley's is so brief as to be little more than an outline. It is Wyatt's much longer description, written for the edification of some unknown person of authority, whom he addresses as Right Honourable, which provides most of the information on the voyage. It is especially valuable for the light it throws on Dudley's intrepid and chivalrous spirit.

His little squadron consisted of four ships. The largest, the "admiral", which he, as "General" commanded, was the 200-ton *Bear*, carrying 30 guns, a fighting ship of sleek design, which was to prove an exceptionally fast sailer. The second largest, the vice-admiral, was the *Bear's Whelp*, of about 100 tons, commanded by Captain Monck. The two remaining vessels, the *Earwig* and the *Frisking*, were pinnaces, intended to serve as tenders. The names given to the two admirals reflected Dudley's ownership, though still he might not properly display the Dudley crest, the bear and raguled staff.

After a month in Southampton harbour, waiting for word from Raleigh down at Plymouth, Dudley, impatient at the delay, and concerned at the ill effects that inactivity was having on his crews, moved there too, arriving on November 19th. It was quickly evident that Raleigh's ships would not be ready to sail for some time.

Among the many vessels in Plymouth harbour was a pinnace commanded by Captain George Popham, who also intended to make for the West Indies. He and Dudley arranged to rendezvous at Trinidad, if circumstances permitted. As Raleigh's start seemed likely to be retarded for weeks, and indeed it was not until February that he and his five ships were able to set sail, Dudley decided to wait no longer, and on November 21st, started off for the Canaries. Whether it was in his mind deliberately to anticipate Raleigh on his Trinidad and Guiana exploration is uncertain, but since he had originally no specific object for the voyage, this may well have become his impulsively adopted intention. Afterwards, Raleigh certainly thought so.

Immediately on reaching the open sea, Dudley's squadron ran into such violent weather that all four ships were forced to turn about. The *Bear* and the *Earwig* contrived to regain Plymouth, but the *Whelp* and her pinnace had to make for Falmouth. Undeterred by this set-back, Dudley sent instructions by land to Monck to rendezvous at the Canaries, or alternatively at Cape Blanco, on the West African coast, and on Sunday, December 1st, started out again.

A strong wind was now full behind them, but as soon as they drew into the open sea, the rough waves swamped the pinnace, and the crew were transferred to the *Bear*. "Notwithstanding all these crosses", Dudley wrote, "all alone, I went wandering on my voyage". The wind held, and his brave craft drew swiftly southwards towards the New World.

At last it had all come about! He was twenty, and in command of his own ship, voyaging to the same fabulous coasts as Raleigh, who was twenty years his senior. They were both making for dangerous seas and uncharted lands. Raleigh's aim was to find gold, to discover El Dorado and the legendary wealth of the Incas. Dudley wrote afterwards that his more modest purpose was "rather to see some practice and experience than any wonders or profit".

But in truth, he was sailing just to find adventure, to see the world, and maybe have a fight and seize some golden galleon. He was moved by the urge which Raleigh himself was to inscribe in a vivid phrase, "To seek new worlds, for gold, for praise, for glory". In young Dudley lived the typical adventuring spirit of the seamen of the Elizabethan age.

CHAPTER VI

OFF THE SPANISH MAIN

Every English vessel that went to sea in Elizabeth's reign was to some degree a man-of-war. Even the fat merchantmen were provided with ordnance and soldiery for self-defence. Whatever its royal commission, however peaceful its declared task, the well-armed ship was always a potential privateer, though whether the potential was realised depended largely on the spirit of the commander.

There was no doubt whatever about Dudley's spirit. Before the *Bear* drew level with the coast of Spain, he was pursuing every vessel that came in sight, irrespective of its size. Because of his ship's unusual speed, he overtook them easily, but unfortunately for his predatory aims, all were English. At length, a group of three ships was seen to "pack on every sail they were able . . . being desirous to give us chase". Assuming they were Spanish, Dudley obliged them by ordering "great drags to be hanged overboard" to reduce his speed. Decks were cleared for action, but again came disappointment, for the pursuers were also English. Their captain, "showing himself a very glad man to meet with our General at sea . . . gave him three pieces of ordnance, the which kindness our General requited with like kindness . . . and so departed, they for Cape St. Vincent, we for the Canaries".

The one vessel they encountered that was not English cheated them by hoisting English colours, and escaping into shallow water. The crew then "began to disclose themselves . . . by taking their English flag from their top and hanging it at their stern most disdainfully. The which our General took mightily offensive, yet at the time could not remedy it".

At Teneriffe, where there were no signs of the *Bear's Whelp*, they were becalmed near a barque from Weymouth, with whose crew they made cheer on Christmas Day. Dudley tried to recruit the vessel as consort on the Indies venture, but they were separated "by the contrary of the wind . . . the weather growing into such a monstrous outrageousness" that they did not see each other again.

Since the sinking of the pinnace, the *Bear* had been uncomfortably overcrowded, with some 140 men on board, and now, with the heat and cramped quarters, sickness began to develop. That this was the only occasion during the whole voyage when serious sickness appeared was a creditable and even unusual achievement in times when the dreaded "ship-fever" typhus, arising from filthy food and insanitary conditions, caused many more deaths among seamen than storms or Spaniards, sometimes wiping out four-fifths of a ship's crew. This immunity was due to the good victualling, and to the health precautions enforced by the experienced Jobson and Kendal.

Dudley was luckily able to relieve the situation by capturing two Spanish caravels, light and speedy ocean-going sailing vessels. One of these was seized close inshore by Jobson in a rowing boat, under a hot fire from troops on the beach, while the other was caught off Palma after an attempt to escape to the open sea "by her swift sailing. In which they were mightily deceived, for our admiral being most singular for her sailing soon overtook her". Dudley had all the prisoners "safely set on shore unspoiled of their apparel or wealth, for which", says Wyatt, "they gave him the greatest commendations, protesting to do him all the service they might, their true dutiful obedience to their natural Prince only reserved".

The caravels, renamed *Regarde* and *Intent*, and manned by the surplus men in the *Bear*, were placed under Captains Wood and Wentworth, and the little "fleet of three sails" made for Cape Blanco. Still there was no sign of the *Bear's Whelp*. Though concerned at Monck's failure to make the rendezvous, Dudley would accept no delay, and on January 9th, began the journey across the Atlantic. The friendly trade winds did not fail them, fair weather held, and with an uneventful passage, Wyatt had little to write about except to praise Dudley's seamanship. His comments, which are the more reliable because they were not written for Dudley's eyes, bear out the good impression which he had already made on everyone, including the toughest rascals of the crew.

This was his first long sea voyage, yet he had not only mastered the inevitable onslaughts of sickness during several spells of rough weather, when the small ship was tossed about like a toy, but had borne himself with both resolution and charity in encounters with the Spaniards. And now, as the *Bear* approached the American continent, he impressed Wyatt by the accuracy of his navigation, which showed him to be in no way dependent on Kendal. As he was to record later, "Having ever since I could conceive of anything been delighted with the discoveries of navigation, I fostered in myself that disposition till I was of more years and better ability to undertake such a matter. In especial, I practised the science of navigation by grand circles with practical longitude." In the result, his voyage provided the first occasion that the practice of great circle sailing by an English ship was put on detailed record.

After a clear run of twenty days, Wyatt noticed that the colour of the sea had changed, and realised they were approaching land, thus "falling most rightly out into the computation and reckoning of our General, who from time to time foretold me by the reckoning of his card when he had taken the height under whatsoever meridian we then happened to be in. . . . 'We shall', saith he, 'if God prosper our proceedings, see land such a day . . . and this was not done once nor twice, but still from the first cape after we were departed from the English coast . . . the which how difficult it is, let those who have been seamen all the days of their lives judge".

"Let me return to that honourable and excellent practiser of the art", continues Wyatt, "that I may admire . . . his wonderful actions, which hereafter will prove to be the world's wonder. I mean our virtuous and careful, honourable and provident General, who seeing the water in the night-time to wax so suddenly white, called unto the master . . . and having caused one to heave out a lead and sounding, found it to be but fifteen fathoms water."

Next morning, on January 31st,[8] it was Dudley who first descried Trinidad. He sent off the caravels to explore the coast, then shortly following them, sailed round the south-western extremity, Cape Curiapan, where Columbus had landed a century before, and anchored "in a bay which our General calls Pelican Bay, from the great abundance of pelicans which we see there".

The eager Dudley next day sent officers to contact the natives, who were of the Arawak tribe, and whom he described as a "finely shaped and gentle people, all naked and painted red". Soon, canoes were swarming round the *Bear*, bringing "neither gold nor pearl, of which there are great store within the island, but tobacco, nuts and fruits, the which they exchanged for knives, beads, fishing hooks and hatchets". Throughout his forty days' stay at Trinidad, Dudley demanded strict obedience to his order that the natives were to be well treated, and their women and dwellings left unmolested. He and Wyatt, profiting from the friendly relations established by this attitude, were able to study the language, and to compile lists of words in the Arawak tongue, which are the earliest known to have been recorded.

Although Dudley had started from England with no set plan, except to enjoy adventure in whatever form it came, he now decided that having reached a land where there was gold, he would be remiss not to try to find some. It was not the fabled possibilities of El Dorado that spurred him but the more practical prospect of winning a moderate and quick reward from some readily accessible mine. Certainly, the Spaniards had arrived here many years ago, and were in control of mines in the north of the island, where they were established under the command of Antonio de Berrio, but the natives insisted that there was also a mine in the south.

Under the guidance of an Arawak who spoke Spanish, Jobson led a party of the soldiery to a site some eight miles to the eastwards, along the coast. There he found a mine abounding in what he took to be gold. Impressed and excited by this news, Dudley landed his "main battle of pyke", marshalled them in military order in case of attack— "If we had been charged with ten thousand Indians, they could not have harmed us", wrote Wyatt—and set out "through deep sands and in a most extreme hot day, our General, unaccustomed God knows to walking on foot, leading the march".

At the mine, as much ore as could be carried was dug out. The return was made next day, and again Dudley led the column "carrying so great majesty in his march, with such unremovable resolution in his proceedings that we all that followed him concluded . . . that he without all doubt would prove the only mirror of knighthood".

Dudley was not the first Englishman to visit Trinidad, for James Lancaster had called there briefly two years previously, and Captain Jacob Whiddon had been sent there only the year before by Raleigh to reconnoitre the area for his present voyage. But both visitors had been repulsed by the Spaniards. Neither had landed troops and erected defences, and marched around in battle array for six weeks, doing, as Wyatt boasts, "whatever it pleased our General to command and liked ourselves best", nor had they taken possession of the island in the name of the English Queen, which Dudley now proceeded to do.

Believing that he had found immensely rich deposits of gold, and unconcernedly ignoring the prior claims of the Spaniards, he caused to be set up, on February 4th, with proper ceremony, on a tree near his mine, a leaden plate inscribed with the Queen's arms and a declaration in Latin of his seizure of the island. "And this, with his sword, God favouring his intent, doth he swear to make good against any knight in the whole world."

"Marching forth in good order", runs Wyatt's description, in which he refers to himself in the third person, as he does throughout his account, "we came to the place where this our service was to be accomplished: first we caused the trumpets to sound solemnly three several times, our company trooping round: in the midst marched Wyatt, bearing the Queen's arms wrapped in a white silk scarf edged with deep silver lace, accompanied by Mr. Wright and Mr. Vincent, each of us with our arms, having the General's colours displayed . . . and after a general silence, Wyatt read it unto the troop, first as it was written in Latin, then in English." He then kissed the plate, and ordered the carpenter to nail it to the tree. "This being ended, the trumpets and drums sounded, the whole troop cried 'God save Queen Elizabeth'. And having thus, as solemnly as we could, accomplished our charge, we marched down the mount."

A few days later, Dudley had Jobson repeat the parade with a second leaden plate, affixed to the tree with even more ritual. Unfortunately these little ceremonies were to have no place in history, for as Dudley was later to discover, his ore was not gold but merely marcasite. The formal action he took to make Trinidad English was to lie dormant for over two centuries until, in 1802, the island came to Britain by the Treaty of Amiens.

But in that February of 1595, he and his men were proud and exultant at their achievement for their Queen and country, so much so that they now looked round for fields for fresh glory. They did not need to search very far. At the other end of the island lay the Spanish settlement of San Paracoa, near where San Ferdinando now stands. Dudley moved his ships to Paracoa Bay, and landed his soldiery under Jobson to seize the town, but while they were still preparing the march a party of Spaniards appeared with a flag of truce, and made friendly overtures.

When Jobson reported this development to Dudley, he received a stiff reply. "I mean to stand upon my guard and have no dealings with the Spaniards", he wrote from the *Bear*. "Let them know I so much disdain the Spaniard and his courtesies in respect of my dutiful service unto Her Majesty as I would they knew I neither trust them nor care for their force, be it never so great . . . Englishmen of worth will never dishonour their Prince, country and selves by faint-hearting unto their courtesy that villainously have sought the life of our most gracious Queen. . . ."

The hostility which he shows in this haughty letter towards those "most bitter foes unto God and his country, and vile enemies unto his Prince and her subjects" was confirmed when de Berrio sent him a letter which he declined even to read, and presents which he contemptuously rejected.

Dudley's attitude was inspired by the several plots against the Queen's life by Spanish-subsidised Catholic exiles from England, and also by de Berrio's treachery the previous year, when some of Whiddon's men had been ambushed and murdered. But in spite of the young leader's fire-eating gestures, the situation ended mildly enough, and San Paracoa was left undisturbed, for the reason which he gave afterwards that the Spanish forces were too strong to risk attacking, and too poor to be worth the looting. Raleigh thought differently, for when he arrived, he assaulted and burnt de Berrio's stronghold and took him prisoner.

Meanwhile, Dudley had profited from the sheltered beach to grave and caulk his ships, using pitch from the strange black hundred-acre lake which they had come across near Cape Curiapan. During this task, the crew lived ashore in a bivouac protected by a sconce of half-moon shape, a precaution thought wise in spite of the success of the policy of treating the natives considerately.

In this, Dudley had himself taken the lead, when, soon after their arrival, he had gone ashore with only six men, unknown to Wyatt, who followed him three hours later. "We found him using the savages with all the kindness he could devise, the which to so good effect that two or three voluntarily went aboard with him, and lodged there all night, where he made them great cheer, and gave them such things as he saw did most delight them." Such methods had won their trust, and as a result, he had learned something about the mainland, of the several kingdoms of the Empire of Guiana, and of the gold and precious stones to be found there in plenty. Though still not moved by any vision of the gilded city of Manoa, the treasure house of the Incas, the abode of vast riches in which Raleigh implicitly believed, Dudley's appetite for gold had been whetted, and the finding of one mine had set him afire to discover others.

It is credible that together with the lure of gold, there was a boyish urge to be a jump ahead of the famous Raleigh, whose expedition, as Dudley well knew, was organised for the express purpose of ascending the Orinoco. Whether or not this was a deciding factor, he could resist no longer when a Spanish-speaking native, whom they named Balthasar, told of an abundant mine at Orocoa, at the head of the Orinoco delta, and was confirmed by other natives who spoke of "how the savages there hanged rich pieces of gold around their necks instead of breastplates".

He decided to attempt to ascend the Orinoco, as yet virgin waters to Englishmen, but he realised the adventure might be costly, for there were tales of how Spanish ships had mysteriously disappeared in these seas, their crews all ambushed and eaten by natives. Such hazards did not deter him, but he did conclude that the risks justified the splitting of his resources.

"Lest I should adventure all occasions upon it only, I sent my two caravels from me the 17 day of February to try their fortunes in the Indies, not appointing any other place to meet but England, furnishing them with all the provision I could spare."

Very quickly, he was to regret this impulsive precaution, for he discovered that the *Bear* was of too deep a draught to be ventured into the shallow channels of the delta, and that, lacking the caravels, the journey would have to be made in the longboat. Undismayed, he accepted the challenge, and announced that he would command the boat.

"This worthy and valourous young gentleman was very anxious to go himself", wrote Wyatt, "notwithstanding the manifold dangers delivered by our master, Abraham Kendal . . . it was generally thought very unfit that the person of so worthy and hopeful a gallant should be hazarded in so small and simple a vessel, wherein could not be thrust any sufficient guard for his safety and defence." On Dudley persisting in his wish, "Captain Jobson, his lieutenant and dear kinsman, was much contradictory and repugnant, desiring and earnestly beseeching the General that it would please him to commit the said service to him".

"The General gave place to his earnest suit", continues Wyatt, "and the good Captain, putting on a very willing resolution (notwithstanding, as I heard him say, in his dream the night before, he did sensibly perceive himself drowning) took unto him" a handpicked crew of twelve men, including the two masters' mates and the boatswain. Dudley's own account of this incident, with proper modesty, attributes the crew's reluctance to see him go to their dislike of the disciplinarian, Kendal, whom he would have had to leave in charge. To avoid possible trouble, he says, he submitted to Jobson's persuasions.

Jobson set off with his crew on the night of February 20th, and having rowed dangerously across the swift outpourings of the Orinoco's many exits, with their swirling currents and unpredictable waves, they struggled into one of the delta's mouths. Pressing up this, they passed by a lateral channel into the main river, Mana (later called by Raleigh, Amana, and today, Manamo), where for four days they rowed slowly and laboriously upstream.

Then, according to the account taken by Wyatt from Jobson and his crew, "having gone fourscore leagues by the true computation of our best mariners, and had passed sundry places inhabited, yet the people differing in language, at the last they came to a place where there was much people of men, women and children. And they were a-making certain very great canoes."

With the aid of Balthasar and the exchange of presents, Jobson made friends with the aged headman, and lost no time in asking for a gold-mine. The headman dispatched a canoe to the neighbouring town of Orocoa—Raleigh's Arriacoa, "where Orenoque divideth itself into three great branches"—whose ruler, Armago came next day with several hundred men in canoes, and offered to trade gold in exchange for the Englishmen's goods. "In token thereof", recorded Dudley, "he sent me three or four croissants or half-moons of gold, weighing a noble apiece or more, and two bracelets of silver. And he told them of another rich nation that sprinkled their bodies with the powder of gold . . . and far beyond them a great town called El Dorado. My men, being satisfied, and thinking their number too few to stay among these savages, and their victuals spent, returned."

But the journey back was not to be easy. "Our company, making great haste to the ship, and finding their labour with the oar irksome in the heat of the day, were desirous to be stirring in the night." Balthasar, who had tired of his task as guide, saw his opportunity, and led them up narrow creeks obstructed by fallen trees, past which the boat had to be carried ashore. During one of these nocturnal holdups, he slipped into the thickets and disappeared.

Left now without guide or food, and with only vague notions of their whereabouts in the maze of crocodile-infested channels, they managed to find their way to a wider stream, where all they could do was to drift with the current and hope to reach the sea. Baffled by the network of waters, they chose a wrong course, and came out on the coast much to the westward. By now they were near exhaustion, for even the last of their water was gone. "At length, with much labour, both in rowing, towing and carrying the boat, they recovered over the indraughts and currents, and got to the windward of a rock called Diabolo", from where they were able to sail to Trinidad.

Dismayed at first to find the *Bear* no longer at the familiar anchorage, they persisted under Jobson's urgings and drove up the coast until, thankfully, but with surprise, they saw not one vessel in Paracoa Bay, but two. The thirteen men had been away for two weeks, and because they had been given up for lost by everyone but Dudley, were received "with great joy and triumph, the which was signified by the shooting of the great ordnance and small shot for the space of a whole hour".

Jobson and his courageous crew had found no gold mine, nor achieved any results of great consequence, and their effort cannot be compared, except for boldness, with that made over the same route a few weeks later by Raleigh, with a flotilla of ships and a hundred men. Yet to Dudley's expedition goes a specific merit, for Jobson and not Raleigh was the first Englishman to navigate the Orinoco.

Inspired by his kinsman's encouraging reports Dudley eagerly proposed to return to Oracoa immediately, this time with himself as leader. But his crew, he records, "were worse than before . . . not one man would go with me, no, albeit I had commission to hang or kill them", and so he had to give up the project.

The second vessel off Paracoa, which had arrived four days previously, was the pinnace of Captain Popham, whom Dudley had encountered at Plymouth. He brought news that Raleigh's flotilla was on its way, and the two commanders decided to wait. "This captain and I", wrote Dudley, "stayed some six or eight days longer for Sir Walter Raleigh (who, we surmised, had some purpose for this enterprise) to the end that by our intelligence and his boats, we might have done some good." Pending Raleigh's arrival, the two captains decided to join forces.

During the longboat's absence, Dudley had made good progress with the "chief Indians of Trinidad, that voluntarily were content to yield their duty and allegiance to Her Majesty . . . a Queen mild and gentle, and the only Christian Prince that doth withstand the cruelty of the tyrannous Spaniard". By these headmen he had been told where the supposed gold was refined into metal.

"Being wonderful desirous to see the end of this discovery, both as well for the service of Her Majesty as also for the good of his country", he decided to inspect the place. On March 8th, the day after Jobson's return, he set out with sixty of his crew, accompanied by Popham with ten. "We marshalled our men in good order, our good General leading the march, Captain Jobson the vanguard, Wyatt the battle of pyke, and Vincent in the rearward. Thus marching into the wood side, we were then enforced, for the more easy passage of our men, to march one after one."

In this single file they progressed "with much toil and extreme travail" for twenty miles through "monstrous thick wood, or sometimes dirty and comfortless valleys, sometimes over high unpleasing mountains, other times through deep and dangerous rivers" until they reached a town, Carowa. The inhabitants had fled, but ore melting pots with traces of gold were found in their huts. These were left undisturbed, for "our General would suffer none of their houses to be rifled or touched".

"The cause that made these people fly from us", explains Wyatt, "was the sounding of our trumpets and drum, with the continual noise of the shooting of our pieces, the which we did of purpose that we might still give notice unto the Spaniard which way we marched, with our colours displayed in honour of England."

Satisfied with this evidence of local refining, Dudley led the return march with even greater confidence that vast riches lay before him. Not until long afterwards was he to admit, ruefully, that "all that glisteneth is not gold".

Meanwhile the time was passing, and on March 11th, as Raleigh had still not arrived (he did so ten days later), and as "Captain Popham and I held it not convenient to stay any longer", the two ships sailed out of the Gulf of Paria by the Dragon's Mouth "to see further of the Indies". They soon separated, probably because strong currents carried the *Bear* off the intended track to Granada, and, in consequence, Dudley set course for the island of Puerto Rico. His appetite for exploring temporarily satisfied, he thought now of capturing a prize. They were soon fortunate, for, tells Wyatt, "it pleased God to bless him so that on the 13th day of March, at four of the clock, we had sight of a Spanish ship, the which we gave chase unto, and by midnight brought her within danger of our great shot, notwithstanding when she appeared first in sight she was some four leagues to weather of us".

The Spaniards made no resistance, for "we had not made three great shot at them but they submitted themselves unto our General's mercy, signifying their submission by striking their sails, and came under our lee". Jobson went aboard to check the cargo, which consisted of wine, linen, hats, and goods for trading with the natives. Dudley then continued towards Puerto Rico, where he caused Wyatt to put the Spanish crew ashore. So quixotic was his attitude towards them that "upon their departure, after their Spanish fashion, they veiled their bonnets in honour of our General". But they made strong complaint to Wyatt at landing them in a remote place, even though supplied with food. Comments Wyatt, "Our General used them so kindly, they forgot they were prisoners".

Dudley did not attempt to man the prize, his complement being far too small, but transferred her cargo and fitments to the *Bear*, and set her alight. "She continued burning all that day and most part of the night." He wanted to waste no further time, for from the prisoners he had learned that early in April the Silver Fleet of 150 sail was due to leave Havana for Spain. Here was his chance to pick up a straggler, and passing between Puerto Rico and San Domingo he sailed northeast towards the meridian of Bermuda, with the intention of placing his ship in the path of the Spanish fleet.

But conditions were against him, for as he wrote, "the fleet I found not, but foul weather enough to scatter many fleets". Flying before the wind, they made for the coast of Florida, then up towards Virginia. The succession of storms gave them no respite, and Wyatt describes indignantly "the extremities of this outrageous weather". Day after day the little ship scudded under the "dangerous gusts" and the "monstrous raging of the swelling seas", accompanied by "dreadful flashes of lightning and horrible claps of thunder" until they were "not far from the coast of Labrador or Nova Francia, which he knew by the great abundance of whales".

Kendal, in his account, records no higher latitude than 40° 10', which took them level with what is now New York. But from her most northerly point, wherever it was, the *Bear* was now forced to run eastwards before another unceasing gale, under which, writes Wyatt, "we expected nothing less than splitting of sails, breaking of shrouds, spending of masts, springing of planks—in a word, the dreadful devouring of us all by some sea-swallowing whirlpool". That the sturdy *Bear* was able to withstand a month of such buffetings spoke well for her builders, for the men who manned her, and for her designer, who was, Dudley later claimed, himself.

At length, on April 28th, they reached the Azores, having made the crossing so swiftly that Dudley and Kendal, deceived for once in their navigation, were some fifty leagues out of reckoning. A day's rest, then they set off for England on a favourable wind. But their hour of adventure was not yet over. On May 6th, Dudley, taking his turn on the quarter-deck, "was the first that scried a sail, unto which, by all the means we could, working warily to keep the wind, we gladly gave chase".

Their quarry, a Spanish galleon of over 300 tons, separated from its fleet by the storms, was soon overtaken by the speedy *Bear*, which, closing to hailing distance, ordered her to dip her topsail in salute to the English Queen, and as token of surrender. But "she very stoutly never budged . . . notwithstanding that we frankly bestowed upon her vollies of shot, both great and small, warmly maintaining the same for the space of five or six hours".

This matter-of-fact audacity against a much larger and better-armed opponent was in the full tradition of Drake, Frobisher and Grenville, for the Spaniard, which returned fire in good measure though without as yet inflicting damage, was no merchant vessel but a man-of-war, "a very fine snug long ship, having in each side six ports open, beside her chase and stern pieces. Her ordnance lying well to pass, she went as upright as a church . . . having fine contrived close fights (*protection along the bulwarks*) with nettings and graplings".

Evening fell, and as "the resolution of our worthy young General was to have a further saying with her", he ordered Jobson to "command the gunners to make ready all such great pieces of ordnance as were not already dismounted, as also to make good store of cartridge against the morning, to give this our proud consort a warm breakfast, keeping them waking in the night now-and-then with a cross-bar shot. And to say the truth, they were not idle, neither did their light go out all the night, but still rummaging, as it seemeth, for their defence."

"So in the morning, by break of day, our good ship being put in her best trim, Captain Jobson caused the colours of our country, and of our General, to be advanced to the tops, poops and shrouds of our ship." Soon Dudley "came forth unarmed, having only his leading staff in his hand, saluted, and took his standing on the open deck, where he might best see and be seen of his enemies".

The Spaniard opened fire, the *Bear* replied, and the exchanges continued "with as great a fury as hath been seen at any time in these affairs". The enemy "made many and dangerous shot, especially exceeding near the very face and head of our General", until at length one "struck the very blade of his leading staff into many pieces, going within a handful of his head, having before torn the sails, cut the shrouds, and pierced the ship very near the place of his standing; yet would he not budge or move by any means".

This was Dudley's first experience of battle at sea, indeed his baptism of fire of any kind, and he bore himself under it with courage and resolution. "Our General fought the galleon always to windward, within musket shot", wrote Kendal. At this range, the enemy fire could not fail to do damage, though miraculously wounding only one man, who was shot through the leg: "which our General perceiving, caused him to be sent down to our surgeon, and did afterwards most honourably comfort him with his promise of an almsman's room in his hospital of Warwick".[9]

One of the heroes of the fight was Dudley's page, "Mr. William Bradshew, whom Captain Jobson ever called his son". This enthusiastic youth, incessantly charging and discharging his musket, eventually broke it. Jobson, observing, took him by the arm to Dudley, indicated the damaged weapon, and there, in the heat of the fight, recited a lengthy verse from a currently popular play, The Spanish Tragedy, beginning, "This is my son, gracious General", and ending " Long may he live to serve my General". This gesture, so much in tune with the consciously intrepid spirit of the age, was greatly to the liking of Dudley, himself so imbued with chivalrous notions. He "honourably acknowledged the most praiseworthy forwardness" of young Bradshew, and gave him "a delicate furniture" (a firearm or piece of armour) "of his own for his better encouragement and well-doing and valiance".

"Having fought this great armada of the King of Spain" for six hours on the Tuesday, and from first light until nightfall on Wednesday, "we gave him seven sound canvasadoes", attacks with every available weapon, and withdrew, with everyone amazed that after receiving so many wounds, she still remained afloat. For her injuries were far more serious than those she had inflicted on the Bear.

This ascendancy was the more creditable because the already storm-battered Bear had held to her running action with only four pieces of ordnance, the remainder having been unfortunately stowed too deep in the hold during the day's stop at the Azores. Only fifteen barrels of powder were usable, the rest having been soddened during the month of storms and heavy seas. "If we had had but two barrels more", lamented Wyatt, "we undoubtedly should have seen their miserable end in short time."

As Dudley, who assessed the galleon at a higher tonnage than Wyatt, afterwards wrote, ". . . a great armada . . . with whom I fought board and board for two days, being in no way able in all possibility with fifty men (*he actually had more, probably seventy*) to board a man-of-war of 600 tons. And having spent all my powder, I was constrained to leave her, yet in such distress, without sails and masts, and hull so often shot through with my great ordnance between wind and water, that being 300 leagues from land, I dare say it was impossible for her to escape sinking. Thus leaving her by necessity in this miserable estate, I made for England, where I arrived at St. Ives in Cornwall about the latter end of May, 1595."

CHAPTER VII

IN THE VAN AT CADIZ

DUDLEY BROKE THE journey up to London by staying with his cousin, Mary Sidney, Sir Philip's sister, and the wife of Henry Herbert, Earl of Pembroke. At Wilton House, their splendid mansion near Salisbury, where Philip had written his *Arcadia*, he first learned that during his six months' absence, his wife, Margaret, had sickened of the plague and died.

This melancholy news heightened the weakness which had come as the result of the hardships of the latter part of the voyage, a not surprising consequence, for a mere stripling did not possess the stamina of such tough sea-dogs as his captains and crew. It was not difficult for the earl and his warm-hearted countess and their two sons to persuade him to stay awhile with them. But Dudley's sorrow, sincere as it must have been, was before long put aside, for not only was he very young, with real love yet to touch him, but he had the distraction of the ambitious plans which already possessed him, to launch another expedition to ascend the Orinoco and reach the land of golden cities that the chieftain, Armago, had described to Jobson.

It might well have been the sixty-year-old earl who, in understanding discussion with this breathless stripling hot from an adventurous voyage, advised him to lose no time in establishing a friend at Court, and who better than the Queen's Secretary, Sir Robert Cecil? From Wilton, therefore, on June 11th, Dudley addressed an appeal for Cecil's goodwill in the deferential, even self-abasing, manner that was obligatory at such levels of society.

"How much I honour you", he wrote, "and how infinitely I think myself tied unto you for your many honourable favours, which I understand by my mother . . . Sir, my true loving and honouring you is all the recompense I am able to make, which though it be not of worth sufficient to countervail the least part of your honour's kindness, yet I humbly beseech you to take it . . . I assure your honour you shall always command more than any gentleman in England."

The favours granted to Lady Douglas Stafford by Cecil, by which Dudley reckons he can lay claim to further favours, were concerned with her husband's work as ambassador in Paris, where he had lined up with the Cecils, father and son, against Walsingham and Leicester. Dudley continues:

"Let me entreat you not to take me as a complimental courtier, but as a plain-speaking sailor, that have learned to love them honestly and unfeignedly that he is so much bound to as your honour. The discourse of these matters I have seen, I leave until I wait upon you, which shall be when I have in some reasonable sort recovered my health, which hath not been altogether the best since I came; I am strong enough, but something dulled with the sea-fare. The best things I know I shall be glad to make known to your honour. So entreating pardon for my boldness . . . Your honour's poor friend to command in all duty and service . . . Ro: Duddeley."

In a cautious post-script he adds, "Let me entreat your honour to excuse my not writing to my lord your father, for I am afraid I should be troublesome to him".

His appeal, made on the ground of affection inspired by benefits received, especially to the hard-headed, and indeed cold-hearted Cecil, was indication of his still ingenuous character. What transpired when he met Cecil in London is not recorded, but it is safe to assume that his approach for ships and the Secretary's backing, supported by the hint as to "the best things I know", which meant where to find gold, was considerably shaken by the discovery that his ore samples were marcasite.

His disappointment at not holding a potential fortune in his hands could have been offset only trivially by the good luck of Captain Monck, who on his way to the Canaries had intercepted two Spanish ships, which he had seized and taken back to England as a more profitable course than scuppering them and following on his General.

Yet there can be little doubt that Dudley had made a certain name for himself. By "divers intelligences out of Spain" he learned that the Spanish man-of-war had indeed sunk. "In this voyage", he wrote, "I and my fleet took, sunk and burnt nine Spanish ships, which was loss to them, though I got nothing." From this summary, it seems that the two caravels, on their way home, took or sank three vessels. All this, and especially the successful outcome of the sea-fight, taken with his Trinidad and Orinoco explorations, showed him to be a resolute youngster of very promising calibre. And although he could not know it, his voyage was to gain him a lasting, if modest, place among the maritime adventures of Elizabeth's reign.

Despite the setback over the pseudo-gold, he pressed on with his scheme to lead another expedition to Guiana, and with some degree of support from Cecil. But before long, he and his recent achievement were set in the shade, for in August Raleigh returned with the tale of how, after destroying the Spanish settlement in Trinidad, and capturing de Berrio, he had then ascended the Orinoco and mapped its main features. And although he had brought back no gold, for he was too astute to be deceived by the marcasite, he presented wonderful reports of the shining golden city that existed by its great lake just a few score miles further than he was able to penetrate.

Although there were some who accused him of invention, he became for a time with a public that normally distrusted him, something of a hero. The Queen, however, was not sufficiently impressed by his deeds to restore him to the favour he had forfeited four years previously for making pregnant a Maid of Honour,[10] Elizabeth Throckmorton, whom, after he had passed a spell in the Tower, he had reluctantly married.

The impact of his achievements may have been in some degree lessened by his having been forestalled. Rightly or wrongly, he thought that Dudley had deliberately stolen a march on him, and his resentment was shown with a littleness of spirit that was unworthy of a man of such brilliant attainment and intellect, especially when directed against so youthful a rival. For he too proposed to lead another expedition to Guiana, and when he heard of Dudley's plans, he wrote disparagingly to Cecil in November.

"What becomes of Guiana I much desire to hear, whether it pass for a history or a fable. I hear Mr. Dudley and others are sending thither; if it be so, farewell all good from thence, for although myself, like a cockscomb, did rather prefer the future in respect of others, and rather sought to win the kings to Her Majesty's service than to sack them, I know what others will do when those kings shall come simply into their hands. If it may please you to acquaint my Lord Admiral therewith, let it then succeed as it will."

Although Raleigh was out of royal favour and office, his views on oversea explorations carried weight, even with such men as Howard and Cecil. His warning was unjust, for as he could easily have learned, Dudley had treated the Trinidad natives with exemplary humanity, but mischief did its work, and despite the goodwill which Dudley had so far found in Cecil, he now met only frustration. And although he could not have known of Raleigh's letter, he did know of his jealousy, and certainly suspected him of being the cause of his difficulties.

This, combined with the deflation of his pride at having his own creditable voyage outshone, is made apparent in the account which he wrote of it, with obvious reluctance, at the importunity of his dead wife's brother-in-law, Richard Hakluyt. This cleric, now the Prebend of Westminster, had begun to collect the stirring records of voyages and explorations that were one day to enshrine his literary fame. Dudley's brief and staid account seems to have been written in a mood of deprecation, as if he wished his journey, and by inference, Raleigh's too, to be regarded as nothing out of the ordinary.

This attitude was doubtless also in reaction to Raleigh's publication, in the spring of 1596, of his *Discoverie of Guiana*, written with much colourful detail and unlaboured skill, which except for one casual reference to "Master Robert Dudley" having confirmed reports of El Dorado, completely ignored his prior voyage, other than in an oblique sneer at anyone who could mistake marcasite for gold.

Dudley's exasperation at this pettiness, and at the negation of his burning ambitions, was the deeper because Raleigh had been a friend and protégé of his father's. As the months went by without the grant of sailing orders for the West Indies, or indeed any commission for any voyage, his hostility inevitably mounted higher and higher. His resentment was in no way lessened by the departure in August of a large expedition under Drake and Hawkins for warlike action against the Spanish Main and Indies. With them went, as navigator, Abraham Kendal, and it is not beyond supposition that Dudley was one of the flood of volunteers who offered their services in vain to the most distinguished captains of the day.

His chagrin at his failure to gain Cecil's active help would have been tempered had he known that Raleigh, despite his friendship with the little Secretary, was meeting with similar disappointment in his efforts to be allotted ships for his own venture. Cecil not only had no great faith in Raleigh's tales of gold and diamonds, but simply could not find the vessels, for the reason that they were needed for an enterprise of far greater urgency and importance.

King Philip of Spain was again menacing England. Since the defeat of his Armada eight years previously, he had built up another immense navy, which Elizabeth and her councillors feared was intended for a second attempt at invasion. By land, he had set about conquering

France, and with such success that he was now threatening Calais. In 1595, therefore, Queen and Council resolved that their country must again possess a powerful fleet, and more, that it must be employed, not defensively, as when the first Armada emerged, but offensively against Spain herself, as Drake and Raleigh had then vainly urged.

Dudley may have realised that the provision of ships for Drake's fleet of twenty-seven sail had helped thwart his own plans, but even more must he have seen the futility of further effort when he learned at the turn of the year of the extensive mobilisation of men-of-war and supporting vessels that the Lord Admiral was directing in readiness for the expected tussle with Spain.

To him had gone the task of organising and fitting out this large fleet, which was to be under the command of two Lords General, himself for naval operations, and the Earl of Essex, more than ever the Queen's cherished Favourite, for land fighting. Seeing here the opportunity to make good his recent frustrations, Dudley threw energy and influence into persuading Howard and Cecil to grant him a place in the expedition.

In spite of his immature years, the experience gained in the West Indies voyage won him, in March, 1596, a commission as a naval captain. To his immense elation, he was appointed to the command of a man-of-war of the Queen's Royal Navy, the 500-ton greatship Nonpareil, which bore the proud record of having been one of Drake's squadron in the defeat of the Armada. The Nonpareil joined the rest of the fleet collecting in the Thames estuary, and here Dudley found that Raleigh too was to take part in the campaign in the role of rear-admiral to Howard. The other flag-officer was Lord Thomas Howard, son of the executed Duke of Norfolk, and Dudley's second cousin once removed.

The enterprise for which such portentous preparations were being made was kept a close secret, and the excitement which the prospect of the unknown generated among the officers and crews of the multitude of vessels now anchored in the estuary came to a climax half-way through April, when news came that Calais had fallen to the King of Spain's troops.

It was at this ugly hour that despatches arrived telling of the disastrous outcome of the West Indies expedition, for not only had it suffered a severe repulse at Puerto Rico, but both Drake and Hawkins had died of disease. The shadow cast over the whole country at the loss of these magnificent captains was to Dudley the deeper, because on the same January day as Drake, and of the same dread pestilence, had also died his comrade of the *Bear*, Abraham Kendal.

This setback, added to the apparent imminence of invasion, all but held the new expedition to a defensive role in the Channel, but towards the end of April, the Queen allowed Howard to sail his fleet to Plymouth. Here were waiting thousands of troops, mostly levies, but also the seasoned veterans whom Sir Francis Vere, ablest of Elizabeth's generals, had brought back from the wars in Flanders, as well as hundreds of gentlemen volunteers and adventurers who had flocked to the banner of the popular Earl of Essex, all spoiling for a fight and even more for plunder.

On June 3rd, the fleet set out from Plymouth for a destination unknown to all but a handful of the leaders. It was organised into four squadrons, each with its admiral and vice-admiral. The Admiral of the Fleet, Lord Howard, was also admiral of the First Squadron in his flagship, the *Ark*, with his son-in-law, Sir Robert Southwell, as his vice-admiral in the *Lion*. The Second Squadron was led by Essex, in *Repulse*, whose captain was William Monson, the vice-admiral being Sir Francis Vere in *Rainbow*. The admiral of the Third Squadron, Lord Thomas Howard in his flagship *Merhonour*, was also vice-admiral of the Fleet, and had as his squadronal vice-admiral, Dudley in the *Nonpareil*. The Fourth Squadron was led by Raleigh in *Warspite*, his vice-admiral being Drake's favourite flag-officer, Captain Robert Crosse, in *Swiftsure*.

Other leading officers included Sir Richard Leveson in *Truelove*, Sir George Carew, Master of the Ordnance, in *Mary Rose*, Sir Conyers Clifford, Sergeant-Major to the Army, in *Dreadnaught*, the Earl of Sussex in *Vanguard*, and Sir Christopher Blount in *Lioness*. There was also a Dutch squadron of twenty-six sail, but this was intended to fill only a supporting role.

The fleet of some 120 men-of-war and auxiliaries, English and Dutch, carried a force of 14,000 English, of whom 6,500 were soldiers, and 2,500 Dutch. Among the soldiery, as Dudley would certainly have known, was Captain Thomas Wyatt of the *Bear*, commanding "a hundred men out of Kent".

Driving south past Finisterre, the fleet seized every foreign vessel encountered, in order to preserve surprise, and arrived without incident on June 18th at a point some twelve leagues off Cadiz. It was not long before every man knew what lay ahead. Whatever the plan, fortified

Cadiz, perched on a steep rock at the point of a narrow five-miles isthmus, was a difficult proposition for an attacking force.

Behind the isthmus lay an outer haven giving approach to an inner haven. Because of shoals and reefs, access through the outer haven, three miles across, was by a channel that narrowed to a half-mile wide passage, covered by the guns of Fort Puntal, and leading to the inner haven. This was the hornet's nest that Drake had so boldly entered and ravaged nine years before, the renowned singeing of the King of Spain's beard that every ardent spirit now longed to emulate.

Plans for the attack had counted on penetrating to the calm waters of the inner haven to land troops on the isthmus for the assault of the city. But as the fleet drew closer to shore, there could be seen, deployed across the channel under the guns of the forts, seventeen galleons reinforced by a group of twenty galleys. This formidable obstacle, announcing that the expected advantage of surprise had vanished, forced Howard and his council of officers to think again. After three days of heated argument, of plan and counterplan, of changes of mind upon whether to land troops from the open sea or force a passage through the channel to the inner haven, Howard, mainly at Raleigh's urging, agreed to fight his way through.

In the temporary absence of Lord Thomas Howard, the opportunistic Raleigh persuaded Howard to let him lead the attack with a vanguard that was to include the ships of Southwell, Vere and Dudley. But Lord Thomas, re-appearing, insisted that as vice-admiral, the honour was his. And because his flagship, *Merhonour*, drew too much water to manoeuvre safely among the shallows that edged the navigable channel, he transferred his flag to Dudley's *Nonpareil*.

Meanwhile, the Spanish fleet had changed its disposition, the galleys withdrawing to the inner haven, followed shortly by the galleons, which took up position in the Fort Puntal waist. On the evening of June 20th, the English fleet advanced and anchored off the entrance to the outer haven.

At sunrise, in spite of the precedencies agreed upon, there was a rush among the leaders to get at first grips with the enemy, followed by brazen attempts to elbow each other's ships out of the fighting line. The instigator of this scramble was Raleigh, the earliest to weigh anchor, who took the lead across the outer haven, followed closely by Thomas Howard and Dudley in *Nonpareil*, Southwell in the *Lion*, Carew in the *Mary Rose* and Clifford in the *Dreadnaught*.

But as the passage narrowed at Fort Puntal, Raleigh saw his way blocked by the four largest galleons of Spain, known from their names as the Apostles, which had moored head to stern across the navigable channel, so as to present their broadsides to the attackers. Disconcerted by his hot reception from these floating batteries, which were supported by the fire of the galleys in rear, as well as by the Puntal batteries, he dropped anchor, and the other leaders, in their first surprise, followed suit.

Then Thomas Howard and Dudley, seeing their chance, weighed anchor and thrust the *Nonpareil* past Raleigh's *Warspite*, and also Vere's *Rainbow*, which had meanwhile arrived from a secondary fight off Cadiz. Dudley's ship thus took up the most advanced position, under the full blast of the enemy fire. But Raleigh, not to be outdone, also weighed anchor, nosed his vessel past *Rainbow* and *Nonpareil*, and slewed her across the channel so that he could only be passed with risk of fouling the shoals.

Then Essex, angry at these high-handed actions by a man he heartily disliked, pushed the *Repulse* through to the front, at the cost of fouling the *Dreadnaught*, until he came level with *Warspite*. Other ships closed up behind, including the *Merhonour*, whose guns were then able to join in the action. Lord Thomas returned to her, leaving Dudley in sole charge of his *Nonpareil*, still among the four vessels in the van of the fight.

No very vivid imagination is needed to picture his pride and exultation at this place of honour among the elite of England's fighting men, commanding his own ship, with his 250 gallant soldiers and sailors, his thirty cannon, and his twenty-two quickfirers. This was indeed fine compensation for his lost Guiana venture, and a more than perfect satisfaction of his longing to bear risk and responsibility.

For the fight was now well joined, with a fierce fire, as hotly returned, coming without pause from the Spanish ships. As Raleigh recorded, ". . . the volleys of cannon and culverin came as thick as if it had been a skirmish of musketeers". The English vessels were at a disadvantage, for as Vere wrote, ". . . they held us to good talk by reason their ships lay athwart with their broadsides towards us, and most of us right ahead, so that we could use but our chasing pieces".

For three hours, from ten o'clock in the morning, the exchange of fire went on. "The ships that abode the fight", recorded Raleigh, "were the *Warspite*, the *Nonpareil*, the *Lion*, the *Mary Rose*, the *Rainbow* and the *Dreadnaught*. To second these came up the Earl in *Repulse*, and the *Swiftsure*, and these were all that did aught against six goodly galleons, two argosies, three frigates, seventeen galleys and the Fort of Puntal."

At length the more accurate English gunnery told, and the Spanish fire slackened. Raleigh, seeing that the time had come to board, tried to get alongside the enemy flagship, the *San Felipe*, and his lead was followed by the more advanced vessels, *Nonpareil* among them. But the Spaniards had had enough. As the English ships edged forward to board, the Apostles slipped their cables and drifted on to the shoals. Panic followed, the crews flinging themselves overboard, "heaps of soldiers, so thick as if coals had been poured out of a sack", wrote Raleigh, "some drowned and some sticking in the mud".

But they had first fired the *San Felipe* and another Apostle, which were soon blazing furnaces. The other two were taken by Essex's troops before they could be set alight. The galleys and other vessels escaped into the inner haven, beyond reach for the present. The Spanish losses in men amounted to many hundreds, but the English had suffered lightly, one of the few casualties being Raleigh, with a shell splinter in the leg.

And now Essex and Vere moved to the assault of Cadiz. The soldiery embarked in the barges and flyboats, and at four o'clock an unopposed landing was made between Fort Puntal and the city. After sharp fighting, the defences were penetrated, and within two hours, Cadiz was taken.

The next few hours were given up to riotous sack, the soldiery, tipsy on unlimited supplies of wine, breaking into houses, markets, friaries, any place where plunder might be won. The lead in the organised spoliation that followed was taken at first by the officers of Essex's army, but soon, Lord Howard, eager to share in the glory and profit of occupying the city, went ashore with most of his flag-officers, followed quickly by other officers and ratings in their hundreds, "all running headlong to the sack", says Raleigh, until the fleet was almost deserted. Raleigh himself was among them, but was so incapacitated by his wound that he had to be carried back to his ship. Later on, the sailors complained that the best of the spoil had been seized by the soldiers, but it is safe to assume that Dudley at least, with his alert and enterprising temper, would not have dawdled unduly.

The looting continued through the night and into the next day, for Cadiz was a rich city, terminal of the West Indies trade. In the palaces and mansions, the churches and convents, the warehouses and shops, booty was plentiful, booty such as ducats and jewels, gold and silver plate, pictures and other works of art, silks and merchandise of every kind. And although Queen Elizabeth was supposed to have the eagle's share of this treasure, there were few of even the highest ranking officers who did not handsomely feather their own nests first.

But such easy winning of wealth demoralised both officers and men, with the result that they failed to respond when the Lords General required their assembly to seize the Spanish ships trapped in the inner haven. Here, in addition to the galleys and other men-of-war, was a convoy of treasure ships and merchantmen, which offered the chance of even richer booty than that of Cadiz. But while the English dallied, the Spaniards acted, and with magnificent self-sacrifice, set fire to them all. Forty greatships, valued with their cargoes at up to twenty million ducats, were soon blazing in a fantastic holocaust, and of all the scores of vessels that might have been won, only the two captured Apostles ever reached England.

Howard now held several conferences on the future course of action. Essex and some of his supporters wanted to garrison Cadiz and hold it as an English possession, or else to sail to the Azores to intercept the Spanish fleet due in from the Indies. The majority, glutted with loot, desired only to get it safely back to England, and this was the course decided on.

But first, in Cadiz, victory had to be celebrated, and on Sunday, June 27th, prior to a service of thanksgiving in the Abbey, Essex and Howard signalled their success by conferring knighthoods on over sixty of the chief officers, including several who had taken little or no part in the fighting. It is difficult to understand why Dudley was not included in the list, not only because the expedition's leaders were his relations by blood and marriage, a sufficient reason in days when nepotism was normal and proper, but because he had played a much more vital and valiant part in the naval battle than many of those who now received the accolade.

It is possible that he was overlooked because at the time of the ceremony he was in the *Nonpareil*, or he might even have been sick, or he may merely have been too proud to push himself forward. Certainly, Essex's generous nature would hardly have ordered the omission because of any lingering animosity over the Kenilworth trouble with his mother, even if Blount had been an adverse influence. Still less would Raleigh have influenced a decision. Yet not until several weeks later were Dudley's services recognised.

Before then came the re-embarkation and the return journey. For days, the fleet, held by calms and hostile winds, was unable to double

Cape St. Vincent. As a diversion, a landing was made in Algarve in Portugal, and the town of Faro sacked and burnt. This inglorious affair left its mark in English history simply because among the loot was the library of the Bishop of Osorio, which was taken by Essex, and later given by him to his supporter, Sir Thomas Bodley, who with it formed the nucleus of the Bodleian Library at Oxford University.

When at last St. Vincent was left behind, contrary winds still delayed the passage northwards. It was Sunday, August 8th, when Howard and Essex arrived at Plymouth with the main body of the fleet, and it was then, after divine service, that the omission of June 27th was made good. Dudley was knighted "in the open street, when the Lords General came from the sermon", with his fellow officers, the soldiery, and the curious citizens looking on. Hakluyt, recording the incident, adds for good measure that Dudley was "of so many good parts of a worthy gentleman as the like are seldom seen to concur in any".

The honour of knighthood, overdue as it was, must have swelled him with a great pride. It was more than a recognition that he had taken a gallant part in England's most important military exploit since the defeat of the Armada. It was a testimony that he had proved himself worthy of the blood that flowed in his veins, the blood of the fabulous Dudleys, and of the glorious Howards, who had given England three Queens.

He had held his own in the forefront of battle at the side of stalwarts such as his blood kinsmen, Howard of Effingham and Thomas Howard, and his relations, Essex, Southwell and Leveson, and others like Raleigh, Vere, Crosse, Carew and Monson. Among this company of England's finest warriors, he had won his spurs. And his years were still not twenty-two.

CHAPTER VIII

"THE *BEAR'S WHELP*"

THE CADIZ ADVENTURE had not only elevated Dudley to the order of knighthood, but had given him a new romantic glamour as one of the select band of heroic stalwarts of the day, headed by those rival cavaliers, Essex and Raleigh. Undoubtedly he spent some little time at Court, sharing in the adulation lavished on the leading actors in this latest English naval drama, but although he was now a more desirable matrimonial prospect than ever before, he managed to avoid becoming involved with any of the flirtatious Maids of Honour, or in the intrigues that swirled constantly around them.

Instead, retiring to Warwickshire, he renewed contact with a near neighbour with several daughters, by whom he was regarded even more than in London as a most distinguished hero. The neighbour was the Thomas Leigh who, with Fulke Greville and other justices of the peace, had a few years previously rescued Kenilworth from the clutches of the Lady Lettice. Now a baronet, Leigh was a wealthy merchant who had once been Lord Mayor of London, and who in that capacity had ridden before Queen Elizabeth on her way to her crowning at St. Paul's. From the Queen, he had acquired Stoneleigh Abbey,[11] on the Avon, some three miles from Kenilworth, and here he and his wife, Catherine, had established themselves among the local quality. They had known Leicester, who once stayed at the Abbey after a fall from his horse.

Despite his illegitimacy, Dudley was an aristocrat, related by blood to the highest families in the land, and the owner of great and historic estates. Now by his service and gallantry he was a knight. To Sir Thomas, he seemed a highly desirable match for one of his daughters, and to the daughters he seemed a no less desirable match because of his dash and elegance and good looks. In return, Sir Thomas could offer not only a virtuous wife, brought up in piety, with a handsome dowry, together with a share of his fortune when he died, but what may have been to Dudley a not unimportant factor, the prospect of financial backing for the seagoing ventures after which he still hankered.

Whether a marriage was in fact arranged in this materialistic fashion, as was customary and entirely seemly, or whether Dudley plunged as impulsively into this new matrimonial contract as he had done into the others, is not on record. But at some time early in 1596, he was married at Kenilworth to Sir Thomas's attractive second daughter, Alice. "She brought him a fair portion", and he effected a jointure in her favour on the timber in the Kenilworth estate, valued at around £20,000.

But the charms of his seventeen-year-old bride, however fresh, did not keep him at Kenilworth, for he was much too absorbed in his maritime interests to remain away long from London. More than ever was he fascinated by the practices of marine navigation, and to such good purpose that he astonishingly invented two mathematical instruments, a new type of compass and a complicated apparatus for finding the ebb and flow of the tides. To add to this achievement, he produced, a year or so later a volume "on the true and real art of navigation, with many curious mathematical and astronomical figures, and other things never before seen, such as nautical instruments for the observation of the variations of longitude and latitude, and others for the horizontal and spiral navigation, and about the Great Circles. Of these, however, common sailors understand little".

Clearly, his fast developing knowledge continued to lift far above the average of the time, especially among the well-born young men whose horizons were limited to fighting Spaniards or playing the courtier in the hope of winning a smile from the Queen. With his enquiring intellect, he not only studied for enlightenment but to probe into fundamentals, to find new ways, to bring out new conceptions. In his learning, he showed that same questing spirit, so much in the temper of the Elizabethan age, that had already thrust him into the West Indian and Cavendish voyages, and was now to impel him to a further enterprise.

For in addition to experimenting with the technical aspects of seamanship, he returned to the active promotion of maritime commerce. The path had been blazed for him by his father and his uncle Ambrose, who by monetary and other support of such seamen as Frobisher, Hawkins and Drake, had played a significant part in launching England towards her destiny as a great seafaring nation. Their example he decided not merely to follow but to better. His voyage to the West Indies had cost much and brought little but adventure, for the gold of the Incas was still but a dream. The squadron he had sent to the

Eastern Seas under Cavendish had failed miserably, and cost him even more. Yet his imagination was still fired by the prospect of vast fortunes to be made, not now by piracy or digging up gold, but by trading with the populous lands of the Orient.

For a century the Portuguese and Spaniards had drawn immense wealth by dealing with the people of India, Ceylon, Burma, Malaya and the Philippines. In recent years, the Dutch had trespassed upon this profitable traffic, to the tune of now maintaining fifty vessels on the India route. Only England had hitherto lagged behind. A solitary merchant, the intrepid Ralph Fitch, had, between the years 1584 and 1589, reached India, Burma and Malaya, travelling overland by Aleppo and the Euphrates valley. But apart from the passages of the circumnavigators Drake and Cavendish, only one English expedition had so far penetrated these eastern seas with the primary purpose of opening up trade. These were the ships led by the experienced sailor, James Lancaster, which during the period 1591 to 1594 had reached Penang, but which had suffered dire losses, all the ships but one being lost, and nine-tenths of the crews, Lancaster [12] himself narrowly escaping death.

The London merchants who had financed the voyage and lost their all, were in no hurry to risk more money in further ventures to the East. But Dudley, as one of the ardent spirits anxious to join the brave new enterprise of winning a share of the far eastern trade, was in no way discouraged by the ugly precedent of Lancaster's failure, nor even that of Cavendish. He resolved to forestall the hesitant merchants by establishing direct trading relations on his own account, not only with India and Malaya, but with the much more distant Empire of China, the still inviolate El Dorado of commerce. It was Cavendish who had planted in his mind the hankering to reach the incredible Celestial Kingdom, the mysterious cities of Cathay. Not even the Portuguese and Spaniards and Dutch had succeeded in landing on these hostile shores. Dudley determined to be the first of all to do so.

He had disposed of the *Leicester* and *Roebuck* used by Cavendish, but he still had his two ships of the Trinidad fleet, the *Bear* and the *Bear's Whelp*, and the records show that he now received the Queen's customary bounty of five shillings a ton as the owner of a newly built merchantman, which he called the *Benjamin*. "There was something touching about these names", wrote an understanding modern historian.[13] "The bear was the family crest of the dead Leicester, the bear's whelp was Dudley, Leicester's son, his Benjamin who could never be recognised, though it was he who carried in his blood the ability and the passionate interest in the country's maritime expansion of his father and grandfather."

The expense of providing and fitting out a fleet of trading vessels for so long a cruise was very high,[14] much higher than for the West Indies expedition, but according to Hakluyt, the voyage was undertaken "principally at the charge of the honourable knight, Sir Robert Dudley", which should certainly have strained his resources, even when supplemented by his share, declared and hidden, of the Cadiz loot. The supposition is reasonable that some portion of the money was provided by Sir Thomas Leigh and other merchants.

Throughout the autumn of 1596, Dudley was well occupied in the transactions of commissioning his ships for their arduous journey. First there was the formal application for a patent to sail and trade, sustained by an estimate of the profits to be expected, and by a vindication of the competence of those in command. This procedure had to be facilitated, as was normal, with the bribery of every official concerned with the granting of a charter, from Cecil downwards. Indeed, the Queen herself would insist on her fair share of the gains.

Greater precautions than on the West Indian trip had to be taken against attack, from both corsairs and Spanish or Portuguese fighting ships. Every vessel had to be well armed with long and short range cannon, and crewed generously with soldiers to serve them, and to resist boarding. Then there was the business of victualling for a couple of years, and of buying a wide assortment of woollen cloths and other merchandise for trading. There was also the matter of finding officers, especially the masters, on whom the fate of the whole expedition depended. Dudley solved the main problem by placing in command of all three vessels the experienced Captain Benjamin Wood, his master of the *Bear*, and with him went two London merchants, engaged as supercargoes. Not so readily settled was the task of recruiting crews, for too many of the far-ranging voyages had ended in disaster, and men had to be impressed largely from the lowest levels of the seagoing community.

The Queen's commission finally granted, the expedition set out towards the end of 1596, its proud hopes attested by the letter, in Latin, which Wood carried, "A Gracious Commendation by Her Majesty to the Great Emperor of China". Why Dudley himself did not lead his venture is nowhere stated, for his restless spirit could have wished for nothing better. Perhaps the fact that his wife was longing for a child may have induced him to withdraw. Perhaps the Queen, just as she had stopped him from essaying the long East Indies trip a little over two years ago, again held a protecting hand over the only blood kin of the man she had loved. If this were so, the day was to come when Dudley would have cause to be grateful for her intervention.

His preoccupation with the despatch of his fleet had prevented him from taking part in another marine enterprise, a naval incursion which the mercurial Essex had induced the Queen to allow him to lead once more against the Spanish King. But this time, the Favourite was in full command, with Thomas Howard, Raleigh and Sir Charles Blount as his vice-admirals. The fleet sailed in the summer of 1597, with the object of attacking the Azores and intercepting the Spanish treasure fleet, but bad luck and bad leadership brought failure. Essex returned from the Island Voyage, as it came to be known, in October, having accomplished nothing but a few destructive raids.

During this fruitless escapade, Dudley was at Kenilworth awaiting the birth of his child. It could have been now that he found time to turn to the pleasures of the chase in which his father had shown such zest all through his life. Over the extensive Kenilworth lands ranged red and fallow deer, against which he may have used the cross-bow, as his father had always preferred to do, and he would have found exciting sport with wild boar and badger. He was adept in falconry and hawking. He used dogs in driving and retrieving game, and long afterwards it was told of him that not only was he a fine huntsman, but he was, in England, "the first that taught a dog to sit in order to catch partridges".

In September, a daughter was born at Kenilworth, and on the 25th she was baptised there in the name of Alice Douglas, an indication that Dudley's mother was in friendly touch with her son's wife and family. For the next few months, Dudley remained at the Castle, attending to his estates, and also expanding them, for in February, 1598, a "Deed of Bargain and Sale was executed by Sir John Throckmorton and others, whereby the Manor of Ladbrooke (*lying to the south-west of Warwick*), was conveyed to Sir Robert Dudley and Dame Alice, his wife, and to his heirs".

That he also passed part of his year in London is indicated by his taking possession of a residence there, Dudley House in St. Giles-in-the-Fields, which had belonged to his grandfather, and for some years to his father, and which came to his hands during this period. Alice Dudley, as she was to show in a later phase of her life, liked the house, and spent some of her time there with him, but Kenilworth probably claimed her more, for she was again expecting a child, and before the end of the year, another daughter, Frances, was born.

That Dudley, with or without his wife, moved in the Court, and also in the associated circles that made up London social life, is certain, if only because of the several blood relations who kept establishments there. Most prominent of these was his uncle, the Lord High Admiral, recently created Earl of Nottingham, whose wife, Katherine Carey, was one of Elizabeth's closest kinswomen and friends, and whose Arundel House in the Strand, as well as his manor at Chelsea, would surely have welcomed young Robert.

At Baynard's Castle, near St. Paul's Wharf, lived the Earl of Pembroke, and his wife Mary, whose sons, William and Philip, both good friends of Dudley, were well to the fore in all that occurred around the Court—"the most Noble and Incomparable Paire of Brethren," to whom the First Folio of Shakespeare's plays was dedicated.

Dudley's aunt, Frances Howard, Countess of Hertford, had a house in Cannon Row, while another Frances Howard, his cousin, who had married Lord Cobham after the death of her first husband, the Earl of Kildare, lived in Blackfriars. Other relations with London houses were his father's sister, Catherine, Countess of Huntingdon, and his cousins of varying degree, Lady Elizabeth Southwell, Lord Hunsdon, Lord Thomas Howard, and Lord Henry Howard. Dudley's mother too, now a Lady of the Bedchamber, had a London residence, for Sir Edward Stafford was both monied and well seen by the Queen.

Of all the great mansions open to him, Essex House, which was to come to him on the Lady Lettice's death, probably drew him most often, with its spacious courtyard, its Great Chamber, and its magnificent Hall giving on to the terrace and elaborate gardens running down to the Banqueting House by the Thames water-gate. The frictions that had followed Lettice's attempt to seize Kenilworth had, so far as her son was concerned, abated, especially since the comradeship-in-arms of Cadiz. Essex was the dashing leader of a group of young intellectuals and aristocrats who met at his house to dabble in the arts, philosophy and politics. In opposition to them was a similar set led by Raleigh, recently admitted by the Queen to her favour and restored to his post of Captain of the Guard, who acted as host at his splendid Durham House in the Strand, once the home of Dudley's grandfather, the executed Duke of Northumberland.

It was to be expected that Dudley would align himself with the Essex House faction, partly because his resentment against Raleigh had still not subsided, partly because he could not fail to be drawn by his step-brother's chivalrous and venturous personality, so much the mirror of his own. At Essex House he would find such gallants as Fulke Greville, Charles Blount, John Harington, Anthony and Francis Bacon, the Earl of Southampton and his protégé, William Shakespeare, as well as other writers such as John Donne, Ben Johnson and Michael Drayton, the last engaged in compiling his lengthy *Polyolbion*, in which he gave due praise to Dudley's West Indian voyage.

Although Dudley's interests lay primarily in science, he continued his earlier trifling with the role of patron of poetry and drama, as was the mode for the sophisticated young aristocrat, though he did not possess the baronial rank needed for authority to maintain his own company of players, as his father and uncle Ambrose had done, and as the Lord Admiral and other relations were doing now.

In addition to these superficially cultural activities, he could hardly have avoided cutting something of a dash at Court. He was no less lively and gay than the boisterous young blades whom he encountered there and at Essex House and the Inns of Court and other meeting places, he had the background of wealth and quality, and also of handsome presence—"A person of stature tall and comely", recorded Sir William Dugdale, "also strong, valiant, and famous at the exercise of tilting."

The miniature (*see* frontispiece) which was painted of him about this time by Nicholas Hilliard shows that he had all of his father's early grace and distinction. He was just as tall and handsome, with a fine open brow, and the stamp of the aristocrat in his features. The miniature shows too that he followed the ostentatious style of attire which was then the hallmark of fashion, reflecting the swaggering spirit of the times.

Yet he seems not to have fallen under the corrupting influence of the Court. That he still avoided entanglement with any of the Maids of Honour is surprising, especially as his step-brother set him a bold pattern of promiscuity during this period. For the splendid Essex was not only adored by the Queen and the general populace, but also by most of the Maids, with four of whom he had affairs at the same time, his equally adoring wife, Frances Walsingham, widow of Sir Philip Sidney, being then pregnant.

When one of the four, Elizabeth Southwell,[15] half-sister of Sir

Robert, also became pregnant, the child, a boy, being taken into the Essex family, the Earl lost face, for the Queen was always vexed when any of her attendant virgins, to whom she stood in *loco parentis*, became with child. However, he was soon forgiven, for Elizabeth doted on him with something of the fondness she had once lavished on Leicester.

But Essex was far from being the only Court philanderer, for morals and opportunities were easy. His cousin, Elizabeth Vernon, was seduced by the Earl of Southampton, who fell out of favour for marrying her without the royal assent. Some time later, Dudley's second cousin, young Lord William Herbert, had no sooner succeeded to the Pembroke earldom on the death of his father than the flighty Mary Fyton produced him a bastard son. He declined to marry her, but was still sent to the Fleet prison. There were adulterous affairs as well, such as the long and open liaison between Sir Charles Blount and Lady Penelope Rich, Essex's sister. And Essex, in addition to his Maids of Honour indiscretions was rumoured to be also the lover of the Countess of Derby, one of Lord Burghley's granddaughters.

That Dudley, in spite of the many temptations that must certainly have confronted him, under conditions when sexual lightness was accepted as an unavoidable human foible, kept clear of scandal is once more emphasised in view of later happenings, for he was no indiscriminate lover like his step-brother.

His easy run of life in London, especially as a member of the Essex set, came to an end early in 1599 through two developments. The first was Essex's impulsive decision to play the soldier once more, this time in rebellious Ireland. He persuaded the reluctant Queen to send him there as Lord Lieutenant, and on March 27th, set out from London as the commander of an army of 21,000 men, with orders to destroy the insurgent forces completely. With him went some of the finest sprigs of the nobility and gentry, but there is no record of Dudley having been among them.

The chief reason for his absence was probably the second development, which was his growing anxiety over the lack of news about his venture to the China Seas. As month after month went by, and no reports were brought by any English or Dutch vessel returning from the East, the possibility of misfortune grew ever stronger. For some time he was buoyed up with the hope that the vessels were merely delayed, that as Hakluyt wrote in 1599, "We have heard no certain news of them since February, 1597 . . . the ships, we do suppose, may be arrived upon some part of the coast of China, and may there be stayed by the Emperor, or perhaps may have some treachery wrought against them by the Portuguese of Macassa or the Spaniards of the Philippines".

But Hakluyt was only guessing. The fleet never returned, not one of the men from any of the three brave ships that had left England so confidently over two years before was ever seen by Dudley again. Not until after 1601 could he have discovered what had happened, for it was then that a Dutch ship calling for water at uninhabited Mauritius picked up a castaway French soldier, the sole survivor. But there is no record whatever of Dudley hearing from this man, or from Dutch informants, and so he could never have learned the full tragic story, for this, lying scattered in various Portuguese, Dutch and Spanish writings, was not pieced together until three centuries later.[16]

The three ships met trouble soon after rounding the Cape of Good Hope, when the *Benjamin* was lost with all hands in a storm. The others, chased by Portuguese men-of-war off Mozambique, crossed to India and Ceylon, where they captured and plundered two Portuguese merchantmen. Arriving in the Malacca Straits in January, 1598, they encountered a Portuguese fleet of six vessels, against which they kept up a running combat for eight days, withdrawing only when an unlucky shot exploded the gunpowder stored below in the *Bear*.

By now, so many of the crews had been lost from fighting and disease that the two ships could no longer be manned, and the *Whelp* was burned near Kedah, on the Malayan coast. The *Bear* set off northwards, but disease was taking daily toll, the victims now probably including Wood and his officers, for the remaining men could not manage the ship, which went ashore. Seven survivors made an incredible journey in a native canoe across the Indian Ocean to Mauritius, but of these only the Frenchman lived.

Ignorant of these grim happenings, Dudley was yet driven after years of uncertainty to the inevitable conclusion that his vessels and their crews had met with complete catastrophe, and disappeared without trace. The extinction of his golden dreams bore heavily on his usually buoyant spirit. The death of his trusted comrade, Wood, and of his officers and crews, was a sore enough blow, but no less cruel was the destruction of all his ships and their cargoes. Even had his father-in-law shared the cost of supplies for trading, the vessels were his, and his was by far the major burden. Yet, in spite of his previous losses in the Cavendish voyage, there is no record of his having to sell or mortgage any of his properties, or of being in monetary difficulties. The wealth he had inherited was very great indeed.

His reaction to this disaster was emphatic, for in spite of his continuing obsession with the sea, he never again financed a seagoing venture. Large as it was, his fortune could not suffer more than two such reverses. Yet although his single-handed efforts to establish trade in the Orient were not crowned with success, he deserved much merit as the first Englishman to try, largely at his own expense, and not once but twice, to breach the Portuguese-Spanish-Dutch grip of far eastern waters. His hope of opening contact with China was particularly bold, for trading relations with that suspicious country were not to be permitted until the end of the seventeenth century. In spite of failure, his name was to live as one of the first pioneers in the drive to trade with the East, that initially modest undertaking that was already blossoming out into the East India Company.

That he too, except perhaps for the Queen's ban, might have perished of some pestilence or in a roaring hurricane, abundantly moderated his longing for further personal nautical experience. Thankfully could he now reflect on the good fortune that had attended his West Indian voyage. And thankfully too could he realise that he had entered that adventure at the right hour, for in these later days the times were on the wane.

This second disaster, in so tempering his ardour, undoubtedly worked to set him in tune with the changing humour of the country. Like thousands of others, he could see that Queen Elizabeth was growing old, and that the vigour and derring-do with which she had fired her people was fading. Many of those who had helped her to create a new England had gone, chief among them her most trusted councillor, Lord Burghley, succeeded in his office by his second son, Robert Cecil. Even that spur to warlike attitudes, King Philip of Spain, had died too, and with him much of his country's implacable hostility. With their going, and the Queen's days numbered, a cold wind seemed to be blowing through England.

For Dudley, this atmosphere may have seemed the chillier because of the several bereavements which the period brought him. He lost an uncle, Sir William Howard, a cousin, Frances, Countess of Hertford, and two aunts, Lady Mary Dudley, and Lady Catherine Howard, whose whole life had been given to serving the Queen in her Privy Chamber. And that stout sea-dog Sir Robert Southwell had recently gone, just before his thirteen-year-old daughter, Elizabeth, "the fair young Mistress Southwell", the Queen's goddaughter, and Dudley's cousin once removed, had arrived at Court as the latest and loveliest of the Maids—to be greeted by her erring aunt, the other Elizabeth Southwell, mother of Essex's child, already back at Court, forgiven, married, and now the Lady Mollins.

The atmosphere of obscurity was deepened by developments in Ireland, where the brilliant Essex had failed. Disclosing himself as not even a second-rate general, he had allowed the campaign to peter out in a futile garrisoning of bases, then, infuriated by the Queen's reproaches, had returned without permission to London. He was soon committed to custody, and not freed until eleven months later, when he was barred the Court: and what was more hurtful, deprived of his monopoly of sweet wines, his main source of income.

Under these and other justified rebuffs, the weaknesses inherent in his character began to come through. Because he had risen to high estate effortlessly, by Leicester's aid and the Queen's favour, he became now the spoilt child of fortune, petulant, insolent and rebellious. Yet such was his charm and magnetism that he drew even solid and balanced men to his side, as well as every kindred irreconcilable in London.

Among his followers was Dudley, attracted partly by those tendencies in his own make-up that responded to his step-brother's head-strong nature, and partly because of his infection with the malaise into which many of the higher classes were sinking. After two years of plague and famine, there had dawned an uneasy apprehension that England's age of high adventure was passing, that young men of quality could no longer win quick gold and glory by piracy, and that disillusionment for all lay ahead.

By the end of the year, Essex House had become a centre not for patronage of the arts, but for those who rallied round the refractory Earl because of their own thwarted ambitions or unjust treatment, and especially those with a grudge against Cecil or Raleigh, Essex's particular abominations. Among this clamorous crowd, with its leavening of swashbuckling adventurers, there were many like Dudley, who had no real grievance with life or authority, but who were intoxicated by the eloquent bravado that transformed Essex into the personification of all that was still heroic and chivalrous in England. Not for a moment did they see him as he had really become, a gatherer of discontents, the victim of his too-demanding ambitions.

During meetings at Essex House and Southampton's Drury House, plots were laid by a handful of the leaders to seize Whitehall Palace and coerce the Queen into dismissing Cecil and Raleigh. Among the full list of conspirators were no fewer than a hundred and twenty earls, barons, knights and gentlemen of rank, ranging from the Earls of Southampton, Rutland and Bedford, and the Lords Cromwell and William and Philip Herbert down to Sir Christopher Blount, now his stepson's most fervid supporter, Sir John Harington, the Queen's god-son, Sir Charles Danvers, Sir John Davis, and somewhere on the fringe, Sir Robert Dudley.

Having made secret contact with King James of Scotland, from whom he had a not unencouraging response, Essex decided that the time had arrived to strike. But the watchful Cecil knew all that was going on, and when early in February, 1601, the imminence of revolt could no longer be ignored, Essex was summoned before the Privy Council to explain his actions. He declined to attend. Instead, on Sunday morning, February 8th, he led out from Essex House some three hundred wildy excited men, all brandishing swords as they rushed headlong into their crazy enterprise.

But the cool-headed Cecil had sent out heralds proclaiming Essex a traitor. When he marched up Ludgate Hill and into the City, con-fidently expecting his popularity to draw thousands to his side, not one man responded. Instead, many of his following, already repenting their rashness, drifted away. Realising he had failed, he set those who remained with him on the return journey. At Ludgate, troops awaited them, and there was fighting, in which the one-armed Sir Christopher Blount is said to have picked out and slain a soldier, Waite, who, recorded Camden, was "a person that Leicester, Blount's rival, had formerly sent into Holland to murder him".

Repulsed and dispersed, Essex and the remnants of the rebels made their way back to Essex House, which was soon surrounded by troops. The Lord High Admiral arrived to demand submission under threat of bombardment by cannon, and later, Sir Robert Sidney, Essex's close friend, accepted the surrender. The leaders were taken to the Tower, the lesser men to the Marshalsea, Clink and other prisons.

Whether Dudley took part in the march to the City is not established, but if he did, it is unlikely that he shared in the fighting. Although he was among the hundred men placed in custody, his association with Essex was regarded as insignificant, for he is not mentioned even in the list of those who were merely fined.

Yet his arrest is on record in a report in which the Florentine resident minister in London, Ottaviano Lotti, described the revolt to his master, the Grand Duke Ferdinand of Tuscany. In this letter,[17] Lotti names only three of those put into custody, Essex, Blount and Dudley, which suggests that he looked on Dudley as one of the ringleaders. As this he was certainly not, it is a mystery why Lotti should have selected his name for mention to the Grand Duke. A possible explanation is that Dudley knew him personally, as the link by which he kept in touch with Sir Thomas Chaloner, who at this time was acting as a special envoy at the Tuscan Court.

The trial of Essex and his closest supporters was carried out speedily. There could be no doubt over the result, and he was beheaded on February 25th on Tower Hill. Three weeks later, Blount and Danvers also knelt to the axe. Only three others lost their heads, but several spent long years in prison, or were released only on paying heavy fines. Dudley was among the remainder who by the Queen's clemency were pardoned. How long he spent in prison is not known. He was probably set free without trial or penalty as soon as it was clear that he was merely one of the impressionable young men who had been drawn into Essex's foolhardy exploit by his vehement personality, and not out of designs of treachery.

He had escaped drastic punishment, but he had had a salutary lesson. The thought that his brave and noble step-brother, despite the favour he enjoyed with the Queen, had gone to the block for a single mad riot, doomed to failure before it began, chastened his own impetuous spirit deeply. He knew he was fortunate not to have fallen into a similar fate. This was an age when life was held cheaply, and he had long proved that he was no coward, no physical weakling, but the sight of the heads of the executed men grinning from their poles above London Bridge, men with whom he had been in friendly talk almost up to the hour of revolt, was a sufficient warning to him then and in the future never to venture his neck within reach of the axe.

CHAPTER IX

"DIVERS FAIR LORDSHIPS"

DUDLEY RODE NORTH to Kenilworth. Subdued, under the heavy weight of the Queen's displeasure, banned from Court, where Raleigh was now the paramount influence, and for some time even from London, he retired into the relative obscurity of Warwickshire. And although after a while he was able to visit the capital occasionally, if only to see his mother, and to contemplate the ruin of his China Seas misadventure, he settled down with his still expanding family, for another girl, Anne, had arrived, and devoted his energies to hunting and the improvement of his estates.

The months passed by uneventfully, with the Queen, her spirit declining rapidly after the death of Essex, and with it her mind and body, seeming to the country and especially to the circles of her Court, to be obviously approaching her end. The close of an era was near, and soon everyone must adjust himself to the uncertainties of a new reign. Dudley had ample time to reflect upon what his own position might be when the change came. Would his possession of the once regal Kenilworth be challenged? Would his rights as his father's heir be contested by some new Favourite because of his bastardy? What would be his state as a mere knight with the smell of treason still about him?

With such uncertainties in the air, he was in every mood to respond when, some time late in 1602, he came in contact with a connection by marriage of his mother, one Thomas Drury, a link, remote as it was, that facilitated the raising of an issue which was to shape the whole of his future life. For Drury assured him that witnesses could be produced who would prove that he was his father's legitimate son, and the rightful heir to the Earldoms of Leicester and Warwick.

Until now, Dudley had not questioned that he was indeed Leicester's "base son". He may certainly have read in the *Commonwealth* that his mother's marriage "were as surely done as Bed and Bible could make the same", and also the reference to his father's Countess Lettice, "I marvel how you call her his wife, seeing the canon law standeth in force touching matters of marriage within the Realm". But these had no value, for he knew that the book was so impregnated with lies and invention that nothing in it could be accepted without confirmation. And if ever he had discussed his birth with his mother, she could only have told him that she possessed no written record of her wedding, that after so many years the witnesses were dead or had vanished, and that she would never mar the contentment of her present marriage by raking up the past.

Had the decision rested with him alone, he might have left things as they were. After all, he had inherited most of his father's estate, and had won distinction and a knighthood by his own efforts. In time he would surely rise high in his country's affairs. But he had a wife who, as later events were to show, aspired to great station. Through her maternal grandfather, she was a distant cousin of the Duke of Sutherland, and she felt herself to belong rightly to the aristocracy. Her father, though a knight and wealthy, was of plebian origin, and, conscious of the social gulf that existed between lords and commoners, would have been delighted to see it bridged by his daughter becoming Countess of Warwick and Leicester. Their rose-coloured ambitions dissipated any doubts that Dudley may have entertained.

This was not the first occasion on which he had been offered evidence of his legitimacy. Some four years previously, Owen Jones, his lackey during his boyhood at Offington, had turned up destitute from the wars, and in return for alms had told a tale of how Leicester, on one of his visits, had said, "Owen, thou knowest that Robin, my boy, is my lawful son; and as I do charge thee to keep it secret, so I charge thee, be careful of him, and forget it not. When time serves, he shall remember thee." But this isolated testimony from a menial, even if true, had no legal significance, and Dudley had paid little regard to it.

Drury's offer was on a different footing, for he was not only a brother of Sir William Drury, who had married a sister of Sir Edward Stafford, but he had come with an explicit and convincing proposition, nothing less than to produce two of the servants who had witnessed Douglas's wedding at Esher. These were the gentleman usher, Henry Frodsham, and one of the gentlewomen, Magdalen Frodsham, now Mrs. Salisbury, whom Drury, in concert with Dudley's proctor, Thomas Ward, soon brought to the Kenilworth estate.

Even when half-persuaded of the trustworthiness of Magdalen

Salisbury's evidence, Dudley hesitated for a while, because of the effect a successful petition would have on his mother's second marriage. But immense issues were at stake, as his wife and her father did not fail to remind him. There were not only the two earldoms, with their secondary titles and dignities, but Warwick Castle, and "divers fair lordships", entails of the Warwick earldom, and also extensive lands escheated to the Crown on the deaths of both the brothers without lawful male heirs. Were all these honours and estates to come to Dudley, in addition to his present possessions, he would rank among the best endowed nobles in England.

Apart from such material benefits, his proud spirit would have gladly seen the erasion of the background of illegitimacy, even though this was a condition that, so long as there was no thought of disputing it, had never greatly affected him. For he was in good company, not only with others of noble blood, but with even Queen Elizabeth herself, who had been publicly proclaimed a bastard at various times by her father, her sister Mary, and Pope Pius V. Yet it would be good to be no longer tolerated because of his blood, but admitted to his rightful place among the peers of England, and able to wield the power and privilege that would then be his.

Swayed by these inducements as the array of evidence supporting his case emerged, Dudley eventually became sincerely convinced that his mother had indeed been legally married, and that he was his father's legitimate heir. From then onwards, he never relaxed in the slightest degree from this view. Because he was sure his case was just, his sanguine temper saw success within easy reach, and he resolved to have his position tested at law. But when his mother refused to be drawn into his petition, or to give evidence, he decided to seek an enquiry not under the common law, but before an ecclesiastical court, where the marriage could be proved by the simple evidence of a couple of witnesses.

At this stage, there entered into the case the poet, Sir William Leighton, recently knighted, whom Dudley or Leigh evidently regarded as a shrewd man of affairs, and also a Dr. Creake, a public notary, who was appointed as counsel. Using them as intermediaries, Dudley wrote to the Archbishop of Canterbury, "particularly desiring him to examine the witnesses himself". This the Archbishop would not do, but he authorised a Commission of the Court of Audience to take their depositions. The date of this award was May 20th, 1603, and that it was executed at Stoneleigh by one of Leigh's chaplains is sufficient confirmation that he was actively behind the claim from its beginnings.

The opening of the Commission was delayed by the plague, then over-running London, with the death roll mounting every day. One of the early victims was the Archbishop of Canterbury, and another was Drury, who died at the Swan Inn at Southwark on August 26th. Because of the ever present hazard, Leighton obtained permission for the enquiry to be held at the Consistory Court at Lichfield, in Stafford-shire, in whose diocese Kenilworth lay.

With this change of venue went a change of plan, for instead of a simple hearing before the Chancellor, an action, which was possibly collusive, was now brought by Dudley against one of his former servants, John Bushell, for having three years previously called him "Mr. Bastard", for which insult the offender had been all but knifed by another servant. The object of this devious course, which must have been devised by Creake or Leighton, for it was out of keeping with Dudley's forthright character, was to have it placed on formal record, as an incidental concomitant of the action for slander, that the Esher ceremony had been a valid wedding under the canon law.

On September 27th, Salisbury, Frodsham and the other witnesses, who were now lodged on the Stoneleigh estate, began their depositions before the Chancellor of the Court, Dr. Zachery Babington. He found nothing in their evidence to which objection could be raised, and the proceedings continued in what must have seemed to Dudley a highly satisfactory manner. But three weeks later, while the evidence was still being sifted, the situation ended abruptly, for on October 18th there rode into Lichfield, Dudley's cousin, Sir Robert Sidney, with a man-date from the Lord of the Privy Council empowering him to stay the Commission's proceedings, to impound the depositions, and to carry them before the Court of the Star Chamber.

This disconcerting interruption was the consequence of Dudley having waited too long, or perhaps of Drury having come too late. Had the case been launched in January or before, when Queen Elizabeth was still in fair health, her support could have been won, for what would have given her greater satisfaction than to see Lettice branded as no wife after all these years? But the death at the end of February of Dudley's aunt, the Countess of Nottingham, Elizabeth's dearest friend, threw her into a deep depression. By early March she was in fever and could not sleep. She rapidly declined and died on March 24th.

When Dudley procured his Commission on May 20th, King James

had been in London for nine days. He and Queen Anne were crowned in Westminster Abbey in July, but they retired at once to Hampton Court to escape the plague, and later further afield to the Pembroke home, Wilton House. But wherever he lived, his accession had transformed the Court overnight, not least for Dudley and his prospects.

If he had gambled on establishing his rightful birth before refutation could be mounted, he was now to find the dice loaded heavily against him. For James, despite his many gross faults, had one quality rare in princes, the redeeming grace of gratitude, especially to those who had secretly declared for him before his succession was certain. High among these long-sighted courtiers had been Essex, whose relations and friends found themselves suddenly lifted high in the royal favour.

First of them all was his mother, Lettice Knollys, buttressed by her brother, Sir William Knollys, Comptroller of the Household, whom James made a peer on the day of his coronation, by her sister, Cecilia, a Lady of the Bedchamber, by her cousin, Lord Hunsdon, the new Lord Chamberlain, and by Essex's widow, Frances, who after his execution had continued to live in Essex House. But more important than any of these was Frances's brother-in-law, Robert Sidney, who had good reason to oppose Dudley's claim, for through his mother Mary Dudley, he was, in default of legal succession to the Earls of Warwick and Leicester, their heir male. With the Lady Lettice, he had already come to regard Dudley as an interloper, appropriating what would otherwise have come to them.

And he was in a most fortunate position, for in 1588 he had the good chance to be sent to Holyrood to convey the Queen's thanks for the denial of aid to the fleeing galleons of the Spanish Armada. He had so ingratiated himself with the young King of Scots, and subsequently kept alive this goodwill that, at his English coronation, James made him Baron Sidney of Penshurst. And now, having won also the liking of Queen Anne, for he possessed great charm and good looks, as well as soldierly capacity, he had been appointed her Lord Chamberlain. It had thus not been difficult for him, as soon as he was alerted to the Lichfield proceedings, to obtain from the Privy Council a command for the enquiry to be brought before the Star Chamber.

Contemplating the impressive list of Court favourites arrayed in opposition, Dudley could hardly have escaped some feeling of misgiving, for behind them was the active backing of the new sovereigns, their partiality sustained by the self-interest of the Crown, which should he establish his legitimacy stood to lose the Leicester and Warwick entails escheated by Elizabeth.

Dudley, too, had his friends and blood relations at Court, particularly the Howards, whom he might have expected to welcome the erasion of a blot on their escutcheon. But some were too busy wearing new honours, such as Lord Thomas, now the Earl of Suffolk, and Lord Henry, now Earl of Northampton, while most of the others, however much they may have secretly applauded Dudley's ambitions, were not prepared to hazard their as yet uncertain standing with a King so clearly behind the Sidney and Essex factions. Among them were such men as Philip Herbert and Robert Carey, who had hastened to join the place-seekers, Scots and English, scrambling to share in the regal spoils, the offices of profit and the flood of peerages, of which James had created more in a few months than Elizabeth in the whole of her reign.

Even the hitherto faithful Chaloner, who, having returned to Scotland, had accompanied the royal family to London, was not outwardly helpful, though doubtless Dudley consulted him. But as he had been appointed only a few months before to the important post of tutor and governor to the King's eldest son, young Prince Henry, he could do nothing without risking everything he had achieved.

There was one good additional reason why Dudley could not expect to enjoy any crumb of the royal favour, for he was Leicester's son, and it was Leicester, with Walsingham, whom James, to cover his own matricidal acquiescence in the execution of Mary, Queen of Scots, pretended to hold mainly responsible for having, as he said, "cut it his mother's throat", and this was a score he might be ready to settle, if only for appearances' sake.

For the next few months, angry and frustrated, Dudley was compelled to wait impatiently for his adversaries to disclose their hand. His uncertainty deepened when he learned that Sidney and Lettice had persuaded the King to direct that their interests should be identified with the Crown's, and so represented by the Attorney-General, the arrogant and unprincipled but astute Sir Edward Coke.

Realising that the handful of witnesses needed at Lichfield to prove only a petty slander would not suffice for a wider hearing in the Star Chamber, Dudley began the search for further evidence. Among the people he approached was Arthur Atye, his father's former secretary, to whom he wrote from Stoneleigh in November. "I am sure you hear of my proceeding to prove my legitimacy, and the Council's authority to proceed in the Arches",[18] he began, and after some circumlocutions, asked if there existed any notarial attestation of the Wanstead wedding, his object being to challenge its legality "were a marriage proved good before it, yet not known". But Atye was committed to the other camp, for he had served under Essex after Leicester's death. He shortly afterwards received a knighthood, but did not enjoy the title long, for he was dead by the time the enquiry came to its close.

Dudley's search for evidence was based on his needs as a petitioner, which he assumed would be his role. But the crafty Coke had other ideas. In February, 1604, under his direction, Lettice Knollys launched a Bill against Dudley, his wife, his father-in-law, and everyone else involved in the Lichfield proceedings, for conspiracy to defame her. By this manoeuvre, he was transformed from a petitioner who had suffered injury into a defendant who had inflicted it.

This was indeed a bitter pill for him to swallow, for he well realised the wire-pulling behind the move. The hatred which Lettice felt for him he could understand, for to her he was the intruder who had inherited most of Leicester's wealth, the rebel who had escaped punishment when her son and her third husband had been executed, and now the bastard who sought to become legitimate at the cost of her good name.

But Sidney's antagonism was another matter. That the chief enemy should be his blood cousin, the man whom his father had knighted in battle, and named to succeed in his son's inheritance should he die without issue, stirred Dudley's hot resentment. Compared with what he, the base son, had at stake, Sidney, already a peer and the husband of a wealthy heiress, would have forfeited little by conceding the claim. But his was an acquisitive temperament, and ever since the death of Ambrose of Warwick he had pronounced himself heir to the main line of Dudleys. He did not scruple now to exploit his influence with the King to ensure that Dudley's pretensions should fail.

At about the same time as Lettice's Bill, an Act was promulgated "to restrain all persons from marriage until their former wives and former husbands be dead". Disobedience was a felony, punishable by death. Dudley could not but be encouraged by the timing and wording of the Act, for it seemed to be inspired by the importance of his petition. And that bigamous marriages, which until now had been merely unrighteous under ecclesiastical law, were sufficiently frequent to call for control and punishment under the common law, seemed to favour the reasonableness of his plea that his mother's marriage had been legal, and that of Lettice bigamous.

He was encouraged the more because at last his mother came to his side. From the first, she, and no less her husband, had been opposed to any effort to prove his legitimacy while she was alive. Even when he was charged with conspiracy, she was reluctant to speak. Not until June, when the Attorney-General insisted on interrogating her at her home at Sudeley in Gloucestershire, did she allow the full story of her thirty-year-old romance to be drawn from her. But once committed, she brought out every painful detail that memory could recapture after so long an interval.

Moreover, for the first time, and then at Dudley's request, she appealed to her brother Charles, Earl of Nottingham, to whom she wrote to protest that the Esher ceremony had truly been legal, and to pray for his support. But the 67-year-old Admiral was too wary to risk forfeiting the favour he had already won from the King, not least by having recently taken as his second wife the young Lady Margaret Stuart, daughter of the Earl of Moray, and great-granddaughter of James's bastard uncle, "the Good Regent".

It says much for Douglas's conviction over the rightness of her son's claim, as well as for her affection for him, that with so much to lose in any case, and with nothing herself now to gain, she should face her ordeal so bravely, revealing her dishonour with honesty and frankness, and holding unshaken to her evidence against all the trickeries and pressures of the Attorney-General's ruthless examination.

Not until June, 1604, did the trial open. In the meantime the plague had petered out, at a cost of 30,000 dead, and the King and Court had returned to Whitehall. Apart from his lavish bestowals of rewards and honours on favourites, James had done little except inflict injury on those he did not like first among them Raleigh, whom he had dispossessed of his posts and possessions, and sent to the Tower. Later, sentenced to death for treason, Raleigh was reprieved at literally the last moment, and sentenced to life imprisonment.

In this trial, "a disgrace to the judicature of England", Coke had played his customary savage and unscrupulous part as prosecutor. That he was giving his personal care to Dudley's case did not portend well. His interest had no doubt been stiffened by the promise of a lavish sum from Sidney, payable on results, for bribes were a perquisite of office to the Attorney-General, as to any other holder of office under the Crown.

Coke, notorious for his insolent bullying of witnesses as well as for brazen falsifications of evidence that did not suit him, had become very rich in his post, but with it he was one of the most skilful and resourceful lawyers in the country, as he was to show by his chicanery in the handling of the trial.

CHAPTER X

STAR CHAMBER MISJUDGEMENT

". . . THE GREATEST CAUSE now of England between Lord Sidney and Sir Robert Dudley for the Earldoms of Warwick and Leicester . . . a very great cause, and many honourable persons interested in the same in blood and right; and for that purpose, there came with Sir Robert Dudley and stood by him within the Court, the Lord Dudley, the Lord Sheffield and the Lord of Effingham."

So recorded Sir John Haywarde, barrister and chronicler, when the hearing opened on June 22nd in the Star Chamber of the Palace of Westminster. The case that had begun so obscurely at Lichfield had become "the greatest cause of England", and that Dudley's second cousin, Baron Dudley, his half-brother, Edmund, and his cousin, son of the Earl of Nottingham, should openly declare for him, did inspire hope that his side of the cause would be given a fair hearing. The Attorney-General, however, with his habitual effrontery, declared that "it was a strange precedent that so great and honourable personages should come into Court to countenance and embrace any cause contrary to the law". At this, Sheffield, "very much offended, took it ill that Mr. Attorney should so indiscriminately tax those who came but to hear and see how the world went". Sheffield's action in standing by Dudley was all the more creditable because he stood to lose the allowance of £1,000 a year which he was in the process of wheedling out of the King.

This opening, with the Crown's assumption of the defendants' guilt, was typical of the one-sided execution of the law at this time, especially in the Court of the Star Chamber, whose transactions bore little relation to modern conceptions of the administration of justice. This Court, whose members were mostly lords of the Privy Council, could still function with a degree of impartiality, provided that no covert interests were involved, but its proceedings were exempt from the rules of common law, and could be readily manipulated to conform with the wishes of the King and his intimates.

The Court took no exception to the Attorney-General assuming the role of judge, and after some petty argument, Coke opened the prosecution by moving "That whereas the Earl of Leicester had named Sir Robert Dudley in his testament seventeen times bastard, whom he had by the Lady Sheffield, Sir Robert Dudley hath stirred up some to call him bastard, and in the Ecclesiastical Court, by the subordinations of Thomas Drury, hath endeavoured to prove himself legitimate, and the Lady Sheffield, his mother, married to the Earl of Leicester, to the great dishonour of that noble and virtuous lady, now Countess of Leicester; and that Sir Robert Dudley hath given the Ragged Staff to his men that work upon the Thames, and calleth himself Earl of Warwick and Leicester; that this was very dishonourable to the King, who is the life and fountain of all honours and dignities; and the Countess of Leicester had complained thereof to the King, who did much dislike the contemptuous and proud courses and attempts of Sir Robert Dudley, and willed the same should be examined and punished".

Incensed by this repeated affirmation of guilt, Dudley intervened to deny that he had ever given the Ragged Staff to his watermen, or published himself as Earl of Warwick and Leicester. He complained with some ire "that Mr. Attorney did cast forth many scandalous aspersions and rumours to prejudice his cause before it came to hearing", and demanded that it be tried publicly. To this the Lord Chancellor agreed, and the hearing was adjourned. To Dudley's surprise, it was not resumed during the Court's current term, but adjourned indefinitely, possibly because Coke had had second thoughts upon the adequacy of his evidence.

The months passed wearily for Dudley, who could set his mind to little until the issue was settled. Then, at the end of the year, learning that his uncle, the Lord Admiral, was about to be sent on a mission to Spain, he sought and was given his permission to go with him, indication that in spite of the difficulties created by the trial, they were still on friendly terms. The object of the Earl of Nottingham's visit was, on the order of James, "to take the oath of the King of Spain for the peace" which, after forty years of war, had at last been signed between the two countries. Dudley desired but a few weeks' respite from the protracted strain of waiting on the tardiness of the Crown, but Coke would have none of this. In January, 1605, during the Hilary Term of the Star Chamber, he intervened, and Dudley "was stayed at the

Attorney-General's motion, because the next term the cause was to be heard".

The Court that assembled on May 1st included, besides the Lord Chancellor, Baron Ellesmere, the new Archbishop of Canterbury, the Lord Treasurer, the Lord Chamberlain, the Earls of Northumberland, Devonshire and Northampton, Lords Zouch, Knollys and Cranbourne, otherwise Robert Cecil, and the Lord Chief Justice and various other justices. That Lettice's brother and Dudley's cousin should sit on the Court was accepted by everybody as perfectly proper.

"The great case between Lord Sidney and Sir Robert Dudley and others, defendants upon the Attorney's information", reported Hay-warde, was opened by the Solicitor-General with an outline of Dudley's claim to legitimacy, with emphasis on the extent of the domain involved—eight hundred families were affected—and an indication of the Crown's line of attack.

"The civil law", he stated, "said that all chamber, clandestine or secret marriages should be confirmed by the oath of witnesses present at the same." Dudley had five witnesses who had attended the Esher wedding, but they had already given their written testimony on oath, and so enabled the Crown to decide how to dispose of them. Coke's tactics were simple.

"There are five witnesses to prove the first marriage" admitted the Solicitor-General, but he added, "all not worth a frieze jerkin." This comparison with a coat of the poorest cloth gave the clue. The vital witnesses were to be shown to have been suborned by Drury, for money reward from Dudley, hence the charge of conspiracy. The Crown intended to so blacken them in character, as debased creatures, capable of any perjury, that their sworn word would be valueless.

And nothing could have been easier for Coke, the bully who had abused Raleigh at his trial as "thou foul and execrable traitor . . . thou viper of hell with a Spanish heart". The man who could transform Raleigh into a traitor had no difficulty in turning inferior servants into rogues. To him, it was child's play to so intimidate and confuse such lowly placed witnesses that their testimonies seemed spurious.

Following the Solicitor-General, Coke announced that he intended to have the depositions of witnesses read in the mass, but to this Dudley's counsel objected, and with some reason, for during several months' search Dudley had collected ninety witnesses, against the fifty-seven of the Crown. When the Lord Chancellor seemed ready to accept the objection, Coke furiously protested that he "conceived it a great wrong offered to him". But Ellesmere refused tartly to be "out-browed", and declared "he knew what he said, and had heard and learned it before Coke". At which, Coke, red in the face with anger, refused to speak again. The whole Court "sat silent for a pretty space", until at last Ellesmere permitted the King's Sergeant to read the evidence that purported to show how Dudley's chief witnesses had been procured for money. All of which was an instructive commentary on the methods used by Coke to intimidate even the Lords of the Star Chamber.

When the Court re-assembled on May 3rd, the whole day was spent in presenting Sidney's case, which consisted mainly of establishing his line of descent from his uncles, Leicester and Warwick, which was never in dispute, and of demonstrating the certitude of Lettice's Wanstead marriage, which was beside the point if the Esher marriage were proved. The Court then adjourned until May 8th.

But on May 4th came further indication of how heavily the scales were weighted against Dudley, for on this day King James created Sidney, Viscount Lisle of Penshurst. The grant of a peerage during the trial was in itself enough to proclaim the royal partiality, but it was in fact much more, for the Lisle barony was one of the subsidiary titles of the Warwick earldom, and should have been Dudley's if he were to succeed in establishing his legitimacy.

Years before, on Ambrose's death, Sidney had disclosed his ambition by petitioning Queen Elizabeth to be granted the Lisle barony as "the next heir male", and she had refused. Now he had gained all he had ever hoped for, except the issues under trial, and these seemed already predetermined by the King's action. But Dudley, despite his ever-mounting resentment, which merely stiffened his resolute spirit, was far from beaten, for he still had faith in the incontrovertible rightness of his suit.

When the Court reopened on the 8th, Cecil appeared now as the Earl of Salisbury, for he had also been among those elevated on May 4th. Cecil was friendly with Sidney, as well as with Coke, and this evidence that he too shared in the royal favour, was no good augury for Dudley.

It was now Dudley's turn to present his evidence, and from the depositions of his witnesses, and especially of his mother, there emerged the full story of her love affair with Leicester, and its unhappy outcome. Her account of the wedding was supported in detail by Magdalen Salisbury, and in general by other witnesses. No question was raised of her having started the liaison before her husband's death, and although one witness declared that a child had been born at Dudley Castle before the arrival of Robert, Douglas denied this, and in Court, her kinsman, the Earl of Northampton, warmly stressed her denial, and demanded the witness's punishment.

But Douglas's evidence, though consistent under interrogation, had little direct support other than from the much maligned Mrs. Salisbury and other servants, and her former friend, Mrs. Erisa, now the wife of Sir Nicholas Parker. For during the passage of thirty years, most of the others who had been closely involved in her relations with Leicester had died, among them her sister, Mary Howard with her husband Lord Dudley, Sir Edward Horsey, Robert Sheffield and his wife, and Sir John Hubard, while others such as Dr. Giulio and George Digby had disappeared.

That those of her surviving witnesses whom the Crown could not easily denigrate, such as Lady Parker, were not always able, after so long a lapse of time, to recall every detail with certainty was made the most of by the Attorney-General. But his chief targets were the servants. Stressing "the baseness and meanness of the defendant's witnesses", he and his aides described them variously as "a base and poor carpenter", "a common drunkard, base and poor", "a lying tailor", and "an infamous instrument of Drury", who was disposed of as "a man of mean condition and notoriously evil character". That every one of these working people, merely because of their links with Douglas's marriage or her son's childhood, should all conveniently be found to be rogues and vagabonds did not seem odd to any member of the Court.

With Douglas's own evidence ignored and her most important witnesses invalidated, the Court was not likely to pay any regard to the inferential confirmation of her marriage contained in contemporary references. Typical of these were the several mentions in *Leycester's Commonwealth*, including the straight assertion that "My Lord of Leicester was contracted at least to another lady before, that liveth, and consummated the same contract by generation of children".

The Crown made much of the lack of any entry of the marriage in the Archbishop's records, though this was of no real significance, for not only was registration not then compulsory, but quite obviously, to have registered a secret marriage would have been to advertise it.

Dudley's case as defendant was continued when the Court sat again on May 10th, and was concluded with the quoting of precedents to justify his action in having the examination of slander witnesses conducted by an Ecclesiastical Court. All these were brusquely put aside later by Coke. "My lords, this is one of the greatest causes that ever came into this Court", he declared in his final speech, and went on to deliver "great protestations of how he dearly affected the honourable Lady, Lady Sheffield, and how willing he would be to speak or do any good for her".

But then, to the surprise of everyone except those already alert to the nature of the King's intervention, he went on to make the astonishing claim that all the evidence concerning Douglas's Esher wedding "should be damned", that her witnesses be "debarred from giving testimony in this or any other Court", and that drastic punishment should be meted out to all the defendants.

This demand formed the basis of the Star Chamber's judgement delivered later in the day. For the real issue at stake was completely ignored. As one commentator, Rowland White, wrote to the Earl of Shrewsbury, "The matter of marriage was not handled at all: only the practice was proved in the proceedings", and by practice he meant Dudley's attempt to establish his legitimacy through the Ecclesiastical Court.

The lords of the Star Chamber accepted Coke's presentation that the possibility of the defendants' innocence did not arise, and that their own responsibility was merely to decide on the punishment for guilt. Some were for giving Dudley a sharp lesson, among them Lord Salisbury, who while admitting "that it was natural for him to want to prove his legitimacy", was for fining him £100 because "he was somewhat indiscreet in his proceedings". Others, including Northampton, thought he had been misled by Drury, and was less culpable than Sir Thomas Leigh. In his final judgement, the Lord Chancellor "acquitted" Dudley, his wife, mother and father-in-law, as also the majority of his numerous witnesses, but inflicted fines on Leighton, Babington, Owen Jones, Magdalen Salisbury and some others of the "base and poor" category.

The imposition of fines was, to Dudley, of minor importance compared with the pronouncement that followed. For in deference to Coke's behest, Mrs. Salisbury, Frodsham and Jones were, on the Court's order, publicly disgraced, and declared for ever suspect in their testimonies. More outrageous still, the Court ordered that all the defendants' depositions and other papers should be "sealed up and suppressed until the King should order the enclosure to be broken". As a final blow, all lands already escheated to the Crown were to remain escheated.

"And so", wrote Haywarde, "was this great cause at six o'clock at night sentenced, but I fear not ended." He was right, for Dudley's mortification and fury at this unjust blow, not only to his hopes but to his pride, were deep indeed. To have set out so confidently on a journey to his rightful place as an earl, only to find himself almost denounced as a rascal, and lucky to escape punishment for the "misdemeanour" of trying to prove his birthright, was a humiliation hard to bear.

But no less insupportable was the suppression of the witnesses who had proved his parents' marriage valid, and of their vital evidence. By its very avoidance of a decision on the validity of the Esher wedding, a decision, one way or the other, which the whole enquiry demanded, the Court had tacitly admitted that it might have been legal. To Dudley, the inference was clear. Coke, who was not only an artful but a clear-sighted lawyer, had seen that in neither common nor canon law could the ceremony at Esher be proved as lacking legal force. On his advice and the King's instruction, the Court, responding with the servility that was normal before the royal will, had arbitrarily smothered the issue of legitimacy, and neutralised the tell-tale evidence to preclude any reopening of the challenge.

Dudley knew well that the law, because of Sidney's influence with the King, had been improperly manipulated against him. He and his family and witnesses had been punished for "conspiring" to redress a wrong with the minimum of scandal. But the real conspiracy lay in the alignment of the King with Robert Sidney and Lettice Knollys, and his constraining of Crown officials, the Attorney and Solicitor Generals, and the Lords of the Star Chamber, for the benefit of a favourite.

At the insistence of his counsel, Dudley, in an attempt to prise slightly open the door so disdainfully slammed in his face, appealed to the Star Chamber on June 7th to amend the judgement on two counts, the first that his vital witnesses should not be branded as "suspected" but "subject to suspicion", and the second that his father's escheated lands should not revert to the Crown, as the Court had directed, but be "supposed to be reverted". These hair-splittings did not prevail. Among the lords who heard the appeal was Salisbury, whose words of rejection overbore the rest.

This crowning closure of his hopes was the last straw for Dudley, for with his essential witnesses condemned for ever as perjurers, he could never reopen the case. The prospect goaded him to desperation. Any advice he might have received of biding his time until events turned his way was thrown to the winds. He was not a man who could easily wear a mask, for his brow was open to all. Now, though seething with wild resentment, he managed to control himself outwardly, but his actions were soon to show his true emotions.

On June 25th, he obtained a licence, produced at Greenwich by the Keeper of the Records, Sir Thomas Lake, "for Sir Robert Dudley to travel beyond the seas for three years next after his departure, with 3 servants, 4 geldings or nags, and £80 in money: with usual provisions". He left England with his party on July 2nd. One of the servants was a page, slim and shapely in his doublet and hose.

Not until they had reached Calais did the news flash round a scandalised Court that the page was no boy, but a nineteen-year-old girl. For Dudley had unbelievably eloped with his beautiful half-cousin, Elizabeth, "the fair young Mistress Southwell", Maid of Honour to Queen Anne.

CHAPTER XI

"GREAT SCANDAL"

THE NEWS OF Dudley's flight with a young Maid of Honour, coming immediately after the sensational revelations of the legitimacy suit, filled London with shocked amazement. This was a flagrant contempt of Court, which could have taken him to the Tower even as a bachelor, and was much more indecorous for a married man. Worse, he had abandoned his wife and bevy of girls, all under eight years of age:[19] ethics are contemporary, but even the indulgent Elizabethans found this difficult to swallow. What was much more intriguing was the complete public unawareness that any love affair existed between him and Elizabeth, the jewel of the Court.

In all the gossipy writings about him during recent months, when his birth and childhood had been exposed to the vulgar gaze, there was not one word of scandal against either him or her, no breath of suspicion of their having formed an attachment. They must have seen each other sufficiently often, and in free enough conditions, to be able to discover their love, yet apart from furtive meetings at Court, where no intrigue could escape notice for long, or possibly at her home under the Argus eye of her straitlaced mother, they seemed to have had no opportunities, especially during the Star Chamber trial, to set alight a passion so strong as to inspire them to face ruin for its fulfilment.

Understandably, Queen Anne was highly indignant at the affront to herself and to the fair name of her Court. Reports on the commotion caused by Dudley's audacity reached most of the capitals of Europe. One of these foreign commentators was the Tuscan minister, Ottaviano Lotti, who wrote to the Grand Duke Ferdinand that "The Queen is much put out because a married cavalier, Sir Robert Dudley, has carried off a Maid of Honour of whom he was enamoured. Strict orders were promptly given out, but at present we have heard no news. This gentleman is about thirty-five years of age, of exquisite stature, with a fair beard and noble appearance. The fact has created great scandal."

Court officials were sent in hot pursuit, and Sir William Monson, one of Dudley's comrades-in-arms at Cadiz, and now Admiral of the Narrow Seas, was "commanded to use the King's ships to stop them in their flight". A few days later, Lotti wrote again. "That Court Lady, niece of the Lord High Admiral, who they say ran off with Sir Robert Dudley, has been stopped at Calais by the Governor of that city: the expedition from here arriving almost at the same time as the fugitives. But as he found she had taken the step not for love but with the object of entering a monastery, and serving God in the true religion, I do not know whether the French will allow her to be brought back by force: on the contrary, it is believed they will allow her to follow out her holy inspiration."

Lotti's information was correct, for both Elizabeth and Dudley, as soon as they arrived in France declared themselves adherents of the Church of Rome. This action staggered London almost as much as the elopement. For Dudley to abduct one of the Queen's Maids was unseemly enough, but for him to boldly recant, and seemingly to persuade the girl to do the same, gave a more nefarious complexion to his misdeed. For though several of the Howards, and members of the noble families, still clung to the Roman faith, they did so in great secrecy, because an overt profession could mean trouble, and even persecution. Dudley was apparently among them, for as he afterwards wrote, "On the point of religion, he was different many years before leaving England, and did not change his opinion as is imputed since his departure".

But in fact, this hasty apostasy, and the foolhardy elopement, were both expressions of his impotent rage at the outcome of the trial. Seized in a tumult of bitter resentments, he could find no swifter retaliation than scornful defiance of the Crown, even at the risk of irreparable injury to himself, a defiance which he himself long after-wards "protested he was driven into with grief of mind".

At the time he did not stop to examine the consequences. In his complex character there were trends of which he was unaware, trends which under the spur of insult or injustice could erupt violently into acts he would never have consciously contemplated. The tragedy was that legitimacy, with all the responsibilities it would have imposed on him, would have stabilised this susceptivity, for as he had shown in his earlier days, especially on his West Indian trip, he was not lacking in steadiness and good sense. Had he been able to pause before taking irrevocable steps, he might have reflected that although his legitimacy had not been confirmed by the Star Chamber, neither had it been legally disproved. With changing circumstances, and the help of his powerful kinsmen, he might in time have gained the essential royal favour, perhaps to the eventual bestowal of the earldom to which he aspired.

But even had such possibilities entered his head, he would have rejected them, for he could never have seen himself following his kinsmen's pattern of patient servility. His temper was too open, his nature that of a man of impulse and action, not of an intriguer. Not for him were the ways of his calculating father, able always "to put his passions in his pocket", but rather those of his grandfather and great-grandfather, whose too precipitate enterprise took them both to execution.

Yet though neither his nature nor his resentment would have allowed him to follow a prudent course, it is not certain that anger at the unjust deprival of his birthright, even when reinforced by disgust at the unworthy King and bitterness towards the malign Sidney, was the only or the chief reason for his rash flight. Confounding these obvious motives was the baffling affair with Elizabeth Southwell. Was this merely an additional inducement for flight or was she the entire cause of his abandonment of England and all it meant for him? Would he have gone into exile had she never existed? Or would he have been content to enjoy her as a mistress in London had he won his suit? There is no positive answer to these questions.

Whether Dudley's flight into exile was inspired primarily by love for Elizabeth must remain a matter for conjecture, but there is no room for doubt that her only possible motive for elopement was her overmastering love for him. She was by every account one of the most beautiful women at Court, as well as gay, spirited, intelligent and well-educated. No word of scandal had ever touched her. She was closely related to the small group of Howards now approaching the centre of power. Her widowed mother had, a few months previously married one of King James's favoured followers, John Stewart, the future Earl of Carrick, and was now a Lady of Queen Anne's Drawing Chamber. In England, Elizabeth was among the elect.

Though she was no heiress, she could have taken her choice of the bachelor nobility of England. And yet, amazingly, she chose to decamp with a bastard knight, already married, a runagate with no foreseeable future, unable to return to his own country except to meet arrest and ignomy. Nor was this surrender the result of some sudden foolish infatuation. Her decision was not that of a kittenish girl such as her fifteen-year-old kinswoman, Frances Howard, now about to marry the fourteen-year-old Earl of Essex. Elizabeth was nineteen, and after four years as a Maid of Honour in a flighty Court, was an adult and sophisticated woman. Something in Dudley's ardent spirit may have touched off a kindred temper in hers. The passion between them, compared with the usual sordid amours of the Court, was not only irresistible but exalted, to the degree that both were prepared to sacrifice everything except each other. And when they fled to the Continent, they became not merely exiles but outlaws without friends or background, blindly self-sufficient in their love for one another.

For a time London buzzed with rumours on their intentions and whereabouts. "There is a bruit that Mistress Southwell is now become a professed nun of the Order of St. Clara at Brussels", ran one report in August, "and was there received with all the solemnity that may be." But the rumour was false, for by early October came reports that they were living at Lyons, "where he is much honoured, and gives it to be understood that he will return to England no more. His young relative is constantly seen with him in public, as a kind of protest that there is no guilty concealment between them."

The next development greatly exacerbated the impropriety of Dudley's conduct, for he established touch with an English Catholic exile, Captain Robert Eliot, who enjoyed familiar relations with the Vatican, and asked him to obtain a papal dispensation from the laws of consanguinity. At this stage, Dudley did not complicate his request to marry his cousin by disclosing that he had a wife and family in England.

News of his intentions created a certain stir in London, for he was now scorning not only the Crown and religion, but the common law. The Statutes introduced during the early stages of his trial, "to restrain all persons from marriage until their former wives or husbands be dead" had specifically declared against "divers ill-disposed persons who, being married, run out of one country into another or into places where they are not known, and there become married, having another husband or wife living, to the great dishonour of God and the utter undoing of divers honest men's children and others".

As a prominent legal luminary, Sir Francis Leake, wrote to the Earl of Shrewsbury, "I am sorry for Sir Robert Dudley's great overthrow, because I was much bound in duty to his father: but if he do marry Mistress Southwell, it is felony by these last statutes". And that the need to introduce this law showed that Dudley was far from being alone in his offence did not lessen either its gravity or the possibility that his punishment could be death.

Eventually the dispensation came, and he and Elizabeth were married at Lyons. He not only set the seal on his misbehaviour by committing what everybody in England regarded as the crime of bigamy, but made his transgression seem the worse by the argument with which he justified it. For he declared that the marriage he had made with Alice Leigh was bigamous under the canon law of his newly adopted faith, because at that time Frances Vavasour, to whom he had been legally contracted in marriage in 1591, was still alive. By the tenents of the Roman Catholic Church, he said, neither her wedding to Sir Thomas Shirley, nor his own to Margaret Cavendish and Alice Leigh, had been valid. Only because Frances had died a few months previously was he now free to marry Elizabeth Southwell.

Even those of his well-wishers in England who had tolerantly thought that in his recantation he had been genuinely moved, began now to wonder whether this was not an act of hypocritical expedience. Yet neither he nor Elizabeth had displayed any such meanly unscrupulous tendencies in the past. Dudley indeed, had always shown, sometimes to his disadvantage, such lofty notions of honour and chivalry that it is hard to imagine that his justification was merely a subterfuge, and that he did not honestly believe, in the temper of the theological hair-splittings normal to the time, that he was indeed free to marry Elizabeth.

But however easily his conscience, and hers, may have been stilled by casuist pleading over religious law, nothing could excuse the sheer heartlessness of their conduct towards those nearest to them. She had inflicted suffering and disgrace on her mother, as well as on her brother and sisters and other relatives. He had left behind the unhappy Douglas, not only wounded morally by the Star Chamber trial, but bereaved of her husband halfway through the proceedings, his death hastened by the disrepute brought upon his name and family. But far the worst of Dudley's sins was his casual abandonment of his young wife and family, and his readiness to see his daughters stigmatised as illegitimate.

Of all the unexpected actions of Dudley's life, his unblushing repudiation of Alice Leigh is the most inexplicable. Almost it seemed as though he were displaying a spiteful relish "in doing what his father, as he contended, had been allowed to do with impunity". Even if his callousness belonged as much to the times as to him as an individual;

even if he were regarded as no commonplace, humdrum type but a being brilliant and volatile, not subject to orthodox codes of conduct; even if he were impelled by a passionate love such as he had never known before; with all these possible excuses, his ruthless renunciation of his family remained as an ineradicable stain on his good name.

There is nothing to show how the rift between him and Alice began. Acute and fundamental breach there must have been for him to leave her, still only twenty-six, with five young girls, one but recently born, when he could, had he wished, have remained in England and the love of Elizabeth Southwell in a discreet liaison, as so many men at Court had done with other women, not least his own father.

Reasons for the rift can only be surmised, for no voice ever explained what caused two such estimable people, apparently happily married, suddenly to break apart. Perhaps their union initially held no depth. Perhaps he married her on too light an impulse, swayed by the physical desires of youth, or by the wish to have children to safeguard his inheritance, or even by hopes of monetary backing from her father for maritime ventures. Perhaps he wanted a boy, and the succession of daughters disappointed him. The breach may have stemmed from a discord of temperament, his impatient and ebullient, hers sedate and self-righteous. She was a good and pious woman, a conscientious wife, a devoted mother. Perhaps she was too good, too self-righteous, for his irrepressible character.

Perhaps, accustomed to having his own way since childhood, he chafed at her efforts, and no less her father's, to dominate him, and not only over the attempt to establish his birthright. Perhaps the Star Chamber reversal had triggered off a long accumulation of submerged frustrations and frictions. Quite possibly she was something of a scold, and he could not face the prospect of a lifetime of lamentations and reproaches over the legitimacy suit debacle. It might even have been religion, for she was a staunch Protestant, greatly given to good works, and her formal piety may have grated on his Roman Catholic leanings.

According to one unconfirmed report, she wrote to him to express her willingness to become a Catholic and to join him with their children. But the source, Anthony Standen, one of Salisbury's roving spies writing from Rome, was only repeating an improbable rumour, for never would the devout and dignified Alice have recanted, nor surrendered her assured state for hazardous exile.

But this last was a plight that Elizabeth Southwell, although of more aristocratic birth and upbringing, faced without hesitation. However much she and Dudley had injured others, they had inflicted greater hurts upon themselves. She had cast away her reputation, her high place at Court, the respect of her friends. He had surrendered the goodwill of most of his blood relations and friends, had rendered himself liable to severe punishment, and had thrown away, as casually as a pair of old shoes, his castle, his manors, his wide estates and his rich revenues.

They had plunged together into the unknown. They did not know where they were going or how they would live. They seem to have decided on flight without premeditation, on the spur of the Star Chamber sentence. Apart from the £80 permitted by the licence to travel, and any gold and jewels they contrived to secret on their persons, their resources were small, for little credence can be placed on a suggestion from an unreliable informant in Paris that Dudley had secretly conveyed abroad some 40,000 scudi or ducats. This was a large sum, transferable only by letters of exchange through merchants, and whether he had time or ready funds to arrange such a transaction is doubtful, especially as there is evidence that before many months had passed he was reduced to borrowing money to meet his needs.

These difficulties did nothing to dampen their spirit, nor weaken their resolution to continue on their path. He was self-sufficient, she was sustained by his sanguine temper, and by his supreme confidence in himself and his abilities, which now, as in the past, spurred him to accept risk with a light heart. This he showed by a defiant assertion of his legitimacy, for he now called himself Earl of Warwick and Leicester.

But in England, interest in his latest indiscretion, no less than in the others, was put in the shade by the tremendous excitement generated by the conspiracy to blow up Parliament. One consequence of the Gunpowder Plot of November 5th, and the subsequent trials and executions, was an intensification of the drive against Catholics, and a harsher treatment of those who declined to pledge the oath of allegiance to the King. By their open professions, the position of Dudley and Elizabeth had become even more parlous than before, should they ever return to England.

But Dudley had no thought of returning, for his eyes were already turned towards a new objective, the Court of the Medici at Florence. Indeed, it was because Lyons was the gateway to the easiest route into Italy that he had gone there. His reasons for choosing the Tuscan State were several. There was the precedent of other Englishmen who had served the Medici with honour, among them the Sir Thomas

Shirley who had married Frances Vavasour. There was the influence of Sir Thomas Chaloner, whose early links with Florence had long ago placed at the back of Dudley's mind the desire to visit the most civilised city in Europe. But the strongest reason was that the Grand Duke Ferdinand, helped by the Knights of San Stefano, was engaged in a fierce naval war against the Turks and their allies, the Barbary corsairs who preyed on Mediterranean merchantmen, and he badly needed someone who could build fighting ships. And in this respect, Dudley held a good conceit of himself.

Some time early in 1606, he wrote a long exuberant letter in French to the Grand Duke, seeking his protection and his permission to settle in Florence. He set out his family background and listed his attainments, especially his practical experience of shipbuilding and naval affairs. And he gave a firm promise that, if taken into the Ducal service, he would build a fleet of superlative men-of-war that would quickly render Tuscany absolute mistress of the Levant.

Several months passed before he received a reply, for the Grand Duke took the precaution to investigate his grandiose claims. From the routine reports of his London Minister, Lotti, he had already learned of Dudley's earlier adventure with Essex, as also of the legitimacy suit and the scandal of the elopement. Lotti had told him, too, of the wrath of both King and Queen at Dudley's contempt of Court. James, declared Lotti, had "expressed himself as disgusted at Dudley's secession from the Protestant faith", but he added, "The chief reason is that His Majesty does not want his subjects to be Catholics, especially when they are brave and worthy men".

This initial opinion was favourable, but in general, Lotti's attitude to Dudley took on some of the hostility which his actions had earned in the English Court, and it speaks well for reports which the Grand Duke, as well as the Duchess, received from other sources, as well as for the persuasiveness of Dudley's approach, that they did not let themselves be prejudiced against him. With the result that, towards the autumn, he received from Florence the summons to Tuscany.

It is uncertain which way he went. The first mention of his presence in Italy is of his arriving at Livorno in the middle of February, 1607, and this suggests that he made the journey by sea, as his maritime bent would dictate. But the movement of travellers by ship between Marseilles and Livorno did not begin until over twenty years later, and then only because of the barrier of war and plague in Northern Italy. There is evidence that he borrowed £200 to make the journey with his wife and two servants, and so large a sum would not have been required for a sea passage, though it would for a journey by coach in good style over the Mont Cenis.

By land, he would have had to start well before the snow came in November, when having passed into Piedmont, he might have lodged for a while in Pisa or Lucca, where Captain Eliot was well known. Whichever way he went, the voyage for his wife, still only twenty, would by sea have been hazardous, with constant risk of corsairs, or by land, a hard and uncomfortable passage over the Alps and the Apennines. Such enterprises, then seldom undertaken by women, were evidence of both her courage and her devotion.

From Livorno, Dudley rode to Pisa, and along the Arno valley to Florence, the city which he confidently expected would grant him refuge. He met with no difficulty on the way, for he had a smattering of Italian and Spanish as well as his fluent if imperfect French. Without any delay, he made himself known at the Grand Ducal Palace[20] on the Boboli Hill, south of the Arno, and was admitted to the presence of Ferdinand I, the ruler of Tuscany.

CHAPTER XII

IN THE SERVICE OF THE MEDICI

Ferdinand I, Grand Duke of Tuscany, was not a man to be put upon by anybody, of whatever race or degree. He had not only reigned supremely well for twenty years, but prior to his accession had, from the age of fourteen, been a Cardinal of the Roman Catholic Church. Had he not come to the Tuscan throne, he would certainly have been elected Pope. His long experience in the Sacred College in Rome had taught him many things not always found in ruling princes, among them the capacity to measure up a man rightly and to judge the value of his words.

But he was a practical administrator of affairs as well as of people. When he succeeded his brother, the tyrannical Francesco I, Tuscany had suffered in every way during thirteen years of misrule. Under Ferdinand's strong but benevolent control, it had found new political standing and economic prosperity. It was now one of the richest, most stable and most powerful of the smaller States of Europe, its ruler everywhere regarded with respect and envy.

This was the man to whom Dudley now brought his story and offered his services. Tall and heavily built, but with a calm and dignified presence, Ferdinand listened gravely. Because he already knew most of his visitor's history and background, he could readily have detected misrepresentations, especially over the degree to which Dudley might have attributed his plight to his open profession of the Catholic faith. But Dudley was too sure of himself to want or need to be deceitful. He made an instant and deep impression. "The Great Duke entertained him handsomely" ran the contemporary record, and by the end of their meeting had agreed to take him into his employment at once, and to give him control of the shipyards and arsenal of Pisa and Livorno.

As a Roman Catholic, Ferdinand accepted that the Esher ceremony between Leicester and Douglas Sheffield was a lawful wedding, substantiated by their subsequent relationship, and that Dudley was legitimate. He therefore recognised without reservation his visitor's right to the Warwick and Leicester titles. But he was impressed that Dudley had not entered Tuscany to ask for charity as Leicester's Catholic son, but to do useful work in return for a stipend.

In a surge of goodwill, he wrote a few weeks later to the Earl of Northampton, referring to "the Earl of Warwick, who has come to our dominions to live quietly in his religion, and whom we have the more willingly received because of his relationship with your illustrious lordship". He declares that Dudley remains still the loyal and faithful vassal of the King, and that, as he regards the Earl as a father, he should be treated as a son, and kept in the King's grace, despite the calumnies of his enemies.

It is doubtful whether Northampton responded to this plea, for though in the past he had shown a benevolent interest in Dudley, and as a lifelong secret Catholic was sympathetic to his acceptance of the Roman faith, he was at this moment engaged in the delicate business of inducing the King to grant him the office of Lord Privy Seal when Salisbury chose to move on to the more lucrative Treasury. This was no time to champion his unpopular kinsman with James, nor indeed with Salisbury, who was already preparing to have the culprit answer for his offences.

News of Dudley's plan to go to Tuscany had reached London some time before, and was passed by Salisbury to Sir Henry Wotton, ambassador to the Venetian Republic, whose responsibilities included keeping an eye on all Englishmen in Italy, whether harmless travellers or Catholic exiles likely to be plotting against their country. Dudley's association with Eliot, one of the most active and dangerous renegades on the Continent, made him the object of particular interest. Wotton wrote at once to Sir Edward Barrett, then on a visit to Florence, and asked him to report on "the arrival of Sir Robert Dudley and his Lady, and the circumstances of their reception". Shortly after, he wrote again to Barrett, this time mainly about Elizabeth Southwell, whom he had known well at Court, and even flirted with, though on a purely chivalrous level.

"I had before understood from the very fountains", he wrote, "how that business was conducted by Captain Eliot, whom the Pope is now likely to charge with surreption, or concealment of circumstances. . . . In the whole matter I do much compassionate the case of the gentle-woman, whose mind, as her blood, was assuredly noble, but deceived. if you chance to see her, which methinks should be worth a step to

Pisa, I pray you to do me the honour to kiss her hand from me; not under the name of her master (as it pleased her sometimes to call me) but now as her fellow-traveller, since we have both tasted of pere-grination."

It was at Pisa that Dudley and his wife had settled, because from there he could readily reach his work in the shipyards at Livorno. He was also seeking a house at Florence, where both he and Elizabeth had been well received by the Grand Duchess Christina, daughter of Charles, Duke of Lorraine. In Florence too, they had met the several groups of Englishmen, the merchants, the travellers and the Catholic exiles. Of these, the most notable at this time was Father Robert Parsons, the Jesuit whom some supposed to have written *Leycester's Commonwealth*. Parsons, briefly in Florence from Rome, was the brain and spur of those exiles who had so persistently conspired to assassinate Queen Elizabeth. Apart from his political intriguing, he never wasted an opportunity to proselytise, and one of his latest converts was none other than Tobie Mathew, son of the Protestant Archbishop of York.

It was concerning the impact of Florence and the Medici Court on impressionable young Englishmen, that Wotton wrote to Salisbury, "I cannot but lament unto you Lordship the danger that I foresee of corrupting many in the Court, whither are drawn of our English gentlemen by the beauty and security of the place and the purity of the language. For there is in that town a certain knot of bastard Catholics, partly banished, partly voluntary residents there, whereof Tobie Mathew is the principal, who with pleasantness of conversation and force of example do much harm . . ."

It is unlikely that Dudley took any part in these pleasant conversations, for he was much too occupied with his absorbing tasks at Livorno. But from him Father Parsons learned that Elizabeth Southwell was one of the Maids of Honour in attendance on Queen Elizabeth during her last illness. He persuaded her to give him a statement of these dramatic hours. Her eye-witness descriptions were so vivid that they have entered into English history, for they have been quoted, often without certain knowledge of the source, in almost every book that has ever been written about Queen Elizabeth.

Her narration described how the Queen, falling ill, looked for the first time in twenty years into a mirror: of how she sat fully dressed on her stool for three days refusing food until at last the Earl of Notting-ham persuaded her to take broth: of her rebuke to Cecil when he urged that she must go to bed, that "the word *must* was not to be used to

Princes. Little man, little man, if your father had lived, he durst not have said so much": of her visions and hallucinations, as when she told Nottingham, "My Lord, I am tied with a stone round my neck": of how her ghost was seen by the Lady Guilford before she was even dead: of how she berated the Bishop of Canterbury and other prelates as hedge priests: and of how, "being given over by all, and at the last gasp", she was asked to indicate her successor by holding up a finger, which she did when they called the name of James of the Scots.

Elizabeth Southwell also told of how, after the Queen had died, and the body was brought from Richmond to Whitehall, she was one of six ladies of the Court who kept watch all night around the nailed-up coffin: and of how the corpse, which had been inadequately embalmed, burst "with such a crack that splitted the wood, lead and cere cloth, whereupon the next day she was fain to be new trimmed up".[21]

The encounter with Parsons for the production of this account, part of which he later published in his theological writings, provided the only significant contact between Dudley and his wife and the trouble-making English Catholics. From then on their interest lay in adapting themselves to a new and strange existence on the fringe of an Italian Court. But they were not to be left undisturbed for long. In Whitehall, Salisbury, whose power under a King careless of State affairs had become so absolute that the Venetian ambassador reported that "he is in truth the Prince of this kingdom", had set in motion the machinery of retribution. In February he revoked the licence to travel and sent out the order for recall. This order did not reach Dudley for several weeks, when Sir Henry Wotton sent messengers under Captain Aubrey Yorke to convey to him at Pisa a Royal Warrant of Privy Seal.

"We granted you leave to travel", complained King James, "in the hope that you might thereby prove the better enable to the service of us and our State, as you pretended. We do now certainly understand that you do bear and behave yourself inordinately, and have attempted many things prejudicial to us and our Crown, which we cannot suffer or endure." Dudley was then commanded to return and "yield and render your body to some of our Privy Council. Hereof fail you not, as you will answer the contrary at your uttermost peril."

Because the messengers were too talkative to all and sundry about their task, Dudley was well aware of the contents of the Seal, but he refused to accept it for the reason that it was not addressed to him as Earl of Warwick. He made his attitude clear in a letter which he sent soon afterwards to the Earl of Northampton, explaining that the Privy

Seal "label of superscription derogating from my due pretenses and right which I claim, being lawful son and heir to my father, I durst not open . . . lest in doing so, it might be prejudicial to my right and title".

He then declared that Wotton's agents had given out that he was being recalled in disgrace in order to be punished, and that "the English merchants were by them chidden for all coming to me, and commanded not to do so in pain of losing what they had. This is a great disreputation for me, to be published over Italy for a traitor and worse . . . I hold the same course not very honourable to have bruited in his Majesty's name such scandals to a subject before trial."

Standing rigidly on his rights, as he saw them, he went on to justify, by comparison with similar actions by other well-born Englishmen, his becoming a Catholic, his marriage with Elizabeth Southwell, and his use of titles to which he considered himself entitled in law. He petitioned that " if these be all the allegations my enemies have made against me to his Majesty, as I presume no man can be so horrible a liar to speak worse against me", he be allowed to remain in Tuscany "to repair my reputation abroad and at home . . . and to give my best assistance and service to the Great Duke of Florence".

By this letter, Dudley showed that he regarded his use of his titles as a vindication of his legitimacy, and that with this stand he intended, whatever the Crown of England might ordain, to re-establish himself by earning new distinction in Tuscany. But Northampton took no more notice of this protest than of the Grand Duke's commendation. To have mentioned Dudley to the King at the very moment when his long laid schemes for his own advancement were near fruition would have been absurd. In truth, Dudley and his *praemunire* had become an embarrassment, and the only course was to ignore all appeals, at least until his own position was secure.

So it was that soon afterwards, news reached Dudley that James had ordered all his estates to be sequestrated to the Crown. Resentful as he was at this step, there was nothing he could do. He was not even greatly surprised, for he had previously expected some such action, and had taken precautions against it. While at Lyons, he had, with the aim of making provision for his deserted wife and family, "conveyed his estates in trust to certain relatives and allies, amongst whom were Sir Thomas Leigh, father, and Sir John Leigh, brother, of the bride". Time would show whether this subterfuge would answer. For the present, he resigned himself reluctantly to inaction.

There were two reasons to account for this restraint. The first was his exhilarating preoccupation with the work at Livorno, where he had hastened to arrange for English workmen to join him as ship-wrights. In April the Grand Duke's secretary instructed Lotti in London to offer Dudley's old instructor, Matthew Baker, master ship-wright at Deptford, double his normal pay to come to Livorno. Lotti replied that he had visited Deptford Docks and gained contact with Baker, who "much to his regret excuses himself from coming, solely on account of his great age, he being 77 years old. . . . Asking me about his old pupil, Sir Robert Dudley, he expressed how willingly he would have taught his profession in Italy to oblige him."

Baker offered to approach a younger man, another of his pupils, and his efforts were successful, for by August it was recorded in London that the Grand Duke was employing English shipwrights to build his war vessels. The first to be undertaken to Dudley's designs was a galleon of sixty-four guns. But he was occupied not only with building ships, but in organising their armament and manning. Lotti wrote of "that naval captain who brought orders from Sir Robert Dudley, and will send everything under his care". By everything, the minister meant cannon and other weapons. As for the crews, they were largely roving English seamen, barely a stage removed from pirates, who liked better to serve for good money abroad than risk the press-gang at home.

The second reason why Dudley showed none of his usual hot reaction to injustice issued from the impact of his conversations with the Grand Duke Ferdinand. In the first furious resentment at his treatment by the Star Chamber, he had cast off all the loyalties of the past, and preci-pitately abandoned his position and inheritance with the vow never to set foot in England again. But Ferdinand not only possessed the traditional Medici gift of persuading those at enmity to live in peace, but from his long wearing of the Purple had acquired an insight into the more subtle promptings of human behaviour. He was a man of nearly sixty, with immense understanding, addressing an impetuous junior of thirty-four, whose ability, character and predicament had all won his interest and sympathy. He realised that however useful the exile might be for a while in Tuscany, his proper sphere was the one to which he belonged in England.

He seems both to have weakened Dudley's resolve not to have any truck with his country, and to have put into his mind the idea of eventually finding a way to return. To help in this, he instructed Lotti to do everything in his power to reassure the King of the runaway's integrity. "Here he is known as a worthy knight", he wrote, "and of the utmost goodwill, and he could not possibly entertain any idea of disloyalty or ill-faith towards King James or his State."

Dudley's sense of ill-usage, and his fierce pride, would not permit him to support these efforts by any open approach to James, but he did abstain from any outburst at the seizure of his lands, and he even opened the door a little through his old friend, Sir Thomas Chaloner, now a minor power at Court as tutor to the fourteen-year-old Prince Henry. For Lotti, referring to a visit to Chaloner, wrote "His Excellency showed me the design for a ship made at Livorno by the Earl of Warwick, and he also showed me another which he said was more perfect than any".

There is something appealing in this act of Dudley's of displaying his skills to the one who had first turned his youthful interest towards ships and their making. But his gesture had practical point too, for Chaloner had established some repute as an authority on the theories of ship design and construction, to the degree that he was appointed to adjudge as a technical expert when Phineas Pett, master-shipwright at Woolwich, was charged with building a faulty vessel.

For a time, it seemed as though the Grand Duke's efforts might achieve something. Later in the year, Lotti wrote "I cannot clearly say, not having official notice from the Court, but I well understand that there are attempts towards a compromise, made by the Viscount de Lisle, the Queen's Chamberlain, who is the party opposing the pretensions of the Earl of Warwick". Shortly afterwards, the minister stated more explicitly that King James had again ordered Dudley to return to England, but this time with the promise of the earldom of Warwick.

Assessed by other information, Lotti's reports were based on false rumour, for Dudley's enemies were much more actively influential than his friends, and his estates were a prize from which several, Sidney first among them, were straining to have their pickings. With such voices predominating in the tight circle in attendance on the King and Queen, the circle which held the virtual council of government, it was clear that Dudley stood no chance whatever of finding regal favour. On the contrary, as Lotti announced in February of 1608, the King disliked him heartily.

"The king of his own accord", reported the minister, "spoke of Sir Robert Dudley, and said, 'If he had been a traitor to my own person and State, I should expect from His Highness the Grand Duke some real sign of friendship; but as he has only erred in lightness and dishonour, I should not wish to drive him out of His Serene Highness's State: yet that he should receive Dudley in his house, and honour him as he does, seems very strange to me. He has a wife and children here, the Pope has annulled his marriage to the woman he has with him, and I for my part hold him incapable of any honourable action' ".

In spite of his displeasure, James, who had consistently cultivated Tuscan friendship as a plank of his foreign policy, would seek no quarrel with Ferdinand, to whose wife he was related through the House of Lorraine, and to whom he owed a debt of gratitude for having eight years previously sent to Edinburgh a warning of a plot of assassination.

The notion that the Pope had changed his mind and now annulled the marriage to Elizabeth was wrong, but it was commonly held, as was confirmed in a letter from that indefatigable gossip-monger, John Chamberlain, who informed Dudley Carlton, "We hear out of Italy that the Pope hath expressly commanded Sir Robert Dudley to forsake his mistress, who they say hath been with child and miscarried five times within the year".

Though from now on, Lotti's reports began to be coloured with such disparagements, symptomatic of the Court's animosity towards Dudley, they had no effect on the Grand Duke, who realising that there was no early prospect of his protégé's return to England, tried to help him in another way. This was late in 1608, when Dudley, becoming anxious about his wife's anomalous position, presented a petition to have the legality of his marriage placed beyond doubt. Ferdinand responded by resorting to his still powerful influence in the Sacred College, as he showed in a letter to Lotti. "It seems to us", he wrote, "that this knight shows himself every day more worthy of our protection, and especially of our efforts to prove in Rome the validity of his last marriage. We will, therefore, that you do your best to elucidate this matter in his favour as far as you can, for truth's sake."

Lotti's "best" accomplished nothing in England, but in Italy, matters progressed better. Elizabeth wrote to the Grand Duchess Christina, pleading her right on the ground of the canonical illegality of her husband's former marriages and on the permission which the Pope had granted for their union, while Dudley supported his suit by producing written verification of the marriage contract with Frances Vavasour which he argued had invalidated his union with Alice. This consisted of an attestation, prepared by his notary in London in November, 1592, and witnessed by two of his old shipmates, Captain Thomas Jobson and Thomas Combley, recording the occasion of the contract in 1591.

The background of this attestation, which was not an original but a copy, could have rendered it suspect, for there was no reason why such a contract should have been legally recorded at a time when Dudley was married to Margaret Cavendish, and Frances Vavasour to Sir Thomas Shirley. Nor it is clear whether this vital evidence was produced when the Papal dispensation was sought through Captain Eliot. It is not out of reckoning that Dudley, driven by the urgency of Elizabeth's situation, as she was expecting a child, for once put aside his integrity and concocted the attestation to enable Ferdinand to vindicate the suit in Rome.

But the Grand Duke was an outstandingly shrewd man-of-the-world, and not easily deceived. An aristocrat of the highest probity, the rectitude of whose Court was a byword throughout Italy, neither he nor the Grand Duchess, a woman of excessive religious scrupulousness, would have tolerated Dudley's union with Elizabeth unless their consciences were satisfied that it was canonically sanctioned. In the result, although there is no record of any official decree confirming the validity of the marriage, it was always accepted as lawful by the Grand Ducal House, by the Vatican, and by the noble Italian families with whom Dudley was later to form family ties.

CHAPTER XIII

SHIPWRIGHT AND ENGINEER

IT WAS IN the tradition of the Medici to have an eye to good business, and that the Grand Duke Ferdinand was no exception was shown both by his family banking house, through which his father and he had built up an immense fortune, and by the efficiency with which he had raised his country's economy to its present flourishing level. And although in engaging Dudley he was swayed by considerations of humanity and religion, he was undoubtedly swayed even more by the benefits the English exile would bring to the Tuscan State.

That his beneficence was a good investment was already proved, for Dudley's efforts in developing the Ducal Navy, by both building ships and finding crews and arms, had borne quick and notable results. In the summer of 1607, Ferdinand was able to send a fleet manned largely by English sailors, to attempt the conquest of Cyprus, and the attack failed only because the Turks were warned. Soon afterwards, another attack, led by the Knights of San Stefano, of whom Ferdinand's eldest son, Cosimo, was the Grand Master, attacked Bona, the chief base of the Barbary Coast corsairs, and took it by storm. The following year, the Tuscan fleet won a decisive victory in a battle with the Turks, when they defeated a stronger force escorting the Alexandrian treasure ships, and "captured 9 vessels, 700 prisoners, and jewels valued at two million ducats".

In this engagement, which gave Ferdinand the firm advantage in Mediterranean naval rivalries, the leading role was played by Dudley's new ship, the *San Giovanni Battista*, because of its fast sailing, its manoeuvrability, and its powerful armament. Launched in March, 1608, this galleon, which was the one whose design he had proudly disclosed to Chaloner, and in which he embodied some original structural conceptions, was in his own description, "a rare and strong sailer, of great repute, and the terror of the Turks in these seas. Alone and unassisted she captured the captain-galleon of the Gran Signore

twice her own size, and valuing a million ducats. She also, with but
little help from others, fought the Grand Turk's armada of 48 galleys
and two galleasses, and set them to flight with great loss of Turks, as
is well known."

The galleon was the standard ocean-going, sail-driven fighting ship,
which as designed in England by Sir John Hawkins to meet the
Spanish Armada, was not intended for boarding, but to out-sail the
enemy, and to out-gun him with broadsides. To gain the necessary
speed and manoeuvrability, the vessel's keel was made at least three
times the measure of the beam. It was because Dudley knew how to
construct these nimble, medium-sized ships, whose defeat of the slower
Armada galleons had earned them great repute throughout Europe,
that the Grand Duke had especially welcomed him.

His first men-of-war, were built to enjoy similar tactical qualities,
to sail closer to the wind than the Turkish ships, and faster, so that they
would keep the weather gauge, choose the range for broadsides, and
engage and disengage action at will. But his fertile inventiveness
ranged not only over galleons but over the whole line of fighting ships,
from the traditional Mediterranean galley, long, low, oar-propelled,
and firing only ahead and astern, to the galleasses, the recognised
compromise between galley and galleon, and to galleons larger than
the *San Giovanni Battista*.

As well as English design, Dudley had, by his engagement of English
shipwrights, introduced English shipyard practice to Tuscany. He had
also enlisted the services of several English master mariners, among
them the renegade Eliot, and a Captain Janvier, who was often engaged,
with Lotti's co-operation, in transporting men and arms from England,
and also Captain Richard Thornton, who had first worked for the
Grand Duke shortly before Dudley's arrival.

This situation caused Sir Henry Wotton some concern. "The Grand
Duke continues to entice English mariners and shipwrights into his
service, has bought ordnance from English ships, and taken English
pirates under his protection. The Tuscan fleet consists principally of
English sailors. There are two English slaves serving in the Tuscan
galleys whom the Grand Duke refuses to release. Also he protects Sir
Robert Dudley and Captain Eliot and other English exiles and
traitors."

When an English Catholic priest arrived at Livorno "to corrupt
English sailors from their religion and allegiance to King James",
Wotton submitted formal complaint to Ferdinand, who received the

letter with unaccustomed ire. Much correspondence followed regarding "the quarrel between England and Tuscany", until James sent a special emissary to the Grand Duke, Sir Stephen Le Sieur, an anglicised Frenchman, who stayed several months in Florence without improving matters at all. He and Dudley were not on friendly terms, and later, in a letter to England, Dudley complained how "the King's agent, Sir Stephen Le Sieur, proclaimed me in his cups for a rebel and I know not what. . . ."

Meanwhile, Dudley's influence continued to grow. It was indicative of the confidence he had won that he was able to inspire Ferdinand, his eyes always seawards, to fit out a 400-ton galleon to continue the exploration of the Orinoco, with the aim of establishing a Tuscan colony in the fertile Guiana lowlands that ran towards the reputed El Dorado. This ship sailed for the West Indies in September, 1608, and although she was commanded by Thornton, it was Dudley who directed the project, and supplied the maps and sailing instructions born of the earlier journey. That this venture was strongly supported by the Grand Duke's First Minister, Belisario Vinta, a man of vital influence in Tuscan affairs, showed that the recognition of Dudley's merits was not confined to the Grand Duke.

Dudley's impact on Tuscany was far from being confined to ship-building and marine undertakings. Indefatigable in both proposals and action, he was a man after Ferdinand's own heart, and one to whom he could confidently give a free rein. The Grand Duke had already undertaken works of public utility, such as draining the Val di Chiana, and had continued the plans of his father, Cosimo I, to develop Livorno into a port. Now, spurred by Dudley's vision and creative energy, and impressed by his engineering knowledge, he embarked on a more ambitious expansion, which consisted of widening and dredging the harbour, and building fortifications, quays and a great mole, all designed by Dudley in the first place, and mostly constructed under his supervision.

Another of his engineering works launched by Ferdinand was the draining of the salty marshes which lay around Pisa and along the Arno valley up to the Val di Nievole, so transforming the whole area into a fertile plain. There is evidence too that Dudley, whose agile mind teemed with constructive schemes for every place he saw, was the instigator of two other projects started by Ferdinand, the first to bring fresh water to Pisa by aqueduct from Asciano, and the second to provide a water link between Pisa and Livorno by diverting part of

the Arno current into a canal, the Naviglio, and so cutting out the
tedious detour by sea. All these achievements were notably in advance
of current ideas and practice in hydraulic engineering.

That Livorno's development as a port was more than matched by
the speedy expansion of its commerce was again due to Dudley's
influence, for it was at his suggestion that Ferdinand added to his
already notable list of fiscal reforms by declaring Livorno a free port.
His decree, the *Livornina*, an outstanding example of despotic benevolence in times when most countries laid restrictions on commerce,
proclaimed the port "a place of universal toleration", with the result
that refugees of many nationalities and religions quickly flocked there,
among them persecuted Jews, to whom the Duke granted a special
charter of protection. The immediate consequence was an extension
of trade to countries beyond the Mediterranean.

In yet one more direction was Dudley's lively inspiration exerted.
This was in the manufacture of silk, which Ferdinand, in his zeal to
develop Tuscan industry, had encouraged by extending the systematic
growth of mulberries, to enable the trade to provide its own raw
material. It was Dudley's alert eye that saw scope for improvement in
manufacture, and in October, 1610, he was granted a patent for an
invention which both facilitated the making of silk and improved the
quality. He was granted the exclusive right to profit from the invention
for twenty years. It is an interesting speculation whether this patent
contributed to the pre-eminence in silk-making that Italy has since
enjoyed.

That Dudley should not only eagerly occupy himself in his several
activities, but should show much pride in all of them, commended him
highly to Ferdinand. This was a time when men of noble blood, if
they could not find profitable adventure or procure an office of gain
under the Crown, preferred to beg for a pension rather than engage in
menial tasks. Shipbuilding and engineering were decidedly lowly
occupations, suitable for worthies like Matthew Baker or Phineas
Pett, but hardly for a gentleman. Yet Dudley for all his high titles,
sought out such work and plumed himself on it. That he earned the
esteem of the merchant-minded Medici is easy to understand.

His several achievements gained him a respected place in the highest
Tuscan circles, but the part he played in helping Ferdinand to strike at
the Turks did him harm in England. This was because London
merchants believed that the reports of an Englishman strengthening
the Tuscan navy "cannot but anger the Turks against our nation, and

they would, if they could, protest to the King". The protest was made, and action followed.

"We are like enough to fall out with the Duke of Florence", commented an official report. "Our merchants are forbidden to trade any more with Livorno, and are minded to translate their traffic to Genoa." But these difficulties eventually passed, chiefly because of Livorno's great advantages as a free port, where merchants and bankers of all nationalities had now settled, and where bills of exchange and letters of credit and other trading documents could be readily negotiated.

This trouble over Turkish trade was a very minor thorn in Dudley's flesh compared with the unfortunate turn which his family affairs had taken in England. First came the death of his unhappy mother. In spite of the shame he had brought upon her by his elopement, especially following on the Star Chamber humiliation, she had held to her love for him, and kept in touch by messages and letters sent through the good offices of Lotti. She had at least some consolation in the presence of her elder son, Lord Sheffield, and his family, though she may have endured further suffering through the loss of her children by Sir Edward Stafford, for there is no later record of them. She remained in affectionate touch with the Lady Alice and her daughters, to whom, when her life ended in December, 1608, she left generous bequests.

Much anguish had been brought upon her by her son's selfish decision to establish his legitimacy, and by his heartless abandonment of wife and family. But his callousness towards her, as well as towards Alice, must be measured not by present-day standards but by those of his times. All their troubles stemmed, in some degree, from the softness in her character, so out of tune with sixteenth-century insensibility. It was not her infatuation for Leicester but her weakness over his renunciation which warped her life, as well as that of the son whose grievances recoiled in turn upon her. Had she been a woman of harder metal, such as her scheming rival, the Lady Lettice, she might have wrested a fairer deal from life.

As for the unfortunate Alice, she had not only lost her husband but seemed likely also to lose her stake in his possessions. For the Crown resisted his conveyance in trust, and sought at law to attach every fraction of his lands for his contempt. Judgement was naturally given in the Crown's favour, and a Commission, headed by Sir Richard Verney, once Leicester's ward, was appointed to assume charge of the estates on behalf of the King.

James was indelicately eager to lay his hands on this booty, for some time previously he had sent Sir Thomas Chaloner to Kenilworth with Officers of Works to examine the Castle and grounds, and to report on what was needed to make good damage and neglect, an indication that Alice had not lived there since her husband's flight into exile. Now, with the Commission taking formal possession of the estate, it seemed that the income she drew from rentals, as well as her valuable jointure on the woods, would be taken from her. And that, at first, Dudley was not alive to this risk may have been due to his preoccupation with the possible hazards that had suddenly fallen upon his own situation in Florence.

So acceptable had he and his wife become to the Grand Duke and Duchess that although he was compelled to spend so much of his time in Pisa and Livorno, he had hastened his search for a house in Florence. This he found in the Via dell'Amore, where he became the tenant of the Cavalier Annibale Orlandini. He and Elizabeth were now frequently in attendance at Ferdinand's small but distinguished Court, contrasting so favourably in its simplicity and dignity with the coarseness and corruption of the Jacobean Court.

Their intimacy there had been undoubtedly deepened when in 1608 Prince Cosimo, now nineteen, was married in San Lorenzo to the sixteen-year-old Archduchess Maria Maddalena, daughter of Archduke Charles of Austria. This was an important alliance for the Medici, for Maddalena's sister, Margaret, was the wife of Philip III of Spain, and her brother Ferdinand was soon to become the Emperor of the Holy Roman Empire. Dudley and his wife attended the celebrations of the marriage, held with extravagant pomp at the Palazzo Vecchio, where a gargantuan banquet was served to the Tuscan nobility in the Hall of the Five Hundred. Around the hall were displayed the treasures and trophies taken from the Turkish fleet by Dudley's *San Giovanni Battista* and her consorts.

The red-haired Maria, when she arrived in Florence to be married, accompanied by her 300-strong train of courtiers and servants, spoke only German and Latin. Elizabeth Southwell, a northerner too, was of an age with the bride, and like her, a stranger, not able to speak the Italian tongue, though as a well-educated girl, as were all Englishwomen of her degree, she was conversant with Latin. It was to be expected that the two exiles should form a friendship, which was to be amply demonstrated later, and which quickly helped Dudley to establish as strong a position with the young heir-apparent as he had done with Ferdinand.

But this extension of intimacy within the Grand Ducal family came, so far as Dudley was concerned, not a moment too soon, for Ferdinand, whose diet was normally sparse, and who was induced to indulge too freely at the several marriage feasts, fell ill, and died in February, 1609. The body lay in state in the Grand Ducal Palace, where Dudley and his wife paid their last tribute to the man who had been so much their friend in need. He was interred in the sacristry of San Lorenzo, next to the magnificent family mausoleum which he had begun some years before, and to which the body was eventually moved.

Ferdinand was by far the best and most enlightened of the later Medici. It was indicative of his humane and beneficent reign that, in a hundred and fifty years, he was the first ruling head of his House against whom no attempt at overthrow was made. His rule had brought order and stability. He ended corruption in the Courts of Justice. He was a liberal patron of learning and art, and revived the prestige of Florence as the traditional centre of the Renaissance, not least by bringing to the Uffizi the superb collection of classic art which, during his long years as a Cardinal, he acquired for his Villa Medici in Rome. In the sphere of music, his encouragement brought about the development of a new form, the Opera, originally called Recitativo, and first performed before him in the Great Hall of the Uffizi.

In the course of his twenty-two years' reign, building on the foundations laid by his father, he made himself the most potent ruler in Italy, and Tuscany the most powerful state, with its standing army and navy, its flourishing industry and its rich commerce, which produced a yearly, income greater than England's, and at least as great as that of France.

He left his son a magnificent heritage, including an immense fortune. That Dudley had notably contributed to some of his achievements, and no less to his wealth, was not lost on the new Grand Duke, nor on his mother, and they did not hesitate to retain their valuable prize in his privileged place and authority. His position was almost stronger than before, because he had made himself indispensable not to an individual but now to the Medici family. He held their liking, and was welcome at their Court, where he and Elizabeth were received as the Earl and Countess of Warwick. His marriage to her was never questioned, and their first child, Maria, born in July, 1609, was accepted as a matter of course as lawfully born. And that her godmother, Mrs. Mary Tracy, was the wife of the most prominent

English merchant in Tuscany, Andrew Tracey, showed that Dudley was on as friendly terms with the sizable trading fraternity as with the Court.

Yet the loss of his proved benefactor, and the consequent change of patron, caused him to reflect that his prosperity, and that of his family, rested on the whim of a young uncertain prince. In spite of all he had gained in Tuscany, his income was small by the standards he had previously known, and he was constrained frequently to borrow money. Inevitably, as he learned what was happening to his splendid patrimony in England, his gaze turned sometimes to the affluence he had abandoned.

Through the ships' captains who worked between Livorno and London, he was in regular confidential touch with his friends in England, and was not long in learning that although Kenilworth and his other estates had been escheated to the Crown, Northampton, prepared to be discreetly helpful now that he was safely in his appointment as Lord Privy Seal, had persuaded authority to adopt a face-saving formula of legality, and have them valued. The underlying reason for this step was for a nominal payment to be made to discharge the trust and jointure. Instructions were clearly given that the valuation was to be kept low, for the first estimate of just under £50,000 for the Kenilworth property alone was rejected. A second was produced which assessed the castle, on which Leicester had spent £60,000, at £10,401, the land at £16,431, and the woods, which had been considered worth £20,000 for the jointure, at £11,722.

Thus for a property worth at least £80,000, a total valuation was made of £38,554, "out of which there is to be deducted for Sir Robert Dudley's contempt, £10,000, and for the Lady Dudley's jointure, whereby she may fell all the woods, £11,722". This report by the surveyors, confirming that, within their purview, the jointure was intact, gave the first recorded indication that Dudley had been fined for his offences, as well as deprived of his possessions.

The exertions of the surveyors were noted with interest by those who hoped to share in the spoliation of Dudley's inheritance. The principal vulture was still Sidney, who not only called for a report on the rents, but bore the expenses of the survey, though not permanently, for King James later ordered the Treasury to pay him some £75 "for sums disbursed by him for the charges of the commissioners, counsellors and others employed for the finding of Sir Robert Dudley's lands".

Even more illuminating was a letter sent by Sidney in March, 1610, to Salisbury, regarding the allocation of Dudley's heritage. "Touching the grant which his Majesty intends to my Lord of Kinclenin and me," wrote the grasping courtier, "I trust his Majesty doth remember as well what he hath heretofore promised me . . . but for me, there had not been anything of Sir Robert Dudley's come to his Majesty's hands." Which was a frank enough confirmation that it was his instigation of the Star Chamber intrigue which had driven Dudley into exile and contempt of the Crown.

But there was another onlooker, more rightfully interested in the disposal of Kenilworth, who kept a close watch on the situation. This was Sir Thomas Leigh, now a baronet, who on behalf of Alice wrote from Stoneleigh to the Commissioners to ask what they proposed to do with the rentals of the estate, which formed his daughter's chief source of income.

These manoeuvrings around possessions that Dudley regarded as still rightfully his, at length provoked him to consider trying to do what Ferdinand had advised, which was to gain the Royal pardon. That he had achieved so much in Tuscany entirely on his merits caused him to reflect that in the elevated spheres in which he could reasonably expect to move in England, provided his transgressions were overlooked, he would be capable of even greater achievement.

He would have pondered on the remarkable advancements that had fallen to some of his blood relations, not only the calculating Northampton, already sufficiently rich from the spoils of office as Lord Privy Seal to be building himself Northumberland House at Charing Cross, but also the much less artful Nottingham and Suffolk, both of whom had found sycophancy under James a far quicker road to fortune than courageous fighting under Elizabeth. Suffolk, particularly, had found wealth so easy to come by that he had already almost completed the vast mansion he was building to Northampton's design at Audley End in Essex.

What they had achieved with their mediocre talents, Dudley may well have thought, he could readily better with the rarer ones he knew he possessed. He realised that there was little hope of propitiating King James, and for a time did not perceive the obvious alternative. Then a sudden change of circumstances pointed his course. For at the end of May, 1610, Prince Henry became Prince of Wales, a dignity which, allied to his precociously intelligent and sensible character, confirmed him, though still a youth, as already a potentially important figure in his country's affairs. And Chaloner was made his Lord Chamberlain, a position of much influence.

It was this favourable situation which, following on Dudley's contemplation of his future in Tuscany, where he could never, however remarkable his progress, climb to the rank and wealth he had so lightly given up at home, decided him to seek a pardon by winning the patronage of the admirable young Prince of Wales.

CHAPTER XIV

"MY MASTER, PRINCE HENRY"

Prince Henry was seventeen years of age, and the time had long since arrived when he should have a wife. This was a problem to which his father had given thought for several years. As a matter of appeasement policy with the great Catholic states, James wished him to marry a princess who was a Catholic, but also one who would bring a very large dowry. Henry was the Crown's most valuable saleable asset, and in view of James's chronic thirst for money, it would obviously be inept to dispose of him to any but Europe's wealthiest regal houses.

For some time the King had tried to arrange a betrothal with the Spanish Infanta Anna, but this plan fell through. There were protagonists for an alliance with a French princess, which ran to inconclusive discussions, and with a daughter of the Duke of Savoy, which James regarded dubiously, for the Duke was nearly as impecunious as he was himself. But there was another project which he had first examined in 1601, when he was still only King of the Scots, and this was a match with a daughter of the Medici.

This earlier plan had foundered because, even more needy then than now, he had asked for part of the dowry in advance, a proposal which evoked no response from the prudent Grand Duke Ferdinand I. Ten years later, dissatisfied with the French and Savoyard propositions, he decided to look again at Tuscany. In October, Salisbury approached Lotti on the possibility of a match with the Grand Duke Cosimo's sister, Caterina, on the promise that she should enjoy freedom of worship, and the hint that wide concessions might eventually be extended to all Catholics.

Cosimo welcomed this advance, for he was already linked by marriage to the reigning heads of Spain, France and Germany, and his influence in Europe would be firmly consolidated if his House were allied also to the Stuarts. But he knew that there would be opposition to the match in England, partly from the stubborn adherents of the

French and Savoyard projects, and partly from the Protestant elements who were fiercely against "their Prince marrying any Papist".

It was here that Dudley found his first opportunity to cultivate the favour of the heir to the throne, for though the young Prince himself declared that he "did not want two religions in his bed", he greatly valued the judgement of Chaloner, and Chaloner was strongly for the Medici princess.

Cosimo knew of Dudley's friendship with the Prince's Lord Chamberlain, and of his relationship with the Lord Privy Seal, and also that his wife's younger sister Margaret, soon to wed Sir Edward Rodney, was a Lady of the Privy Chamber to Queen Anne, and so in an advantageous position to ensure the Queen's support for the match. Official negotiations went on through Lotti, but Dudley was the unofficial link through whose agent, a Mr. Yates, the hidden inducements could be secretly conveyed by way of Chaloner to Prince Henry and Queen Anne.

Meanwhile, the claims of the two alternative young women were being pressed by the other self-interested intriguers of the Court, including the remaining members of Henry's own Household, with the result that competing negotiations dragged on spasmodically from month to month. The Prince watched these manoeuvres with some amusement, for he was in comprehension in such matters a good deal older than his years, partly because he had but recently relinquished a mistress whom, in spite of his youth, he had enjoyed for some time. This was none other than Dudley's kinswoman, Frances Howard, Countess of Essex, whose too-early marriage had proved a failure. The Prince had shown his customary sagacity in withdrawing from her favours when he saw her ready to transfer them to his father's newest favourite, the handsome but not very literate, twenty-year-old Robert Carr, now Viscount Rochester.

In Florence, the good reception given by Cosimo to Cecil's proposals was reinforced by the approval of the Grand Duchess Christina, who recognised the important benefits the marriage might bring to her co-religionists in England. Acting at once, she sent her own confessor to Rome, who presented the plan to a commission of cardinals, and judged from their reaction that Papal consent was certain. On this news, Cosimo formally offered James a dowry of 600,000 ducats. In London, this overture was well received as a basis for bargaining, and Lotti was congratulated by the Privy Council for his good work.

And then came trouble, for Pope Paul refused his sanction unless Prince Henry changed his faith and every English Catholic enjoyed unrestricted liberty of worship. Cosimo realised that such terms would never be accepted, and so he began a succession of pleas and arguments with the obdurate Pope, meanwhile engaging in temporising manoeuvres with James and Henry.

In these delicate exchanges, Dudley played his discreet part. But he was far from relying on this service alone in his bid for Henry's good-will. He had learned that the King had been suddenly moved to bestow Warwick Castle, which would have been his had he proved his legitimacy, on Sir Fulke Greville, who was busy restoring and extending it. Helpful as Northampton had been since confirmed in his office as Lord Privy Seal, there were limits to what he could do in his erring kinsman's interests, and if King James were again suddenly moved, but this time to bestow Kenilworth on Sidney, the fact of possession would settle every argument. Dudley had to act quickly, and he contrived, through Chaloner, for Northampton was not *persona grata* with Prince Henry, to interest the Prince in the idea of acquiring the Kenilworth estate for himself. Henry inspected the Castle, liked it, and told his father he wanted to take this once royal residence as his own. At first James demurred, but much to Sidney's exasperation was eventually persuaded by his son's persistence to give his approval.

From subsequent happenings, it is clear that Chaloner enlisted Henry's interest not only in Dudley's castle, but also in his talent, his achievements, and his uncertain condition, and that the Prince was prepared to do as much for a Dudley exiled in Tuscany as he had for a Raleigh imprisoned in the Tower. For when James, after escheating Raleigh's estates for supposed treason, granted his Dorsetshire home, Sherborne Castle, to Lord Rochester, Henry, a friend and admirer of Raleigh, whom, in one of the strange paradoxes of the times, he frequently visited in the Tower, and who contributed much to the shaping of his accomplished character, demanded the house for himself. The reluctant James submitted, but had to present Rochester with £20,000 as compensation.

Everyone realised that Henry intended to keep the house only until Raleigh's release, or his own succession. Some similar subterfuge was contemplated over Kenilworth, for there can be little doubt that Henry's interest in Dudley was inspired in part by the extraordinary similarity in character and background between him and Raleigh.

Both were proud and overbearing, conscious of their superior powers, and yet frustrated, and both had run into trouble in consequence. Both were men of action, adventurers, explorers, courageous seamen and fighters, yet both were men of intellect and learning, of science, mathematics, physics, philosophy. Their restless brains seethed with projects which they had the energy and capacity to carry out. And both were especially concerned, as was Chaloner, with the lore of the sea, with opening up the oceans, with navigation, with shipbuilding, and with naval tactics and strategy.

These last interests, Prince Henry, through the influence of Chaloner and Raleigh, had come to share keenly, for in contrast with his timid father, he leaned to the heroic Elizabethan maritime spirit, and so was readily led to extend a benevolent patronage to Dudley. Of Raleigh, he had said, "None but my father would cage so fine a bird", and he may have felt that Dudley was another "fine bird" encaged in foreign exile. From now on he worked, tactfully but persistently, not only to save Kenilworth for Dudley but to help him win a pardon, and return home.

For his years, Prince Henry was astonishingly forward in both mind and character. Although hankering after martial pursuits, he was an avid student, well versed in affairs, conscientious over his duties, kind and amiable, and a far better judge of men than his father. He was, indeed, so different from James that there were many who, reflecting on Queen Anne's frivolities, and the amours of Mary, Queen of Scots, questioned his paternity nearly as much as they questioned that of James himself.

Prince Henry's first step was to suspend the sequestration of Dudley's estates, on the grounds that his offence was not treason, the usual excuse for such drastic action, but only contempt. In consequence, he insisted that all Dudley's properties must be paid for. With little delay, he sent one of his factors, John Wyatt, with a notary, William Dyneley, to Italy, where Dudley, primed by Chaloner upon the Prince's intentions for the future, showed uncharacteristic readiness to accept a low price. The progress of these negotiations is well illuminated by extracts from relevant State Papers.

The first is a warrant, signed by Sir Francis Windebank, the Chancellor of the Exchequer, authorising the payment of £50 expenses to Wyatt, "employed as a commissioner to Sir Robert Dudley in Florence, to treat and compound with him for the Castle and Manors of Kenilworth". Wyatt did not get his expenses refunded until 1616, but a contract was prepared which was signed by the Prince in November, 1611, when the agreed price was stated as £14,500, to be paid within the year. This was an inordinate reduction on the already eroded valuation of £38,554, but it was not low enough for James.

According to a later Privy Council Register of February, 1617, "John Wyatt and William Dyneley have been long suitors for satisfaction of charges and moneys disbursed in the execution of a commission concerning the concluding of a bargain on His Majesty's behalf with Sir Robert Dudley, Kt., for the Castle and Manors of Kenilworth and Rudfen, in the county of Warwick, and for passing the fine and conveyance of the same. For the performance of this service, they went twice to Livorno, in Italy, where Sir Robert Dudley then was, and by their care and travail reduced the price from £38,000 to £7,000."

This fantastic drop was in the nature of a bribe for a pardon, for as was stated in a paper written much later on, unsigned, but obviously by Dudley, he "asked Prince Henry to tell the King that no other motive induced him to pass so rich a castle at so low a price, except to give the King satisfaction for his contempt". The paper also declared that "Prince Henry was so confident that the King would pardon the contempt that he sent Mr. Attorney to make ready a pardon for when it should please the King to grant it". This confidence was misplaced, and the Prince sent a messenger to Dudley "to let him know that it was not his fault that the condition of the pardon was not performed".

But because of complications arising from Alice's jointure on the estates, and the several parcels of land bequeathed to Lettice in Leicester's will, negotiations proceeded slowly, and not until another year had gone could Prince Henry write to Sir Julius Caesar, then Chancellor of the Exchequer, "Sir George More hath acquainted me from you that the King my father is willing that the Castle and lands of Sir Robert Dudley should be inserted and settled in the entails of lands to the Crown . . . this is my first purchase, and no ill bargain, as I conceive . . . you will be careful to provide the other £3,000 which His Majesty is content to bestow for buying in of the Countess of Leicester's estate in some things near adjoining".

The considerate Prince did not forget Alice's needs. A few months later, an order from the Chancellor of the Exchequer declared that "In consequence of Lady Alice Dudley's distressed state", King James was pleased to grant her "£300 yearly revenue and allowance out of the rents and profits of the Castle and Manor of Kenilworth, seized into our hands for contempt, to be paid half yearly".

The decreased price agreed for Kenilworth was confirmed by a warrant of a later date, with the King's own sign manual, and countersigned by the Chancellor of the Exchequer, "for payment of £500 to Thomas Stone, merchant, on account of Sir Robert Dudley, part of the sum of £7,000 which King James had bestowed towards the purchase of Kenilworth and the parks thereto belonging". Prince Henry appointed his Receiver, Sir George More, to collect £3,850 of the total, out of which the £500 was given to Stone "to be paid to Sir Robert Dudley now beyond the seas".

The unsigned paper had mentioned that Dudley "had three manors worth £30,000 yet to sell". Irrespective of whether Kenilworth might one day be restored to him, and anxious to have a sizeable fortune in his hands, he was trying to dispose of these manors. He arranged to convey to his agent, Yates, and to Chaloner's close friend, Sir David Foulis, the Prince's Cofferer, "all such lands remaining unsold", in order that their disposal could be easily negotiated. But the greedy Sidney considered that these properties should be his, and used his influence to get possession of them. Writing later to Foulis, Dudley asks that Prince Henry "protect me in the sale of the manors of Itchington and Balsal, that I might settle my estate, for without the sale thereof, I shall be in far worse case than I was before".

Following the practice of the times, he adds that Yates, to whom "I have given warrant to undergo all my business whatsoever in my behalf, in my absence . . . can assure you that on the sale of the lands, I have proportioned a thankful gratuity for you, as testimony of my thankfulness".

The reasons he was in need of money were twofold. Generous as was his yearly pay from the Grand Duke of around 2,000 scudi, it was not sufficient to provide suitably for his fast growing family, for Elizabeth had delivered a second child, Cosimo, in July, 1610, a third, Anna, in October, 1611, and a fourth was in prospect. The house in the Via dell'Amore was no longer adequate, but he was unable to rent a larger one, and he knew he would ultimately have to find the funds to buy or build his own residence.

Neither was his salary enough to enable him and his wife to take part with proper dignity in the elegant Court life to which they were now so often invited, for Cosimo was more given to gay entertainment than his father. They were much in favour with the religious-minded Grand Duchess Christina, who extended to them her special protection as persecuted Catholics, and in probably even closer intimacy with the Grand Duchess Maria Maddalena, as was demonstrated when she became godmother to the fourth child, born in December, 1612, and named after her. In similar fashion, the Grand Duke had endorsed his friendship with Dudley by becoming godfather to the boy baptised in his name.

Cosimo had been faced with a difficult task in following his father, for the success of Ferdinand's reign had rested entirely on his commanding, shrewd, and mature personality. Though well trained by both father and mother, and sustained by an exceptional wife, the nineteen-year-old ruler could not be expected to possess either Ferdinand's authority or his wisdom, and he was still somewhat under the sway of his strong-minded mother. Nevertheless, he continued in his father's steps, there was no immediate change in Tuscan affairs, and he and his wife, a handsome couple, were well liked by their subjects.

So far as Dudley was concerned, the shipbuilding and other projects begun under Ferdinand, Livorno harbour and the Mole, the Naviglia Canal, the Asciano aqueduct, continued without interruption under Cosimo. And one angle of his constant efforts to keep the Tuscan Navy in full fighting trim was reflected in a letter to Carleton in Venice, in which John Chamberlain mentioned that "the pirates have refused the King's pardon that was offered them, and it is said, have gone to Florence to be commanded by Sir Robert Dudley".

It was about this time that Dudley became engaged in compiling two large volumes, in English, the first on "the fortifying and ordering of ports", the second on "naval architecture", as he always labelled his ship designing. In the course of an examination of some 34 symmetries, or classes of vessel, he avers his preference for the 12th symmetry, the most perfect for two-deckers, the proportions being in thirds, the keel three times the beam, board, and draught. He plans a galleon of 1,200 tons, carrying 90 demi-cannons, as compared with the largest English galleon carrying 18 demi-cannons. But he adds that "These vessels are chiefly fit to be Royal galleons of a great King's settled Navy, not to be employed but upon great occasion, to defend the State or such like".

Although it was probably Dudley's pleasing ambition to build so grand a vessel, with its batteries of 30-pounder demi-cannons, it is unlikely he ever did so, for there was no role for it in the Mediterranean. Instead, he provided Tuscany with the type of fighting ship she needed, chiefly of the galleass breed, with both sail and oar, a powerful broadside, and nearly the seaworthiness of the galleon, though low and snug in the water. With her batteries of long-range demi-culverin firing 9-pound shot, she could, with even the lightest wind, outfight any number of galleys, and also the kind of unwieldy galleons and galleasses which the Turk then employed.

In this volume on shipbuilding, he explained how "curiosity made me more painfully search into the depth of this art, and with good success I have accomplished my desires and promises by practice herein, both in the time of Ferdinand, Great Duke of Tuscany, of famous memory, as also his worthy son, Cosimo, now Great Duke, from both of them having received more favours and obligations than I could merit".

Suffering from no false modesty over his writings, he concludes, "Not to divert the reader, I will only secure him that whatsoever is contained in this work is different from all others, and not taught by any, but invented (by God's assistance) by the practical experience and knowledge it hath pleased the Infinite Goodness to employ in me, and afforded by my practise, contemplations and studies herein".

Dudley's repute in marine affairs, already high enough to give him undisputed eminence in Tuscany, was expanded even further when, soon after Ferdinand's death, Captain Thornton returned from the West Indies, having closely explored the South American coast between Trinidad and the Amazon. "The said Captain went and returned prosperously", wrote Dudley afterwards, "and though he had never been in these parts before, nor yet in the West Indies in any wise, yet by means of the charts and instructions in the author's own hand, he by the grace of God, achieved his voyage without loss except one man who died of sickness. And he discovered the coast of Guiana more exactly than had ever before been done, and he discovered, moreover, the good port of Chiana, which is a royal port and safe."

Entering the mouth of the Amazon, Thornton "found a bore, a dreadful tide and perilous in the days of the new and full moon, noted here in the said chart by the author in the words 'Beware of a bore at six hours and a quarter'. And with these few words of warning, the Captain saved his vessel and the subjects of his Highness. As the Captain testified to his Highness, without the warning he would have known nothing of the peril; and he would have been lost if he had not warped his vessel with cables in a safer position, so as to receive the bore with his prow, and thus the vessel did not founder."

Thornton stayed some time at Chiana, later the French port of Cayenne, where he made friends with the natives. He brought back samples of commodities of commercial value, including cotton, sugar canes, pepper, rosewood and balsam, and even persuaded half-a-dozen natives, "who were", wrote Dudley, "of those Caribs who eat human flesh", to return with him to Tuscany, where they were presented to the Grand Duke.

Although it was a disappointment to Dudley that Cosimo did not follow up his father's hopes of settling a colony in Guiana, the presence of the Caribs in Florence, a constant advertisement of his former prowess, was a source of pride to him. In the course of many talks to them, he learned more of the fertility of their kingdom, of its silver mines, and even of the elusive Manoa, situated by its great lake, and the capital of the legendary Emperor. Unfortunately, most of these men did not last long, for they fell easy victims to smallpox, "which in them is more virulent than the plague itself, because in those countries they have no knowledge of a like disease". After a few years, only one had survived, and he, having learned to speak fluent Italian, stayed in service at the Court.

But the satisfactory interlude of Thornton's safe arrival, and his confirmation of all the strange places and people which Dudley had seen seventeen years before, soon passed, and he gave his attention once again to his design to go back to England. His hopes of receiving a pardon, which had mounted steadily over the year, were sensibly strengthened when news arrived early in June of the death of the Earl of Salisbury, whose formidable disapproval had always blocked his way. Now, Chaloner's influence over Henry, and through Henry, over the King, should be much stronger, an expectation that was to be substantiated a few weeks later.

CHAPTER XV

"GRACIOUS PARDON"

Richmond Palace, the place where Dudley was born, was now the residence of the Prince of Wales. It was from here, at the end of July, 1612, that Chaloner sent a long letter to Livorno, with which for the first time were presented specific conditions for the grant of a pardon. In this letter, Chaloner adopted an unusual note of admonition, which, taken with the importance of his message, indicated that it had been phrased to pass the scrutiny of both the Prince and the King.

"Since you took a course to repair your offence by submitting yourself to his Majesty's grace", he wrote, "and resolved therein to use the mediation of his Highness, Prince Henry, I have not failed to do you all the good offices that lay in my poor ability: and as it beseemeth a friend to deal plainly with him to whom I profess friendship, let me persuade you to apply yourself to such actions as may rejoice those that wish you well, and have sorrowed much for your late misfortune.

"The means, in my opinion, to effect this, consist chiefly in giving evident tokens of your loyalty, and to make good by your service what by your neglect you have forfeited. Which point being happily won, and his Majesty's favourable conceit gained, it followeth next that to your Lady's friends and allies here in England you endeavour to give present satisfaction, to the end that both herself and your children may have portions allotted to them, or some such assurance thereof as you, in your fatherly care, are found to produce for them."

Chaloner's concern for the welfare of the Lady Alice in England was matched by a discreet consideration for the future of the Lady Elizabeth in Italy.

"Neither am I unmindful", he went on, "to put you in mind of what I presume you will not omit, that before your return to England, you will take order that some with you who have suffered loss of friends, and other prejudices, for your sake, be honourably settled with a convenient estate.

"By these endeavours", he promises, "you shall return a welcome guest to all your country: and the Prince, whom you vow, next only unto the King, to honour and serve, shall not be ashamed to have such a servant. To which purpose, it hath seemed good to his Majesty and his Highness that I should enclose the articles herein, to the end that, upon notice given by you of your humble readiness to give way unto your own happiness by subscribing dutifully thereto, you may forthwith receive that gracious pardon which you so much thirst for.

"And as you have received through my Lord of Northampton's especial care (as I may justly term it) the life of your estate, which through your debts and other intricacies was ready to perish, so let me advise you to acknowledge it with the best terms and fashion you may.

"I will end", concludes Chaloner on a less chiding note, "though not end to be a friend to him that shall apply himself to all loyal duties."

The terms laid down in the document enclosed by Chaloner, were, judged by the pointers in the letter, not unreasonable, but unfortunately they did not go on record. Nor is anything known of the manner of Dudley's reply. Assuredly, his greatest problem, which thus far seems never to have been faced by anybody, even himself, was what would happen in England to Elizabeth and her children. The idea of abandoning one whom he unquestionably loved tenderly, and who showed him no less a devotion, could hardly have entered his plans.

Though there is no trace of the correspondence that resulted from Chaloner's letter, Dudley seems to have had the effrontery to do some bargaining, probably through Northampton. He was fortunate to have this disinterested aid from his normally egocentric kinsman, but even more to possess a friend such as Chaloner, who could write to him frankly, and whose reproaches he could accept without loss of face.

That their understanding was not prejudiced by the situation was shown by their continuing co-operation over the proposed royal marriage, for in spite of Papal obduracy, negotiations had persisted, and soon after Salisbury's death reached a stage where Prince Henry, to disarm Protestant apprehensions, was compelled to deny rumours that he was already betrothed to Caterina. To help quicken the conversations, however, Chaloner sent his elder son with the agent, Yates, to Florence, where as Dudley's guest, he was warmly welcomed at Court.

Another visitor to Florence at this time was Lord William Roos, son of the Earl of Exeter, and a cousin of the late Salisbury. He was against the match on religious grounds, and wrote to Sir David Murray, Groom of the Stole of Prince Henry's Household, who also opposed the marriage, "This morning, the resident of Venice being with me told me that Yates, which came hither to see Sir Robert Dudley, had a conference with the Grand Duchess of three hours long —they have plotted which way to place the bribes. They make court here to Sir Thomas Chaloner's son. They would build upon his father for a chief foundation to this match". Then followed a cautionary note for the Treasurer of the Prince's Household. "The Great Duchess is advertised that Sir Charles Cornwallis is a great dissuader of the Prince from the marriage".

Roos had dealings with Dudley, and his letter to Murray continued, "It is advertised by Sir Robert Dudley that you have been for my Lord Lisle against him in some business between him and the Prince. Therefore you must look for all the ill offices he can do you. I love many good points that are in Sir Robert Dudley, but dislike many evil ones. He hath undertaken here by his credit with the Prince to persuade him by discourses to be firm in this match."

This letter not only reveals that Sidney had vainly tried through Murray to deter Prince Henry from buying Kenilworth, but also that by now Dudley had established himself in Henry's estimation. And in spite of the fears of English Protestants and the difficulties created by Pope Paul, plans for the marriage had arrived at a footing when Cosimo could confidently dispatch his prospective brother-in-law a gift of "three coursers and twelve brass figures of Hercules".

The ill-will of Lord Roos did not endure, for a few years afterwards, following the pattern of Dudley's own misadventures, he fled from England because of family scandals, left his estates in disorder, rejected the King's command to return, and after entering the Church of Rome, died twelve months later in Naples.

Dudley was now in good fettle at his prospects. Writing to Foulis, whom he thanks, on information given by Yates, for "the increase of your extraordinary good respect unto me, which now at his coming to Florence, he hath so fully confirmed (affirming you to be a principal agent in the speedy effecting of my business with the Prince, my Master)," he continues, "it cannot be unknown to you that I have given his Highness my estate of Kenilworth for a small matter, considering its worth. I have only reserved to myself and my heirs the Constableship of the Castle, so that I may have some command there under his Highness whenever I shall happen to come to England."

With this letter, which he signs "Warwick", and which gives clear enough indication that he felt himself within reach of a pardon, he encloses a copy of a treatise, again over the Warwick signature, that he has sent direct to Prince Henry, in the hope of engaging his interest still further. He may have been inspired to do this on learning that Raleigh was pleasing the Prince with similar papers on the same subject, the need for England to maintain a strong and well-organised navy.

This treatise, "*A Proposition for Prince Henry, Prince of Wales*", was divided into two parts. The first, prompted by the decline in naval efficiency since King James's accession, enjoined the Prince to give his care to the Navy as the most certain way to sustain England's power and authority. Beginning "What King is most powerful by sea hath the means to secure his own greatness", Dudley gives historical examples to prove his argument, among them the English and Dutch resistance to Spain, and the operation of Venetian and Tuscan sea-power in the Mediterranean. "For England", he declares, "their good and safety hath always been upheld by their sea-forces", and, using the word patron in the sense of master, he concludes with the then novel dictum, "Whosoever is patron of the sea commandeth the land".

That he and Raleigh, almost alone among their contemporaries, should so plainly enunciate this principle is sufficient indication of Dudley's insight into the strategic importance of sea-power, an insight gained like Raleigh's, partly from his own experience of sea fighting, and partly from an alert study of the experience of others, and of the far-reaching consequences of recent maritime campaigns.

In the second part of his essay, he set forward a proposal for an ideal navy to outmatch any other fighting force afloat. He knew that the deterioration in the English Navy was due in part to a return in design to two-and-a-half beamed ships, which were easily outsailed by the longer foreign galleons. In this situation, he saw his opportunity, for he was accustomed to building long vessels, his shortest galleon being now four beams in length, and the secondary vessels up to six and seven beams. In these proportions lay the secret of their speed and manoeuvrability.

One such vessel that he now proposes is what he calls a gallizabra, armed with 30 demi-cannons and 20 demi-culverins,[22] yet light, and only 10 feet in draught, and thus usable in shallow rivers and ports for invasion. Swift in sail, especially on a tack, it could evade any other ship. Only 150 sailors and 110 soldiers would be needed to man her in action. A fleet of 30 of these gallizabras, averred Dudley, which would cost no more than £70,000 to build, could "affront in battle the armada of any other potent State".

The gallizabra design had been adopted by Spain for her treasure ships, but was an untried proposition for the English Navy. It was a compromise between the galley and the zabra, a small, speedy sailing boat used on the coasts of Spain, though it is not clear how such light vessels could carry the heavy armament Dudley proposed. The older naval ships displaced by the gallizabras should, he shrewdly recommends, be sold cheaply to the "merchant adventurers of London and other port towns, who would keep them in good order, and form a naval reserve, strong in defence against pirates".

His second proposal was for a *Gallea Reale*,[23] which though of similar draught to the English galley, could row no less swiftly, sail faster, and fight with much greater force, for she could carry 60 pieces of ordnance. Such a vessel, he boasts, would beat off 20 ordinary galleys. But he warns that a fleet of these galleys, because of their lightness and speed, "would require a particular command, with other officers for their government, being greatly different in all orders from those of gallizabras and other ships".

Whether either the gallizabras or the royal galleys could have displayed the extraordinary qualities Dudley claimed, their specifications at least showed his readiness to produce original designs to confer new tactics, while the successes won by the vessels he had already built for the Grand Duke proved that he did possess the technical skills to give his ideas practical shape.

He concluded his treatise to Prince Henry, "Whereas I have found no friendship nor favour in England but from your Highness, so do I renounce all other obligations (his Majesty excepted) but yourself. And when it shall please God, I may, with my honour, return to serve you, I can then promise divers other services, not inferior to this, as well as for your profit".

The assurance which Dudley now displayed over the prospects of being once more in England was mentioned in a letter sent by Sir Dudley Carleton, who had relieved Wotton as ambassador in Venice, to John Chamberlain. In this he writes of an English visitor to Livorno, Sir Thomas Glover, who had reported that Dudley "entertained no small hopes of returning to England by means of the Prince's favour, and to be employed in some special charge about the King's Navy".

But his high expectations, so painstakingly built up over the past two years, and all so completely dependent on Prince Henry's patronage, were destined not to be realised. As had happened twice before at critical hours of his life, Fate had already intervened, was about to shatter his buoyant aspirations at a blow. The treatise which he wrote on November 12th was never to be seen by the Prince's eyes, for on the day after its despatch came news from England that just over two weeks previously he had been struck down by a malignant fever, and after a short illness in St. James's Palace, had died on the sixth of November.

This shocking anti-climax for some time left Dudley stunned with disappointment. Yet his was an extraordinarily resilient nature, and by now he had become inured to such cruel blows. That he had, before the Prince died, taken a pardon for granted, indicated that the terms were not too onerous, and it is possible that at first his sanguine temperament led him to consider taking advantage of them, despite the disappearance of his patron and protector.

But if the idea did occur, he would hardly have entertained it for long, for there were too many deterrents, all revolving around whether he could trust the King's word. According to English notions, he was guilty of bigamy, a crime in common law, as well as of contempt, a crime against the Crown, and of apostasy, a crime against Church and State. Because of his association with renegades like Parsons and Eliot, he had been openly deemed a traitor. Even if absolved of these offences, enemies such as Sidney, freed now of the curb of the Prince's eye, might soon conjure up a royal decision that he should, on second thoughts, answer for one or other of his crimes.

He had before him the example of Raleigh, guilty of nothing but the King's dislike, yet immured for years in the Tower. He could consider the unhappy Lady Arabella, also in the Tower, merely for marrying Lord William Seymour against James's wish, and being rapidly driven insane by her misfortunes. Nor would his wife fail to remind him of the fate of her father's cousin, the Jesuit priest, Father Robert Southwell, tortured ten times during his two years in prison before his sufferings ended on the scaffold. Dudley could reflect that though no plotting Jesuit, yet he was a recusant, and on entering

England would have to swear the oath of allegiance to King James, or take the consequences, and these, added to penalties for his other misdemeanours, might be dire. Inevitably he recalled the skulls grinning on their poles on London Bridge after the Essex revolt, and his vow never to put his own head within reach of the axe. And he decided that the risk was too great. With Prince Henry gone, the backing of Chaloner and Northampton would count for little, and even a formal pardon might soon rank for nothing with a King indifferent to his dead son's solemn intentions.

Especially as the suddenness of the Prince's death had produced the usual crop of rumours, but this time so serious that they had to be whispered. It was widely said that Henry had been poisoned at the instigation of James himself, jealous of his son's growing authority and popularity. In her first grief, Queen Anne had cried that Henry had been murdered by the Favourite, Rochester, and his secretary and adherent, Sir Thomas Overbury. Fingers pointed to the unconcern at the Prince's death shown by James and Rochester a day or so after the funeral, in opening negotiations for the marriage of Henry's younger brother, Charles, to a daughter of the Queen of France, and in cementing the betrothal of their sister, Princess Elizabeth, with Frederick V, Elector of the Palatinate, which was followed by the marriage three months later.

These suspicions of James's complicity, though completely unjust, were widely held and persistent, and they were neither stilled when a post-mortem gave the cause of death as fever, nor forgotten three years later, when another great scandal burst on a disapproving people.

Drastic and frustrating as were the effects of Henry's death on Dudley's prospects at home, they were far more serious for Raleigh. For the Prince, prior to his illness, had extracted from his reluctant father the promise to release Raleigh by Christmas. Now the unfortunate prisoner saw his hopes of freedom vanish, and with it, his Sherborne Castle, which reverted to the King, who promptly sold it to Rochester at a profit of £5,000.

But even Dudley's and Raleigh's interests were of minor significance compared with what was lost to England by the deprivation of a youngster of such promise. The course of English history would scarcely have run to civil war had this intelligent and judicious prince lived to restrain his father's political bunglings, and to succeed to the Crown instead of his weaker brother, Charles.

Unaware of these profounder consequences of the death of his patron, Dudley could see only its effect on his own fortunes, that there would now be no future for him in England, and that he must be content with Tuscany. Not that this was in any way a hardship, for there he had security, honour and domestic happiness. It is possible that his disappointment was not untinged with relief as he turned anew to his work at Pisa and Livorno.

CHAPTER XVI

AN ADVANCE TO KING JAMES

It was fortunate for Dudley that Cosimo, though a man of pacific nature, drew the line at displaying this tendency towards the Turks and corsairs. On the contrary he adhered firmly to his father's policy of keeping the Tuscan Navy strong, and of employing it whenever opportunity offered, such as when he sent it with the Knights of San Stefano to help the Druses in their struggle for freedom from Moslem domination. Because Cosimo not only wanted fighting ships, but also a larger mercantile fleet, the shipyards at Pisa and Livorno worked to capacity, and the stocks were never empty for long. So renowned had Dudley's master-hand become that shipbuilders in the ports of other States sought his designs and specifications in order to work by them.

Although the pressure of these activities, together with the continuing development of Livorno harbour and the engineering projects for Pisa, kept him largely tied to this area, he contrived to pass frequent spells in Florence. His standing at the Grand Ducal Court had steadily mounted, because he and his wife had become greater favourites than ever with the two Grand Duchesses, and hardly less so with Cosimo, who in spite of a too amiable and unassertive character, was conscientious over his responsibilities and impelled always by good intentions. A minor but significant symbol of his attitude to his position was his closure of the lucrative family banking business, as derogatory for a reigning monarch.

Dudley's now recognised place among the Florentine nobility was manifested by his role at a Tilting Tournament held in February, 1613, in the Great Salon of the Grand Ducal Palace, a chamber about twenty-five yards square. Here, opposing bodies of knights contested at the tourney before spectators in boxes and on raised seats around the room. "Senators were deputed to elect twenty gentlemen as umpires, among whom Sir Robert Dudley, famous in all knightly exercises, was one." These umpires, who sat in a box of honour opposite the Grand Ducal party in a similar box, included the General of the Tuscan Army, the Master of the Horse, the Constable of San Stefano, the Ducal Secretary and Treasurer, "and other cavaliers of the same order". After the tournament, all the participants made a torchlight procession through the city.

Other celebrations held about this time, indicative of the high-spirited outlook of Cosimo and his lively young brothers and sisters, and attended by them as well as Dudley and his wife, were a Game of Calcio, the current Florentine version of football, in the Piazza Santa Croce, a Court Ball at the Palace which continued into the middle of the night, and a torchlight masquerade.

But though Cosimo, like most of the Medici rulers, was fond of show and entertainment, he was actively interested also in the arts and sciences, a quality which Dudley welcomed, for in consequence, his own technical projects met always with understanding. Cosimo had, as soon as he succeeded, taken a step which was to throw lustre upon himself in history. In 1609, he invited to Florence, with the offer of an appointment as Court Mathematician and Philosopher, the illustrious Galilei Galileo, whose genius had first been recognised by Ferdinand with a professorship at the University of Pisa, but who had been forced by Jesuit opponents, who declared his teachings heretical, to flee to Padua, and there pick up a living by teaching.

Cosimo, who had been Galileo's pupil at Padua, built him a villa at Arcetri, on the southern slopes just outside the city's gates, near where he was erecting his new palace of Poggio Imperiale. His protection quickly produced results, for Galileo, constructing the first astronomical telescope, became the first human being to see the mountains of the moon and the satellites of Jupiter, which he named Sidera Medicea, in honour of his benefactor. So began that astonishing succession of discoveries which were to revolutionise man's knowledge of the universe.

Cosimo, deeply interested in these epoch-making developments, frequently visited Galileo at his villa with a few selected friends, Dudley among them, and here they shared in the astronomer's triumphs, and saw with their own eyes the discoveries revealed by his telescope. Although he was ten years older than Dudley, the two would find common ground, not only because both were mathematicians, or because Dudley had, through his practise of marine navigation, an instructed acquaintance with astronomy, but also because of their mutual interest in military fortification, on which Galileo had written a treatise twenty years before.

Contact with so stimulating a personality undoubtedly acted as a challenge to Dudley's own considerable intellect, and it was unfortunate that there was no chance for him to direct his enquiring mind into new channels. Instead, about this time, he began once more to devote himself to his writings on maritime matters, but now with the object of building up more comprehensive and erudite works. These he himself illustrated, for he was a skilled draughtsman and artist.

But he did not allow these activities to interfere unduly with his social relations in Florence, which were by no means confined to the Court or to Italians. Apart from the well-to-do English traders, led by the Traceys, who lived in the city, there was a constant flow of travelling Englishmen passing through on the customary *Giro d'Italia*, now more than ever part of the education of the young aristocrat.

Some of these travellers took care to avoid meeting an exile whose company, if reported back to King James by one of his numerous spies, might prove embarrassing. But others had no such qualms, and even recorded their encounters. One of these, Lord Herbert of Cherbury, the philosopher and historian, wrote how, riding to Florence from Rome, he "saw Sir Robert Dudley and the handsome Mrs. Sudel, whom he carried with him out of England and was there taken for his wife. I was invited by them to a great feast the night before I went out of town: taking my leave of them both, I prepared for my journey the next morning: when I was ready to depart, a messenger came to me and he told me, if I would accept the same pension Sir Robert Dudley had, being two thousand ducats per annum, the Duke would entertain me for his service in the war against the Turks. This offer, whether procured by the means of Sir Robert Dudley, Mrs. Sudel or Signor Lotti, my ancient friend, I know not, being thankfully acknowledged as a great honour, was yet refused by me, my intention being to serve in the Low Country war."

Another visitor whom Dudley undoubtedly arranged to meet was Inigo Jones, on the fruitful tour with Lord Arundel which brought Palladian architecture to England. As surveyor of works to Prince Henry, Jones had inspected Kenilworth on his behalf during the negotiations to purchase, and could thus have brought news for the man who still regarded himself as the rightful owner of the estate.

For the contract signed between Dudley and the Prince was rendered inoperative because the funds set aside for payment were frozen at

his death. Prince Charles, as his brother's heir, had inherited Kenilworth, but he was still only a boy of fourteen, and much younger for
his years than Henry. He had neither the interest nor the authority to
complete the transaction, and so far as Dudley was concerned, ownership of the property had reverted to him.

So much so that he exploited his expectations from Kenilworth in
order to borrow money, a course to which he was again impelled at
this time. Although his yearly salary was twice that of Galileo, the
sum was even less adequate than before to match either his pretensions
or the increasing expense of his ever-growing family, for Elizabeth
had by now given him five children. One of his largest creditors was
William Dyneley, the agent sent by Prince Henry to negotiate the
transfer for Kenilworth, to whom, even before this date, his debt had
mounted to £1,649 14s. 6d.

In spite of these persisting monetary embarrassments, he seems never
to have received any grant from the King of Spain, though there was
nothing discreditable about doing so, as most Catholic exiles were on
the King's pay-roll, as well as public men in England, including even
the late Salisbury, who had taken an allowance in return for supposedly
confidential information passed to the Spanish Ambassador.

In no way deterred by his financial difficulties, Dudley at last decided
that his expanding prestige and family demanded that he acquire his
own residence in Florence. In April, 1614, he paid 4,000 scudi to the
prominent Rucellai family for three small houses on a wedge-shaped
piece of land in the Via della Vigna Nuova, and on this site he erected
a four-storied mansion of his own design and construction, the ground
floor being occupied by merchants. In spite of the awkward trapezoid
shape, the house was large, for the principal frontage measured 45 yards,
and had ten windows to each story.[24] It is not clear how he met the
cost of this building, but later indications suggest that the Grand Duke
himself came to his aid.

Originally, Dudley conceived and planned his home with every
intention of spending the rest of his life in Tuscany. But early in 1614,
something not manifest occurred that caused him once more to think
of trying to win a pardon from King James. There was no evident
reason for this reversal of view, but despite past rebuffs, his was a
persistent and always optimistic nature, and it is likely that he acted
on the impulse when events in England took a turn that offered an
unforeseen opportunity.

This new situation lay in the powerful position that the Howards had won since the King's dismissal of Parliament, for they virtually ran the country. The Howard phalanx, consisting of Northampton, Lord Privy Seal, the most sagacious of them all, Suffolk, Lord Chamberlain, Nottingham, Lord Admiral, and their several sons and sons-in-law, had been powerfully reinforced when what had started as a casual affair between Suffolk's daughter, Frances Howard, and the Favourite, Rochester, became an overwhelming mutual passion.

This situation the insidious Northampton hastened to exploit, for nothing would better confirm the predominance of the Howards than to have Rochester married to one of them. With the help of some highly improper rigging of the Divorce Commission by the incorrigible King, more flagrant even than his intervention in Dudley's legitimacy suit, Frances gained her freedom. In December, 1613, she married Rochester, on whom James conferred the Earldom of Somerset as a wedding present.

It was doubtless Northampton who alerted Dudley to the opening that existed through his relationship with the Countess, whom he had known as a child, and who was now almost as much in favour with James as her husband. The result was that, despite all the factors which had previously held him back, and though Suffolk and Nottingham had never shown any eagerness to help him since his flight into exile, he decided to approach James again, and this time direct. But that he prudently pressed on with the building of his house indicated that he held no great hopes of real success.

His decision was made when news of the Rochester marriage arrived in Florence, and he launched his first attempt in the following month. Knowing how inefficient the English Royal Navy still was, he offered to build yet another fighting ship of unparalleled speed and power. No copy of this treatise exists, but he refers to it in "a letter to a friend", sent also in January, the friend being Chaloner.

His new vessel, he writes, is "of so wonderful a consequence of force and swiftness as I dare boldly say the like was never known to the world, and wonderfully far beyond those I mentioned in my discourse to the Prince, my master, of famous memory". This "counter-galleass" as he calls it, is designed for use against the Turks, and not only is the Grand Duke pressing him to build it, but also the Venetian Republic. However, "out of my affection to my country and duty to his Majesty" he wishes James to have the first refusal of the design. "No three of the King's greatest ships royal is able to endure the force of one counter-galleass", he concludes. "To have but ten of them would make a Prince absolute patron of the seas."

He asks Chaloner to ensure through Foulis, "now at the Court", that if the King declines the design, he shall at least grant its creator permission to exploit it to his own best advantage. James saw the treatise, and a demand for further information was sent which Dudley answered on May 8th, giving his pledged word "to be able to perform what is here written". But this time he wrote to Foulis, for Chaloner's star had set with Prince Henry's death, and from now on he disappears from the circles of the Court. To Foulis went a fuller description of the new vessel, and of the power a fleet of them would possess. Then, rather too precipitately, but in characteristic style, he goes on to make stipulations.

"One thing I resolve you that if it pleases his Majesty to hearken to this greatness to himself", he writes, "I must pretend to desire to be general (with a title) of such a squadron of these vessels, and to be a command and government by itself, not to be under the Admiral of England, but as the galleys is in France, a different command at sea, nor hazard the reputation of my own works under the discretion or skill of another."

A few days later, feeling that he should not delay in exploiting his relationship with Frances Howard, he wrote to Somerset, sending him also a copy of his treatise. "My Very Good Lord", he wrote in a letter which, in the polite usage of the times, was both fulsome and condescending, "I have heard by many, but especially by one that respecteth you much, of the worthy courses your Lordship taketh for his Majesty, his country's honour and good." He then refers to the treatise sent recently to the King, "wherein my worthy friend, Sir David Foulis, can inform you particularly".

The paper accompanying describes a vessel of under 600 tons, yet with a laden draught of only 10 to 11 feet, and compact enough to be kept under cover at little cost. She would carry 100 pieces of cannon, the lowest tier at midships, be well conditioned for rough seas, yet swift enough to outsail any ship in England. She could be rowed when becalmed, with condemned men or watermen. This vessel, built by new but proved methods, was a far better proposition than the galleass, stated Dudley, any two of which she could outfight.

"Though unknown to your Lordship", he continued, "I am bold to encourage your willingness to walk in such worthy steps, to your perpetual fame, and the comfort of them that thirst after nothing more than all happiness to his gracious Majesty and his seed for ever."

This unconvincing effort to solicit Somerset's interest surprisingly produced a not unpropitious response some months later, in which the Favourite stated that if the claims "prove as you promise, I shall be ready to employ myself to procure you such favour and reward as shall be suitable to the service, as upon the return of this messenger, and his Majesty's satisfaction by his report of this business, you shall more particularly understand. So wishing the good event of so great a project and much contentment to yourself, I rest, your loving friend, R.S."

In June came news that the Earl of Northampton had died. In spite of his duplicity and other dubious qualities, which were largely a natural self-protective reaction to the executions and other savage punishments suffered by members of his Catholic family, he had often been kind to Dudley, and since achieving authority, had tried to guard his interests. His loss at this time came as a depressive setback, but did not deter Dudley from his purpose. From then on, he was dependent on Somerset and his wife, whose father had now been appointed Lord Treasurer, and on the Herbert brothers, for they had held to their old friendship with him even though both were in good favour with James, who had years before created Philip Earl of Montgomery, and was soon to give William, Earl of Pembroke, the appointment of Lord Chamberlain.

Meanwhile, nothing had transpired from Dudley's letter to Foulis. Without doubt, his astute but presumptuous demand that his squadron should enjoy an independent role at sea, and that his vessels' tactical merits should be properly exploited by himself as commander, had not met with the approval of his elderly kinsman, the Lord Admiral, to whom his proposals were referred.

Growing impatient at the delay, he sent a reminder to Foulis in July by the hand of Yates, who had again visited him on business. "It is nearly two months since I wrote you full answer to satisfy his Majesty of my ability to make these forcible and swift vessels offered him . . . touching the same, I wrote something to my Lord Somerset. . . ." He then went on to refer to another treatise which he encloses for transmission to the King. This related not to shipbuilding but to the frequent opposition the King had encountered from the House of Commons, culminating with the suspension of parliamentary rule.

To Dudley, the troubles which James had experienced through stubborn and unruly parliaments contrasted strangely with the equable and popular rule of the Medici Grand Dukes, exerted unhindered as a benevolent autocracy through a professional secretariat. This rule, which never met with any kind of opposition during Dudley's lengthy service in Italy, had made Tuscany one of the first States of Europe, with a standing army of 20,000 trained troops and the strongest fleet in the Mediterranean, a rich and flourishing domain, respected by her neighbours, and pre-eminent in the arts, sciences and literature. In fact, Dudley could certainly have reflected, a model State.

It seemed logical that a polity which the Tuscans found so acceptable might well solve King James's problems in England, and to introduce it should be all the easier now that he had taken positive steps towards autocracy, for he was ruling entirely through Somerset, the Howards and a subservient Council. Seeing here a promising opportunity to ingratiate himself, Dudley prepared a treatise showing how England could be run, like Tuscany, free of trouble as a military dictatorship.

This he presented in his letter to Foulis, where after saying how, trying to devise a way to be of use to the King, "I thought of some application for his service of much I have seen and had extraordinary means to learn, from the school of the Great Duke Ferdinand, of famous memory", he goes on, "I thought it not amiss at this present to write you a word of some importunate matter for his Majesty's good, upon the occasion of the thwartness I understand of late that Parliament useth towards him. . . . Certain designs of mine, which if followed in England by his Majesty, I know may make him secure against all these rubs, and make him safe to do what he please with his own (absolute monarch as he is), without dangerous resistance, and free from the possibility of foreign invasion, if any such should ever be attempted, and keep the bridle in his own hands." As an additional attraction, he promises schemes "to increase his revenues to a much greater value—I hope double".

With questionable sincerity, he adds that he recommends the measures out of love and duty to his Majesty, and not out of any desire to leave his present home for England, where he has "received so many discourtesies from my friends and kindred, which are the greatest in the Kingdom". He was indicating Sidney, Nottingham and Suffolk.

The treatise was titled, *A Proposition for his Majesty's Service to Bridle the Impertinences of Parliament*, and was divided into two parts, the first to establish autocratic control, the second to produce additional monies.[25]

Under the first head, he urges that a fortress be built in every large town, which he points out "commonly has a ruinated castle, well seated for strength, whose foundations and stones remaining may be quickly repaired for this idea". The cost of maintaining a fort with 3,000 garrison he estimates would be "£40,000 charge per annum or thereabouts, being an expense that even inferior princes undergo for their necessary safety".

The governor and garrison of trained troops for each fortress must not be inhabitants of the place. All main highways must be routed through these fortress towns, so constraining travellers to pass through them. Gates must be shut at night, travellers made to carry tickets of identity, and innkeepers ordered to deliver the names of unknown voyagers who lodged with them. No one was to carry arms or weapons, save the King's enrolled men.

By these and similar measures, already proved in Tuscany, argues Dudley, the people could be kept under constant check and control, and no rebellion could succeed. Parliament would be "forced to be conformable to Your will and pleasure, for their words and opposition import nothing where the power is in Your Majesty's own hands. . . . This being indeed the Chief Purpose of this Discourse, and the Secret Intent thereof, yet to be concealed from any English at all, either Counsellors of State or other.

"In policy", declares Dudley with matter-of-fact effrontery, "there is a greater tie of the people by force and necessity than merely by love and affection, for by the one the Government resteth always secure, but by the other no longer than the people are contented."

After pointing out that the garrisons of trained men, assembled together, would provide a standing army against invasion, he turns to the second part of the treatise. In view of "the great expenses that Princes have now-a-days, more than in times past, to maintain their greatness and the safety of their subjects", he recommends "A Decimation, being so termed in Italy, where in some parts it is in use, taxing a tenth of every man's estate, to be paid yearly to the Crown as rent". In particular, he blandly suggests, there should be an imposition on lands owned by Catholics.

He further proposes that the salt monopoly be rented out at a profit of £150,000 per annum, that weights and measures be inspected and sealed yearly at sixpence a time, to procure £60,000 a year, that a 5% rate be placed on all offices in the King's grant, including notaries and attorneys, "whose fees and gettings are expensive in England", and that "a 7% tax, as in Tuscany, be laid on dowries and marriage portions and the alienation of lands". There should also be licences for inns and taverns and alehouses, and on people who wish to eat eggs, cheese and white meat on fasting days, "at 10/6 the rich and 1/6 the poor".

From all these levies, Dudley reckons the King should draw over two million pounds per annum. Then, after suggesting that his Majesty could save £60,000 a year by "reducing the Royal Household to board wages, as most other princes do", he goes on to his most easily productive scheme, to make "earls and grandees pay for their privileges, as in Italy and Spain. For example, barons to be made earls at £19,000 apiece." The King should also "ennoble 200 of the richest commoners, as in Naples (the ancient nobility to precede them): for a duke, £30,000; a marquis, £15,000; earl, £10,000; baron or viscount, £5,000. This should raise a million pounds or more."

Dudley concludes by asserting that other ways of raising money are available, which he will disclose "if Your Majesty resolve to proceed on the former courses". But he advises that his "counsel, if I may without presumption so call it" should be examined "by some one most trusted by his Majesty, which I conceive of, or rather wish it may be, my Lord of Somerset".

Although the Proposition did reach the King, through Somerset, to whom Foulis passed it, Dudley's temerity was evidently not appreciated, for he received no reply, not even a formal acknowledgement. In spite of his demonstrated tendencies to absolutism, James, whose "standing army" consisted of a handful of Yeoman of the Guard and Wardens of the Tower, could not see himself progressing very far along Dudley's road to military control. It is possible too that he was uncertain whether Dudley might not have written his treatise with his tongue in his cheek, as has been since suggested. But preposterous and even iniquitous as some of the proposals might have seemed at that time to Englishmen, many of them, as later generations were to find to their cost, came eventually into common usage.

The scheme for drawing revenue from titles lay in a different category, for James had peddled knighthoods since the day of his coronation, though only for modest sums. The gibe, "forty pound knight" did not exist for nothing. Since 1611, he had revived the rank of baronet, and put it on sale at £1,080 cash. But Dudley's propositions opened up more ambitious vistas, and soon led him to expand the business on a much higher level.

As for the *Proposition to Bridle the Impertinences of Parliament*, nothing more would have been heard of it but for a comedy of errors some fifteen years afterwards which was to provoke an astonishing commotion in England. But Dudley's offer to build an all-conquering navy, though backed by his proven expertness in creating ships to beat the Turks, drew not the slightest response. For King James was no more able to appreciate Dudley's undoubted talents than he was the even rarer genius of Raleigh.

CHAPTER XVII

"MY SIGNORE, THE GRAND DUKE"

THE EPISODE OF Dudley's attempt to ingratiate himself with an ignoble and faithless King marks a distinct modification of his outlook. If his proposals to install a military autocracy in England were not written as "a kind of Machiavellian satire", as has been suggested, but as a description of a proved constitution in Tuscany and most other States of Italy, then some of his recommendations, and his cynical arguments for them, come unexpectedly from one whose chivalry and generosity has been so amply displayed in the past, with the single exception of his attitude to his abandoned family.

The whole *Proposition*, taken with the persuasions of the naval papers, point clearly to the changes that were evolving in Dudley's nature. He had come to realise that a rebel could never win when both his King and Fate herself were against him. And under the pressure of the sharpest reality in his exile, the need for money to live and to keep his family, some of the high mettled independence in his character had wilted away.

That Raleigh was also reduced to the ignominy of ingratiating himself with King James by writing his *Prerogative of Parliament*, an essay on the divine right of kings, could not be set against Dudley's approaches, for he qualified his ideas with criticisms of worthless favourites. Moreover, he was in prison, living close to the axe, while Dudley merely aspired to improve his lot. His endeavours to gain the help of Prince Henry, through Chaloner, had carried an atmosphere of amicable negotiation, but his efforts to curry favour with James, and especially through his amoral kinswoman, Frances, and her upstart husband, all showed that he had come to terms with the hard fact that he would get nowhere without the favour of the monarch.

This was no less so in Italy, for his existence, and that of his family, depended entirely on the continuing beneficence of the Grand Duke. But his sycophantic overtures to James were on a very different level from his role of courtier with the Medici. His privileged position in

Tuscany had been won and held by his skill and labour in shipbuilding and engineering, while the intimacy which he and Elizabeth enjoyed with the Grand Ducal family was a matter of domestic concord. Yet even though these warrantable reasons existed for his good fortune in Tuscany, it seemed that even there, age and vicissitude had brought a mellowing of outlook, together with a readier disposition to bend the knee than he had ever shown in his earlier days.

But, as the building of his house indicated, his advances to King James were half-hearted. He did not really expect to gain a pardon, except perhaps to the extent of being allowed to visit England occasionally, and such a possibility was of the shadow, while in Tuscany he and his family enjoyed their reasonable fill of substance. To them, Florence was no longer an outlandish place of exile, but the centre of the world. They had long since come to regard England, as did the Florentines, as a remote and primitive island on the edge of Europe and of civilisation.

To the capital of the Medici came men of learning, art and commerce from all the chief cities of Europe, drawn by the work of scientists such as Galileo, or by Ferdinand's art collections, which Cosimo had judiciously augmented, or by the new buildings, typified by the Grand Ducal Palace extensions and the Chapel in San Lorenzo, which were conferring on the city fresh architectural prestige, or simply by the opportunities to trade, and to enjoy a secure, friendly and civilised metropolis.

Florence has become a livelier place in which to live. Since the previous year, 1614, when Cosimo, after an attack of malignant fever, had relapsed to the level of an invalid, and so been deprived of an active outdoor life, he had more than ever encouraged not only the arts and sciences, but also spectacle and entertainment, both in public and in the new courtyard at the Palace, which he had created by lengthening the front and adding wings to the rear. Jousts and tournaments, horse racing, theatrical and musical spectacles, were frequent, and the populace enjoyed their city as seldom before. This new spirit reached a climax in 1617, when Cosimo's sister Caterina, she who might have been Queen of England, was married to the Duke of Mantua, amid brilliant ceremonies and public rejoicings.

To Dudley and his wife, the prospect of never returning to their native hearth was thus ceasing to inspire any deep regret. He surely realised that the England of the present was a very different country from the one he had left ten years before. Gone was the lustre of

Elizabeth's reign, and the achievements of the spirited men her leader-ship had fostered, among whom he himself could claim a notable place. The conditions which bred them had vanished, and their suc-cessors were of different metal. The enterprising young aristocrat of today could no longer rush off to the Spanish Main, as Dudley himself had done, "to seek new worlds, for gold, for praise, for glory", but had to be content to tour Italy with a tutor.

Well might Dudley have considered the contrast between the Courts of Florence and London: the one cultured, harmonious and dignified, ruled by a gentle high-principled young prince, an active patron of art and science, and like his father, well able to appreciate an exile's talents: the other, corrupt and cut-throat, centred by a weak king of gross habits, publicly fondling his male favourites, incapable of judging character, incapable of recognising real talent in anyone.

And recent events had rendered England, to Dudley, even less inviting than before. The wretched Lady Arabella had expired, a madwoman in the Tower. Chaloner too, had died,[26] embittered by his eclipse. And an ugly tale had come to light of how Sir Thomas Overbury, Somerset's secretary, had been poisoned in the Tower two years before, at the instigation of Frances Howard and her husband.

The lengthy developments of this scandal put paid to any hope that Dudley might still have held of returning to England. In the spring of 1616, when the Somersets were placed on trial, the King's anxiety to protect them, added to Somerset's veiled threats of ugly revelations if he did not, revived public suspicions that James had connived at the murder of Prince Henry, suspicions that strengthened when, after the pair were found guilty and sentenced to death, they were merely confined in the Tower, from where the King, a few years later, released them, with the grant of an annual pension of £4,000.

The trial revealed the dubious part which Northampton had played, by his share in procuring Overbury's imprisonment, but his death had absolved him of retribution. The Suffolks, less culpable but in none too secure a situation, were unwise enough to earn the enmity of the King's new favourite, George Villiers, later Duke of Buckingham. Eighteen months afterwards, at his instigation, a Star Chamber enquiry was held into corruption at the Treasury, an ironical turn in a Court and Government where every office-holder, led by Buckingham himself, looked upon peculation as a rightful perquisite.

Although Lady Suffolk had taken bribes, Suffolk's fault lay no deeper than laxity in supervision, but they were punished by a spell in the Tower, and a fine, later reduced, of £30,000. A threat of a similar enquiry into the Admiralty's financial affairs precipitated the resignation of the elderly Earl of Nottingham.

A humiliated country thus witnessed the great Lord Howard of Effingham, conqueror of the Armada and captor of Cadiz, as well as that hardly less illustrious sea-dog, Lord Thomas Howard, brought to their knees in disgrace by their contemptible King's latest semi-illiterate favourite, who to crown their abasement, was appointed Lord Admiral. Their eclipse, together with that of their sons and sons-in-law, saw the end of the political ascendancy of the Howards, the vesting of virtually all power in the hands of the twenty-two-year-old Buckingham, and as a remote consequence, the end also of Dudley's notions of exploiting his Howard blood.

If, after these sinister events had unfolded, he had clung to the slightest glimmer of hope of one day retrieving his position, it was brusquely extinguished in August, 1618, when news arrived that his old adversary, Robert Sidney, had been created Earl of Leicester, and that the earldom of Warwick had been conferred on the wealthy Lord Robert Rich.

This was a blow that must have mortified and infuriated Dudley almost beyond sufferance. That Rich had paid £10,000 for his Warwick earldom, the very figure for the rank that its rightful incumbent had suggested to James in his *Proposition*, might at least have been received with no more than a wry smile, but that his father's title should go to the crafty intriguer, who, solely by James's favour, had after a succession of triumphant preferments, now usurped his every birthright, was nothing less than an outrage. Yet neither the jealous hatred which he certainly felt for Sidney, nor the resentment which consumed him at the King's affront, with its derisive dismissal of his claim to his father's honours, found expression at the time, though there was to be an unexpected dénouement later.

Dudley's long experience of unpleasant slaps in the face from Fate had by now sufficiently hardened him to take this latest reverse with outward composure. Indeed, he might even have been able to reflect that amid all his adversities, there remained one consolation, that Kenilworth was still his. More, he was again negotiating for payment of the amount agreed with Prince Henry. His chances of achieving this end were not great, for his only friend now at Court was the Earl of Pembroke, and he as Lord Chamberlain, had to be extremely circumspect. Dudley had learned, two years previously, how easily such plans could go wrong, when the arrangements for the sale of his remaining manorial lands were at last put through, for Alice's father, the alert Sir Thomas Leigh, had laid a petition before the King to stop the proceeds leaving England.

In this application, he pointed out that Dudley, "having taken to wife his daughter, Alice, and cohabited with her for the space of ten years, had sired seven daughters,[27] five living and four now grown to woman's estate", remained overseas "in contempt of his Majesty's laws and express commandment, signified under his Highness's Privy Seal". He had, the appeal complained, not only "disloyally forsaken his said wife and daughters, but also now endeavoureth utterly to defeat them of all means of livelihood from him by selling all such lands of his as are left unsold within the realm".

King James, instructing that "some course be taken for the restraining of his intended purpose", referred the petition to the Lord Chancellor and Mr. Secretary Lake. "They have this day ordered Sir David Foulis and Mr. Yates, who have the inheritance of several manors conveyed by Sir Robert Dudley, to attend and show what estate they have, whereupon their Lordships will further advise what is yet to be done. And in the meantime, they are of the opinion that neither the £800 yearly rent, nor the £8,000 ready money, shall be conveyed out of the Kingdom, either in specie or exchange, to Sir Robert Dudley, whereby to encourage him to persist in the continuance of his wilful contempt and disobedience. The money is to be stayed in this Kingdom, to the end the Lady his wife (who brought him a fair portion) and children may be relieved and provided for."

Much the most difficult facet of Dudley's character to comprehend is this unrelenting indifference towards the condition of his wife and daughters in England, which contrasted so strangely with his exemplary conduct as husband and father in Florence. The reason could hardly have been only that he could not forgive those he had wronged. There must have existed some deep and inexplicable bitterness in his relations with Alice that held him permanently to so unnatural an attitude to his daughters. As Leigh pointed out, four of them were now of marriageable age, and the eldest, Alice Douglas, was already betrothed. Yet Dudley showed no interest in their future, nor took any share in providing the dowries that were essential to advantageous marriage.

One of the excuses which he might have produced, at least to himself, for his neglect, and for the decline of his interest in affairs in England, could have been the increasing pressure of his work as Head of the

Arsenal at Livorno and Pisa. For Cosimo, despite his delicate health, had never ceased to add to the strength of his navy and merchant fleet. One of the more recent vessels Dudley had built was the *St. Cosimo*, an oar-propelled galley, which was better suited for Mediterranean coastal work than the sailing, ocean-going galleon or galleass.

Letters[28] which he wrote in 1618 to the Grand Ducal secretary, Bali Cioli, throw an interesting light on these labours, and also reveal that his ships did not always pass without criticism. For it was reported by some ill-wisher that one of his newest galleys had so failed to answer the helm that its owner left it behind at Marseilles. He learned that it had been overladen with ballast, probably out of spite, but when complaint was made to Cioli, and passed to him, he answered mildly, compared with what would have been his tone in earlier days.

"I doubt not that they will write even more and worse things about the new galley, for I know their intentions. I am ready to assert in their presence that the new galley floats as well and is swifter than the *St. Cosimo*, but if they want it to answer the helm, they should not overweight it with more stones and sand than they put in the other boats. I do not believe they do this from ignorance. When a boat is once proved to float well and answer the helm it does not lose these qualities, therefore they must account for it in this case.

"And further, I reply that even if it were true that it sinks so deep as to impede its speed, I certify his Royal Highness that in two days I would remedy the defect by a stratagem of my own which has never been revealed."

Proceeding from this bold covenant, he turns to a certain "Madame", a potentate of a neighbouring state, who has criticised the *St. Cosimo*, of which a replica has been built in her yards. He protests that the *St. Cosimo* "though it is my own building, I say with truth is the very best work, and her shipmasters could not do better than imitate it. I, who know both one and the other, and have seen them both tried, assure you that if the *St. Cosimo* is good, this new one will never be bad. True, the *St. Cosimo* has this advantage—I watched over the building of it until the hull was perfectly finished, while for this new ship I merely gave the design, and only inspected the work when it was ready for trial."

He reminds Cioli that even the *St. Cosimo* "attracted such jealousy and hindrance that it was kept on the stocks for two years before it could be brought to perfection: and so we must have patience also with this new one, and let the envy and ill-feeling work off a little, until people better recognise the quality of the ship".

These criticisms were evidently of small account to Dudley, who continues serenely on his way. He writes to Cioli again in May from Pisa, where he has been detained while superintending the construction of another ship, and refers to two of the Ducal vessels, the *Sassaja* and *Petaccia*, which after suffering damage the year before in Livorno harbour, had been placed in his hands for repair.

"You may tell his Serene Highness, my Signore, from me that the new vessel will be all that I wished it to be. I have thought of a curiosity in the matter of a new form of oar, which rows with more force and yet facility. I have sent oars of this kind to be tried on a galleon at Livorno, and they write me word that they succeed very well. Before returning to Florence, I shall go to Livorno to see the effect, and also inspect the *Sassaja* and *Petaccia*, as lately commanded by his Serene Highness."

Writing ten days later from Livorno, he reports on two new galleys he has just completed there, then says that the new oars are a success, as they are less fatiguing to use, and make more way. "The galley slaves, who are the best judges of the mysteries of the art of rowing, oppose no difficulties of any kind, but I have given orders that the trial be fairly continued all this year."

He goes on, "The vessel I have in the docks at Pisa is not far enough advanced to permit my immediate return to Florence to attend to other business of his Serene Highness. I pray your Excellency to procure me from his Serene Highness the loan of one of his carriages for the journey thither, which if graciously conceded I desire may be sent to Pisa on Saturday evening next". The carriage came, but four days later, Dudley writes to excuse himself for not having come to Florence, but he has been ill of a fever, and the doctor would not allow him to travel. The fever he himself cured with a powder of his own compounding.

This curative powder, which he had first produced some four years earlier, acquired so great a reputation that about this time it was the subject of a book written by a Professor of Medicine at Pisa, Dr. Mario Cornacchini. Dedicated to "The Illustrious Don Roberto Dudley, Count of Warwick", the book's introduction[29] sings his praises as a benefactor of humanity.

"You are living with the Grand Duke of Tuscany upon terms of friendship and affection", writes the doctor, "and all men wish you success and prosperity in whatever you undertake. For what other object have you in building pinnaces and rowboats upon new principles of construction but that of deterring the pirates who assail our coast; by capturing and overthrowing them you not only protect the land of Italy but the whole of Europe. And hence it has arisen that so many enjoy safety and tranquillity who might have been dragged into most wretched slavery.

"But how much greater is the blessing of being delivered from premature death! And daily by your invention is this deliverance effected." For the Powder, declares the doctor, provides a wonderful way of rescuing the sick from death, and of giving hope to those who despair of existence, and he praises Dudley for allowing it to be used freely for the benefit of mankind.

Cornacchini writes of "peccant humours", for which the physician normally resorts to blood-letting or to medicines "which overturn the stomach, produce griping, constrict the bowels", whereas the Powder is at once safe, speedy and pleasant. "When the Earl told me some four years ago that he had cured 600 persons, all at that time alive, I openly answered that it was fiction, that it overthrew all the maxims of the ancient physicians.

"About the close of last spring, when travelling from Livorno to Pisa taking violent exercise on the road by hawking and hunting, he was seized with an attack of pleurisy, with acute fever. He returned to Pisa, took to bed, took his powder three times, and recovered without any bleeding or medicine. The Earl's wife and daughter, and Philip, purveyor to his household, also suffered fevers and boils, and were cured with only one dose. Since when, convinced of the powder's efficacy, I have used it regularly, and with every success. Its use is supported by the Chamber of Medicine of Pisa."

The Powder, which was a blend of scammony, tatar and antimony, is named in the pharmaceutical lists as Pulvis Comitis Warwicencis, the Earl of Warwick's Powder. Its existence indicates the practical interest which Dudley took in medicine, but it also betrays how, for lack of scope at higher levels, such as an active naval command or a governmental ministry, his ranging mind sought outlet in things of minor consequence.

The Powder provides yet another example of the similarity of his gifts with those of Raleigh, who in the constraints of the Tower had turned his equally versatile mind to producing a "Great Cordial or Elixir, a Balsam of Guiana", a quinine preparation whose composition he kept secret, but which was said to cure all diseases except poison. It was reputed to have saved Queen Anne's life, but was given too late to Prince Henry.

In October, 1618, King James, to propitiate Spain, basely contrived the luckless Raleigh's execution. So ended the parallels of character and life between him and Dudley. One of these similar paths in recent years had been their writings on naval matters, for although Raleigh's mind moved easily on elevated levels, such as humanism and philosophy, he wrote with authority also on technical subjects, and had already published essays on maritime affairs.

Dudley did not have Raleigh's profundity, but with the advantage of his practical experience of shipbuilding, he did share the other's expert appreciation of the problems involved in relating warship design to specific functional and climatic needs. By independent study and reasoning, he arrived at similar conclusions to Raleigh's on the tactics of fighting ships, and the vital role of sea warfare to a maritime nation. These views he regularly committed to paper, but now only for Italian consumption, for one consequence of King James's repulse was that he wasted no more time on treatises for unappreciative regal consumption in England.

He had, for the time being, put aside the cogitative writings of five years ago, and turned again to practical aspects of seamanship, which he covered in two manuscript volumes, both in an Italian that was far from perfect. The first was a companion to the two volumes in English written ten years before, and, dealing chiefly with the design of ships, was not finally completed until some time later.

The second was a book of instructions for the edification of officers of the Tuscan Navy. Entitled *Direttorio Marittimo*, this work consisted of information in an abridged form of the kind he had put into the four volumes so far produced, and included navigation, great circle sailing, the administration of ships at sea, and tactical manoeuvres in battle. The introduction consisted of a description, from which excerpts have already been quoted, of his qualifications, in terms of background and experience, for issuing such a book.

As the year 1619 drew ahead, he did not continue his writings so assiduously, for much more important matters were afoot. Although he had refrained from open outburst over Robert Sidney's Earldom of

Leicester, he had certainly not taken the provocation meekly. But experience had at last taught him to hold his hand until the situation was favourable to him, and this stage arrived out of the sympathy which the Grand Duke, and his wife and mother, showed over his humiliation. In this sympathy, he found a new way to express his defiance of the English Crown.

CHAPTER XVIII

ITALIAN NOBLEMAN, FLORENTINE COURTIER

Dudley's first palliative for his scurvy treatment by King James came shortly after the event, when the Grand Duchess Maddalena appointed him as her Grand Chamberlain. Her example was shortly followed by the Grand Duchess Christina, and so Dudley could flatter himself on being Chamberlain to two regal personages, against Sidney's one.

The next move was made by the Grand Duke, who conferred on Dudley the life use of one of his country mansions, the Villa di Castello,[30] by Quarto, a few miles to the west of Florence. This fine house, with its elaborate gardens, studded with fountains and statues, immediately adjoined the ducal Villa della Petraia, originally a castle of the Brunelleschi beseiged by the great English *condottiere*, Sir John Hawkwood, some 250 years earlier. For Cosimo to invite Dudley and his family to become such close neighbours was a generous indication of the personal liking in which he held them.

But these gestures, although of signal value in proclaiming Dudley's standing with the Ducal house, were but secondary salves to his hurt. A much more significant step had been taken by Maddalena, whose brother, Ferdinand, the Hapsburg Duke of Styria, had only a short time before been elected to succeed his cousin Matthias as Emperor of Germany and of the Holy Roman Empire. To him she put Dudley's story, and appealed that the wrongs done should be in some measure righted.

The Emperor of the Holy Roman Empire was the fount of authority, law and honour wherever his seal ran, as it did in a large part of Catholic Europe. And this was no weakling prince, giving way tolerantly to his young sister's persuasions, for the forty-two-year-old Ferdinand, already one of the dominant figures of Europe, was entirely the reverse of tolerant. Swayed by a fanatical hatred of all Protestants, his efforts to suppress them in Middle Europe launched the succession of conflicts that was later to be known as the Thirty Years' War.

His clash with the would-be leader of the Protestants, Frederick of the Palatinate, Princess Elizabeth's husband, had drawn King James reluctantly into the struggle, and his ambassador was now at Vienna trying vainly to mediate on Frederick's behalf. Ferdinand had many problems and many opponents, and he had already disconcerted the English King by seizing the Palatinate through his Spanish allies, and putting Frederick to flight. He was not therefore greatly concerned at disconcerting James further by helping Dudley, whom he accepted as a persecuted Catholic.

This then was the man who, on March 9th, 1620, issued letters patent which, affirming that every person ought to possess what was his own, and even when in exile, should be secure in his just and lawful distinctions of honour, proclaimed Dudley's right to the Dukedom of Northumberland "throughout the Holy Roman Empire and all the provinces and dominions of the same". He worded the patent to make it clear that he was not creating the title, nor conferring it, but recognising Dudley as the legitimate heir of his grandfather, whose attainder he put aside, and ordaining that the title should continue to descend by the male line.

In a preamble, Dudley's "singular integrity of life and morals, his prudence, knowledge of affairs and rare ingenious inventions" were emphasised, as well as the deprivation of estates, and other penalties suffered by him in consequence of his adherence to the Roman Catholic faith.

The material for this preamble was no doubt supplied by Dudley himself, and indeed he may well have suggested the approach that led to the Emperor's edict. His notable sway over the two duchesses derived partly from their concern over his misusage as a Catholic, and whether or not he sincerely attributed his misfortunes to his change of religion rather than to his indiscretions, he took full advantage now and in the future of his credit in the Roman Church.

But even if he did manoeuvre for the lawful authority to be designated a duke, and even if his chief reason was to confirm his legitimacy, his right to the title was now incontestible, for no one, not even the Protestants, could ignore the Emperor's writ in such a matter. Had not Ferdinand's uncle and predecessor, the Emperor Maximilian, by his edict, transformed Cosimo I, Duke of Tuscany, into a Grand Duke and reigning monarch? Much less exalted was the authority needed merely to recognise an abeyant title.

Whatever King James thought of the move, he was in no position to protest, for he was engaged in pleading with Ferdinand to return the Palatinate to his erring son-in-law, pleas which were futile, for after a time Ferdinand gave the province to Bavaria. Nor could he easily challenge the Emperor later by giving some favourite the Northumberland dukedom, or even by lifting Henry Percy, the Earl of Northumberland, to ducal status. Thus Dudley remained in secure possession of at least this one titular distinction.

The sympathy felt for Dudley at the time of Sidney's elevation was shared by the Tuscan minister in London, Amerigo Salvetti, for as Lord Cherbury's letter indicated, Lotti had been recalled to Florence. Notifying the Grand Duke's First Minister, Curzio Picchena, who had replaced the defunct Vinta, that the two earldoms had been conferred "to the prejudice of Sir Robert Dudley, Earl of Leicester and Warwick", Salvetti expresses regret that Dudley is at "a great disadvantage now because he has no one to take his affairs in hand for him".

At the time Dudley did not follow up this opening. He may not have seen the letter then, or may have been content with the services of Mr. Yates. But two years later, he became alive to his opportunity, and asked Salvetti to act as his agent, in conjunction with Yates, which was arranged with the ready consent of the Grand Duke. The only task that Dudley gave him was to try to obtain the money due for Kenilworth.

Meanwhile, in Florence, there was great apprehension over the continuing decline of the Grand Duke, and it was clear that he had not much longer to live. Perhaps because of this, in 1620, he hastened the marriage of his youngest sister Claudia, then aged sixteen, to the even younger son of the ageing Duke of Urbino, a union that was later to produce mischievous consequences.

A few months afterwards, in February 1621, Cosimo died of consumption, at the age of thirty. He had ruled as rightly as his capabilities allowed, and Tuscany had continued to prosper and to sustain her external authority, especially at sea, but he was much handicapped by weak health, and even more by his deference to the preponderance of his mother and wife, particularly in matters involving religion.

Following a magnificent funeral, the full ceremonial for which was the responsibility of Dudley, as Grand Chamberlain, the much-liked young prince was buried in the New Sacristy, for the Medici chapel was still under construction, and his remains were not be taken there until two generations later.

He was succeeded by his eldest son, Ferdinand II, then ten years of age. Cosimo had appointed his mother, now aged fifty-six, and wife, aged thirty, as Joint Regents, assisted by a Council of Four Ministers. In his will, he ordered that no foreigner should hold any office of State, or even of domestic service at the Court. He may have taken this precaution because he feared that Dudley's influence might become too great, but in the result, the two Grand Duchesses overruled his wishes, for they valued their Grand Chamberlain much too highly to lose him just when his advice was needed. In this situation, Dudley's standing was immensely lifted. Where before he had been a favoured but relatively minor functionary, he now became, as Cosimo had reluctantly anticipated, the confidant of the Duchesses Regent, rulers of Tuscany.

This was a position which could have made him many enemies, but it did not do so. He showed an unusual discretion in his handling of the old Florentine families, those who in republican days had provided the *gonfalonieri*, the elected short-term rulers of the city. Their traditional dislike of seeing foreigners in positions of power was dispelled by his charm and ability, and so far from exciting their jealousy, he won them as well-wishers and allies.

There was something in Dudley's make-up which, in spite of his flashes of arrogance, and his good conceit of his blood and talents, enabled him to find friendship at every level. From the tough ship-mates of the West Indies voyage, and solid workmen like Matthew Baker, through such differing types as the sterling Chaloner and the unprincipled Northampton, to Medici Grand Dukes and Duchesses whose regard for him was intimate, sincere and lasting, he never found it difficult to make far more friends than enemies.

Only in relation to his own family in England was this aptitude lacking, for nowhere is there any record of him softening in his inexplicable harshness towards Alice and her children. Not even the death of his eldest daughter, Alice Douglas,[31] in May 1621, at the age of twenty, could outwardly soften him. That she was able in her will to bequeath to her mother, "to lay out for pious and charitable uses" the sum of £3,000, could have brought him little but self-reproach, for the money had been left her by his own mother. As is shown by entries in the Stoneleigh Register, part of the bequest was devoted to augmenting the pay of the vicars of local parishes.

His unnatural obduracy towards his English family was periodically stiffened by the legal actions which Alice and her father were compelled to take to safeguard her rights, of which the latest came in the spring of 1621. This concerned her marriage jointure on the Kenilworth woods, and began with a special Act of Parliament, laid at the request of Prince Charles, who was now interested in Kenilworth, to enable her to alienate the rights of her jointure to the Prince as if she had been a *femme sole*, so disposing of Dudley as dead or non-existent.

The woods were valued at £14,000, but the sum Alice was offered was £4,000, and the promise of certain annual payments drawn in part from the Kenilworth rental roll, and in part from the Exchequer. These payments were never made. The patent authorising the capital sum specified that it was in consideration of all her interests in the Kenilworth property, though it permitted her to "quietly enjoy the goods, chattels and pensions, whereof she, or others to her use, now are possesssed, without claim by his Majesty by reason of any contempt or forfeiture by Sir Robert Dudley".

But Alice had never resumed residence at Kenilworth, whose upkeep was certainly beyond her resources. Only a portion of the cash for the jointure was paid, but she had sufficient means to move to London, to Dudley House, adjacent to the Church of St. Giles-in-the-Fields, then well in the countryside. Here she established herself as a philanthropist, active in the service of charity and the Protestant religion. She contributed generously to the rebuilding of the church and later provided most of the interior furnishings. The death of her father in 1625 was an additional reason for relinquishing the link with Kenilworth and with Stoneleigh, now occupied by her nephew, Sir Thomas Leigh, for her brother John had died some years previously.

Other deaths in England about this time signalled the completion of an era, both for Dudley personally and for the country. In 1624, the Earl of Nottingham died, the close of his long and splendid career tarnished only because Buckingham did not like the Howards. March, 1625, saw the end of James, murdered it was credibly rumoured, by the Favourite because he had now gained the affection of Prince Charles, and the maudlin, decrepit King had become a nuisance. So ended a reign which had lowered the Crown to a disreputable level of which all knowledgeable Englishmen were ashamed.

The following year saw the death of Robert Sidney, Earl of Leicester, and so, too late, Dudley's spiteful rival vanished from his path. But Sidney's son, Robert, had his father's covetousness, which he showed by exploiting some legal uncertainty in Leicester's will, and taking possession of Dudley's two remaining Warwickshire manors, Long

Itchington and Balsall. Soon, Dudley initiated legal proceedings to regain these properties.

The new King, shortly after his accession, granted Kenilworth to Robert Carey, Earl of Monmouth. Among the first honours which he conferred was the Earldom of Mulgrave on Dudley's half-brother, Edmund Sheffield, who had suffered a grievous loss some years previously, when his three sons were drowned while crossing the Humber.

Meanwhile, from Dudley House, the Lady Alice was arranging matches for her three remaining daughters. The second eldest girl, Frances, married Sir Gilbert Kniveton, Baronet, of Bradley, Derby, who was later to hold influential office under the Crown. The next eldest, Anne, wed an able young lawyer, Robert Holburne, afterwards to be knighted by King Charles. The third, Katherine, born at about the time Dudley left England, became the wife of Sir Richard Leveson[32] of Trentham Hall, Staffordshire, a kinsman of the sea captain of the same name, husband of Dudley's cousin Margaret Howard, and his comrade-in-arms at Cadiz.

That these three daughters, handicapped by the background of an absconded father, were able to make good marriages with such personable men indicated that Alice was far from distressed over money, for they would have needed sizeable dowries. Like their mother, the girls probably benefited under Sir Thomas Leigh's will. Whether Dudley contributed to their portions is unlikely, if only because of his impecuniosity. He probably never even knew of the negotiations for the marriages.

But he was in regular contact with Salvetti, who had now, after several years of effort, became thoroughly bored with trying to drag the balance of the Kenilworth money from Charles, both as prince and king. One of his handicaps was Dudley's assertive attitude over his titles, for as Salvetti had written to Curzio Picchena long before, he "wonders at the strange humour which causes him to style himself Duke of Northumberland, a whim which very much militates against his chances of success in England". He adds later that he is "sorry this vanity for titles so misleads Dudley that he loses the real for the unreal".

Concerned about protocol, he asks Picchena, "I beg your Excellency to inform me on a point I am desirous to know, whether in your Court he takes the name of Duke Dudley, as he has for the past few months in writing here". His uncertainty was understandable, for Dudley variously signed himself Duke of Northumberland, Duke Dudley, Earl of Leicester and Earl of Warwick.

Salvetti's letters make constant complaint over the difficult task he had so incautiously undertaken, and the fruitless results of the efforts which, under Dudley's frequent urging, he had made to have the Kenilworth debt paid. Like Lotti before him, he had now come to accept the English Court's adverse view of Dudley, though well alive to the significant role he occupied at the Tuscan Court.

One consequence of Dudley's improved status was that his patience grew shorter. The continuing failures, year after year, of Lotti and Salvetti, which he had previously been compelled to suffer without effective complaint, now became insupportable to the holder of his high rank and important appointments. His resentment mounted with each negative report from Salvetti, until at last he resolved on a course so extreme and injudicious that it seemed as if all the courtier's tact and pliability which he had acquired over the past years had dropped away like a cloak, to reveal his inborn spirit of rebellion, his capacity for rash and extravagant defiance.

But before the hour arrived when he could confidently embark on this demonstration, two important changes had to develop, the first being the transfer of his main sphere of activities to the Court. That his duties as Grand Chamberlain reduced the time available for work at Pisa and Livorno was not inopportune, for most of his engineering tasks were finished, chief among them the harbour mole. Of this structure, concluded in 1621, he was particularly proud, because as he afterwards wrote, he "completed the mole at no great cost and within a period of twelve years, when similar works undertaken elsewhere cost millions of scudi, and took twice as long to finish". To the prestige which this and the other engineering achievements brought him, he could add not only the dignities pertaining to his Court appointments, but also the extraordinary credit which he had established with the hierarchy of the Roman Catholic Church. This last situation was due to the second notable development since the death of Cosimo.

Viewed in the perspective of time, it is clear that Tuscany was unlucky to have two very young rulers in succession, both overborne by women, who although high-principled, devoted to duty, and intensely religious, were not of the stuff of which capable rulers are made. During the years of illness, Cosimo, unable to devote himself adequately to State affairs, left them largely to his mother and his ministers. Now, under a Regency of two not very clever women, assisted by a Council of hardly more able ministers, whose pay was no higher than Dudley's, Tuscany began again to enter on a recession.

But as yet, the country seemed stable and prosperous enough, with abundant harvests and active commerce, and with the blessing of peace at a time when war flamed everywhere around. Florence showed little outward change, except that the Court exhibited a greater magnificence than ever before. This was because the two Grand Duchesses, realising that so young a Grand Duke could have no personal impact on the people, thought it right to emphasise the importance of their Regency by an augmented public show of pomp and splendour. For this reason, they were now escorted everywhere by a retinue of richly costumed officials, Dudley at their forefront.

Over an eight-year minority, this and similar lavishness began to eat into the fortune left by Cosimo, but these extravagances were of minor account compared with the financial drain resulting from the seeds of decay which the two Duchesses had introduced into the organisation of the State. For Christina, since her husband's death, had become blindly subservient to the Church of Rome, an attitude which she symbolised in her dress, for she wore a nun-like garb, with widow's peaked cap, flowing black veil and black robe, and affected no rings or ornaments, save for a large gold cross. And Maddalena, although busily occupied in bringing up her eight children on sensible lines, including tuition by the heretical Galileo, stood staunchly by her mother-in-law in all matters of religion.

Christina gathered around her a body of ecclesiastics, chiefly Jesuit and Dominican, to whose every demand she bowed her head. With so favourable an opening, a flood of other churchmen followed, with the result that Tuscany saw hundreds of priests and monks establishing themselves, with the backing of the two Duchesses Regent, into positions of authority at every level of the State administration. Christina bestowed immense sums for their maintenance, and for the pensions awarded to thousands of so-called converts to Catholicism. Despite the resentment and resistance of Florentine officials, the priests were virtually gaining control of Tuscan affairs, and it was a direct consequence of their bigoted and often corrupt intervention that the Tuscan economy began to falter, and her proud and strong position in Europe to be undermined.

This ominous change, so harmful to the Tuscan people and to the Medici regime, though nobody could see it then, was one which presented no problem to Dudley. For not only had he himself become a pillar of the Church, either in all sincerity or partly in support of his role of Catholic martyr, but he had concluded that he could do no better than to follow the example set by his patrons, the two Grand Duchesses, and even by young Ferdinand, now approaching his sixteenth year, and already committed to obedience to pontifical authority.

Dudley's decision to swim with the tide meant acquiescing in all the infringements of the independence and sovereignty of the State which the churchmen perpetrated at every opportunity. But even had he wished otherwise, he could have done nothing, except remonstrate with the Duchesses, and so hazard his standing with them, for his post of Grand Chamberlain afforded him no voice in government, least of all with the ministers of the Council.

But so far from opposing the priestly hierarchy now so well established in Florence, he surprisingly gained its esteem, a course made the easier for him because of his background as one who had been victimised through his Catholic faith, and even more so because of his wife's relationship with the truly martyred Jesuit, Robert Southwell. That he succeeded well was shown by the understanding which he reached with the Vicar-General in Florence, the bishop Pietro Niccolini, and by the consequences of this relationship yet to be seen.

It was because of this changing pattern of power in Tuscany, by which he was able to extend his importance by aligning himself with the ecclesiastical structure, the only such course open to him outside the Court, that when the continued frustration of Salvetti's efforts to obtain the Kenilworth monies at last forced him to resort to desperate action, he was emboldened to embark upon what was probably the most melodramatic episode in his career. This was nothing less than the launching of a private economic war against England.

CHAPTER XIX

DUDLEY'S PRIVATE WAR

IT WAS IN the autumn of 1626 that Dudley let it be known in London through his friend, the Florentine merchant, Andrew Tracey, who during his periodic visits to England, acted as contact with Salvetti, of his firm intention to wage economic war. At this stage, he did not disclose how he intended to implement his challenge, but that it carried some weight was shown by a letter sent by Salvetti in October to one of the Grand Duke's Council, Dimurgo Lambardi.

"There are rumours whispered of some sentence which that Sir Robert Dudley, or Duke, as he calls himself", wrote Salvetti, with less than his usual formal courtesy, "has procured from the Ecclesiastical Forum, declaring him the creditor of this Kingdom for £200,000. I hope this is not true, or it will prevent merchants from putting into port at Livorno with their ships and effects."

Salvetti's concern was understandable, for Livorno was now a great international port, with a large community of prosperous English traders. The Council replied reassuringly that "the English merchants of London need fear no surprises". But Dudley's threat was not an empty one. Already he had obtained from the Curia Ecclesiastica of Florence, presided over by his friend the Vicar-General, a decree authorising him to take reprisals against non-Catholic English merchant ships entering Livorno, and also against the English mercantile houses there, in order to recover the full value of his lost estates, with interest since his dispossession, all owed to him by King Charles of England and Scotland.

Dudley must have used much persuasiveness and plausible argument to win this edict, for no direct question of religion was involved to justify ecclesiastical intervention. No doubt he traded on the immense fortune he had been forced to sacrifice because of his recantation, and he also played on the customary Jesuit objection to granting commercial privileges to heretics.

No result having come from this introductory effort, Dudley wrote

"From my house, January 2nd, 1627", to Balli Cioli, now the Grand Ducal Secretary. "Most Illustrious and Respected Signor", he began, "Seeing no hope from England of my affairs being settled, even though so often through your kindness recommended to King Charles by His Serene Highness, we must now come to the last remedy to obtain justice, which as High Highness denies it to none, he may the more readily concede to me." After a statement of his demands, he promises that if his measures succeed, Cioli may be certain of a gift of 400 ducats for himself, while Madame Cioli will also receive a handsome present from Elizabeth Dudley "as soon as High Highness has consented to the restitution demanded".

This letter was followed by another from Pisa in March, in which he reiterated his determination to obtain full authority to carry out his reprisals. But the Grand Duke, now seventeen, was not to be burdened with this problem, for he set out on a tour, first to Rome to see Pope Urban and then to Vienna to see his uncle, the Emperor Ferdinand. Cioli let Dudley know that his proposals could not be accepted. He may even have pointed out that the Grand Duke would hardly risk sacrificing Tuscany's profitable trade with England, and possibly even finding himself at war, merely for the private benefit of an individual.

But Dudley was at this hour more irrationally obstinate than he had ever been as a young man. No doubt encouraged by the Vicar-General, he sent off to Rome, and there put his case before the Camera Apostolica. This august body promptly endorsed the Florentine decree, and in October published one of its own.

"This letter of Gregorius Navo, Auditor-General of the Camera Apostolica, commands by the same the Grand Duke Ferdinand and all the Ministers of Justice under him, under pain of 1,000 gold ducats, that they shall confiscate and sell all or any of the goods of English Parliamentarians and English people conjointly, excepting only professed Catholics: to the end that they may give and repay to Robert Dudley, Duke of Northumberland, to Cosimo Dudley, Earl of Warwick, his son, and to Elizabeth Southwell, wife of the above mentioned Robert, and to all other children which are or shall be born to the above consorts, 8,000,000 ducats with other 200,000 ducats as interest for the same: by reason of the unjust occupation and confiscation made of the above-named Dukedom: and this according to the decree promulgated by Pietro Niccolini, Vicar-General of the Archbishop of Florence, and confirmed by the before-mentioned Gregorius Navo."

This dogmatic document was now affixed by a member of the Florentine Curia to the main door of the Duomo, the Cathedral of Florence. Its appearance, and especially its dictatorial tone, excited the anger of every Florentine citizen who saw it, or heard of it, not least the members of the Court and Council, and later, on his return home, of the young Grand Duke. Only the two Grand Duchesses Regent accepted the decree, because of its source, as being just and proper, and it was chiefly by their intervention that Dudley's temerity did not bring him to disaster.

Earlier events had demonstrated how easily he could act precipitately first and reflect on the consequences afterwards, but now he was older and wiser, and had learned the discrimination and tact of the courtier. It seemed extraordinary that, having taken so much care during the past decade to avoid exciting the jealousy of the important Florentine families and officials, he should not have been alive to the possible consequences of his present action. He could have expected nothing less than the loss of both Court and Pisan Arsenal appointments, and had he and his family been obliged to leave Tuscany, their predicament would have been grave, for never could he have found an equivalent asylum. If he duly appreciated these risks, he must have felt a remarkable degree of confidence in the loyalty of the two Grand Duchesses to put his fate to such hazard for so impracticable a cause. As it was, his enterprise came to nothing, for the edict was ignored by the Council, no action was attempted against English ships, and the whole episode petered out ingloriously.

It may have been because of the high-flown climax of this scheme, the Apostolic Chamber's peremptory order to a sovereign potentate under pain of fine, that Ferdinand, on his return from Vienna, decided or was persuaded that he had reached the age when he should terminate the Regency and take over the reins of government. But such was his dutiful affection for his mother and grandmother that he insisted on their retaining some measure of authority as his counsellors, and this indulgent gesture unfortunately confirmed the churchmen in their all-pervading influence.

Astonishingly, Dudley lost none of the goodwill and prestige he had so painstakingly built up with the Medici Court and the noble Italian families with whom he now associated. Among these was the former owner of his property, his neighbour, Orazio Rucellai, "at whose house all the nobility meet", and with whose daughter his son Ambrogio had vainly fallen in love at an early age, an example of how completely his family had fused with their Florentine background.

When, soon after Ferdinand's assumption of rule, his sister, Margharita, was married to Edouardo Farnese, Duke of Parma, Dudley took his normal post as Grand Chamberlain during the nuptial ceremonies, and he and Elizabeth participated fully in the subsequent celebrations in the Ducal Palace. We may picture his tall, bearded, and still elegant figure in embroidered doublet and silken hose under a purple robe of rich velvet, bearing the Medici crest, moving in stately fashion among the members of the Court, his wand of office in his hand, his sword supported by a broad sash, his head covered with a plumed felt cap. His distinction was the more notable through his height, which lifted him above most of the shorter-statured Italians.

Evidence of his standing with both Court and Church was plainly seen in a ceremony held in June, 1628, in the Baptistry of San Giovanni, on the occasion of the christening of Elizabeth's new-born baby, for the infant was held by Cardinal Francesco Barberini, a nephew of Pope Urban VIII, and by Ferdinand's twin-sister, the eighteen-year-old Princess Maria Christina, in whose name the child was baptised.

The unshaken regard with which Dudley and his family were held by the Medici was described in a statement which he prepared soon after the baptism in order to obtain a privilege for another of his sons. The revealing glimpse given by this document can be accepted as correct, for among those to whom it had to be submitted were members of the Court who were familiar with all his circumstances.

Dudley points out that he had, at that date, five sons, another having died young, and five daughters. The eighteen-year-old Cosimo, the eldest, "attends His Serene Highness on horseback on festal occasions, and so well comported himself at the marriage of the Duke of Parma that he was made head of the Grand Duke's Squadron. He attends His Serene Highness always, and has the entry to the Chamber, being much esteemed and favoured by his patron".

The other sons, declares Dudley, "are well brought up in letters, and every sort of *virtù*. They are taught the arts of delineation, dancing, riding and other knightly exercises." Turning to his daughters, he says of his nineteen-year-old Maria, "The condition of the eldest girl is known to everyone, as also her deportment at Court, where she is invited by their Highnesses to all their fêtes, and is much respected by them. She is a great favourite with the Princesses, especially the Duchess of Parma, now married." He goes on to declare that Maria's dowry "will be in accordance with the person with whom we treat, and will not be less than that of the highest persons in Florence, or that which the Prince of Massa gave his daughter. She is under the protection of Madame Serenissima (the *Grand Duchess Maria Christina*) who is seeking a good match for her, and favours her very much."

Turning to himself, Dudley says that the Grand Duke treats him "as his equal with much respect and courtesy, as a *Signore* who has rendered him great services". He explains how, by his plans, "Livorno has been rendered not only the key of Tuscany for commerce, but also of Italy, to the extent of eight millions of scudi of merchandise now annually brought there".

The esteem held for Dudley by the Grand Ducal family continued to be matched by that of the Church. That Cardinal Barberini had played the part of sponsor to the infant Maria Christina was significant, and this friendship may have provided the link which culminated two years later in Pope Urban enrolling Dudley among the Roman nobility. In a Papal Bull issued in 1630, as noted in the Ceremoniale di Roma, Urban not only created Dudley a Patrizio Romano, a Roman Patrician, but conferred on him the authority to form an Order of Knighthood. Nowhere is it recorded why this honour was given, who instigated it or recommended it to the Vatican, or even whether Dudley had ever encountered the Pope in person.

Whatever lay behind the edict, nothing could have better pleased his self-esteem, and he at once set about devising comprehensive rules for the Order. These were recorded in a manuscript book, in which he drew representations of himself as Master of the Order, robed, armed and crowned. He ruled that there should be seventy-two members, elected solely for their military merit and bravery, and that the Grand Master should be the Holy Roman Emperor, thus allowing the name to be the Imperial Military Order.

Dudley amused himself by working out the structure of his Order, in grades ranging from princes to cavaliers, in whose service he provided, on paper, a force of 300 footmen and 100 horsemen. He designed an elaborate insignia, centred by the double-headed eagle of the Emperor, and laid down that a rich habit should be worn, with velvet gowns, cloaks lined with ermine, Spanish silk breeches, swords borne by scarlet sashes, the whole topped by ducal coronets.

It is unlikely that this institution ever passed beyond the planning stage, but that Dudley should take so much active interest in devising so stillborn a ceremonial provided yet another of the several examples to emerge during his time in Tuscany of a talented man applying his gifts to insignificant tasks for sheer dearth of work of real responsibility and honour, such as possession of his rightful standing in England would have afforded.

But no sort of honour was attached to his name in England at this moment, for apart from the odium he had earned over his private war, he had come to public notice through a fantastic development of an entirely different nature. In the autumn of 1629, Sir Thomas Wentworth brought to the attention of the Lords of the Privy Council a pamphlet then in furtive circulation entitled *A Project How a Prince may make Himself an Absolute Tyrant*. The Privy Council declared that this paper "pretended to be written for his Majesty's service", and that it "proceeded from a pernicious design, both against his Majesty and the State". This was a time when King Charles, after the assassination in 1628 of Buckingham, the man who had virtually ruled England for the previous five years, had run into fundamental conflict with a parliament rebellious over his denial of their rights and privileges, and especially his impatient dismissal of two preceding parliaments. Not without reason, the Privy Council wrote that "the business bred by these writings proves a matter of much moment, importing his Majesty greatly in honour".

A special commission was appointed by King Charles, which examined numerous people. As a result, on November 15th, information was filed by the Attorney-General in the Star Chamber against several eminent people, among them the Earls of Clare, Bedford and Somerset, the elderly Sir Robert Cotton, renowned as an antiquarian and book collector, and "sundry other persons of inferior quality". They were charged with distributing copies of the pamphlet with the object of bringing odium on the government by suggesting that it proposed to adopt the measures advocated, measures, declared the Attorney-General, "such as are fitter to be practised in a Turkish State than among Christians".

The accused were put under house arrest pending further investigation. But the exposure of the pamphlet and its theme set alight a fierce flame of parliamentary and public anger and suspicion, for it seemed to propound exactly what the King, with his dictatorial ways, aspired to do. The commotion travelled swiftly to the provinces, to Yorkshire, where Sir David Foulis was engaged on protracted judicial duties. He at once wrote to the Privy Council.

But not until May 1630, when the trial reopened, was he able to testify that the pamphlet had not been written recently, as the Attorney-General assumed, but sixteen years previously. He explained that it was none other than the *Proposition to Bridle Parliament*, sent to him in 1614 by Sir Robert Dudley, and passed by him to the Earl of Somerset, who in turn had presented it to King James, since when he had never seen it. In some underground way it had been abstracted from the official archives, and acquired, unknown to Cotton, for his library, where it had lain for years until copies were made by a mercenary clerk, and sold.

On Foulis's evidence, the King ordered the defendants to be released. "The *Proposition* was ordered to be burned as seditious and scandalous, and the proceedings taken off the files." But this was not to be the end of the delayed outcome of Dudley's sixteen-year-old essay. The unfortunate Sir Robert Cotton, a man of the highest standing, took so much to heart the disgrace of having guards put on his house at Westminster,[33] and of seeing his library locked against him, that he died a few months afterwards.

A no less extraordinary outcome was to appear eleven years later, when Wentworth, by then the Earl of Strafford, was impeached by Parliament for encouraging the King's autocratic ways, and summarily executed. A copy of the *Proposition* was found in his study, and this was printed and published by the King's opponents with the title "Strafford's Plot Discovered and Parliament Vindicated in their Justice executed upon him by the late Discovery of certain Propositions delivered by him to his Majesty, entitled *A Proposition for the Bridling of Parliament*".

Well may Dudley, when he heard of all this furore over his long forgotten effort to portray the living Tuscan way of government, have pondered on the ironies of inconsequence, especially if he read Dr. Andrew Kippis's description of his *Proposition* in the *Biographia Britannica*, as being "in all respects as singular and dangerous a paper as ever fell from the pen of man".

It may have been the knowledge that his name had been brought to King Charles's notice over the *Proposition* that prompted Dudley, whose streak of persistence reasserted itself at the slightest incentive, to endeavour once more to collect his Kenilworth dues. But now he tried a new approach, for he persuaded his wife to send in an official claim, though for a sum very much more modest than the astronomical amounts demanded in the Apostolic edicts.

In several letters, sent through Cioli to Elizabeth towards the end of

1630, Salvetti thanks her for money sent for his expenses, but warns her that "this is an old and worn subject which will be extremely difficult to revive, and I cannot promise you any hope of success". Later he writes that "the affair becomes every day more difficult. Treating as it does of extorting from the Royal Exchequer the sum of 12,000 scudi, which her Grace claims, I confess I have not the courage to demand it, knowing the straitness of means in these parts". He points out that with the death in April of the Earl of Pembroke, the Lord Chamberlain, her husband has now lost his last friend at Court, especially as his continued intractability over his titles has almost deprived the debt of any legality it possessed, Salvetti promises not to abandon the negotiations, though he "has but the faintest hopes of winning out with honour".

While Salvetti reluctantly pursued this unavailing business in London, a dark shadow had descended upon Florence, and with it, tragedy for Dudley and his wife. For plague broke out in the city, and one of the first victims of the pestilence was their lovely eighteen-year-old daughter Anna. She was buried in the Church of San Pancrazia, where the inscription on her tomb told of "A Northumbrian virgin Princess Anna concealing her beauty, grace and virtue beneath this stone".

The plague flooded with great fierceness through Florence, and brought the normal working of the city almost to a standstill. Ferdinand responded nobly, not only lavishly distributing provisions and money to the poor, but with his younger brothers going daily among the victims to organise their care. He established hospitals and lazarettos, and also a special Council of Health to enforce hygienic regulations, not least in the crowded monastries and convents, whose members were ordered to share in the work of receiving and caring for the sick. But these sensible precautions were too much for the priests, who denounced them as in conflict with the will of God. Ferdinand was forced by the Pope's orders, compliantly supported by the Grand Duchess Christina, to disband his Council of Health, whose members were made to do penance, and to cancel his sanitary measures. As a result the plague lasted thirteen months in and around the city, at a cost of twelve thousand dead out of a population of seventy thousand.

When a couple of years later, the plague again afflicted Florence, there was this time no Council of Health, no hygienic precautions. Instead, religious processions were held frequently, which by assembling large crowds caused the pestilence to spread the more swiftly through the city, and produce an even greater incidence of fatalities than before.

The death of Anna marked for Dudley the beginning of a period that was to contain more than its fill of family joys and sorrows. The series began with the first wedding in his family, for the Grand Duchess Christina had kept her promise, and found a suitable husband for Maria in the person of Don Orazio Appiano Aragona, Prince of Piombino, a port and terrain opposite the Isle of Elba. The Duchess had not only arranged this admirable match, but certainly provided a large part of the dowry, for this would have been well beyond Dudley's resources, in spite of the confident pretensions in his statement on his family, and in spite also of the additional income he now received in the form of gifts and bribes, the customary perquisites to his Court appointment. Soon after this wedding, Maria's younger sister, Maddalena, took her place in attendance at Court, where the Grand Duchess began to look round for a husband for her also.

The next happening, in April, 1631, was the birth of Enrico, Dudley's thirteenth child, all except Anna and the fourth son, Giovanni, lost in infancy, then still living. But this glad event was followed three months later by a most grievous blow, the more so because it came about through the terms of amity which his family quickly established with the Appiano household, shown outwardly in their exchanges of visits. Towards the end of June, his eldest son, Cosimo, was staying at the Piombino castle when he fell sick of a virulent fever, and within a week, shortly before his twenty-first birthday, was dead.

The loss of so promising a youngster inflicted the deepest sorrow on the whole Dudley family, but especially on his parents, for not only were they excessively proud of a gay and gallant son, the great favourite of the Grand Duke, and Captain of his Bodyguard, but they loved him for his affectionate and responsive character, so much in contrast with that of the next eldest brother, Carlo, an unruly and ill-natured boy, already giving them trouble and anxiety.

The shock of this sudden bereavement bore heavily on Elizabeth's resolution, for she had still not fully recovered from the birth of Enrico. She fell ill herself, probably of the pestilence still lingering in the city. In September, at the house in the Via della Vigna Nuova, where she had borne eight of her children, she died, leaving her husband utterly grief-stricken. She had still not passed her forty-fifth year. A day or so later, her body joined that of her daughter Anna in the Church of San Pancrazia, where in time, Dudley erected a noble sepulchre to her memory.[34]

The loss of this wife who had been so loving and steadfast a partner through all their twenty-six years in exile cut Dudley to his inmost soul. At first, it seemed that the whole purpose for existence had vanished. He would look back over the years to the day when she had fled with him from England, consumed by a rapturous love, sacrificing her good name, her family, her chance of a splendid marriage, all to be with him. For his sake, she had plunged without thought of the consequences into a life of uncertainty, in which she had shared his every trouble, and sustained his resolution through every setback and humiliation.

She had given him her youth and beauty, a beauty retained in later years in spite of frequent childbearing and the cares of bringing up a large family in a strange land with never enough money to spare. But she had attractions beyond beauty. She had great courage, she was uncomplaining of her lot, she had faith in him, she had patience and level-headedness, she was a loving mother to his children, and she had a sweetness of disposition that had won her the intimate friendship of the Medici family, and helped him to establish his unique position with successive Grand Dukes and Duchesses.

And she had been a virtuous wife always, for in spite of the headlong rashness of their elopement, their love had endured. Nowhere in any record, or in the gossip of even the sourest and meanest critics, is there to be found any suggestion that either of them had a moment's thought for anybody else.

At the beginning, her elopement with a married man had exposed her to censure, yet through all her time in Florence, she was respected and honoured for her untarnished life. A woman of high moral character, she sincerely believed that by the doctrine of her Church, Dudley was not wed when she joined her life to his, and that their subsequent marriage was right and lawful.

Though Dudley had loved her tenderly all through their romantic existence in Tuscany, he could not have been an easy man with whom to live. His impulsiveness, his restless spirit and his pride, his assertions of his legitimacy, and his constant concern over matters of rank and blood, must sometimes have compelled wonder at the world of make-believe he created to help compensate for the high estate they had thrown away in England. And his self-assurance and self-centredness were such that her personality inevitably became submerged by his, to the extent that in the everyday run of her life in Florence, she seems to be but his shadow.

But against these qualities were his manly courage, his engaging ways, his openness and innate lack of guile, his boy-like enthusiasms, his generous kindness and good intent, and the charm that gained him so many friends. That he could win the lifelong devotion of a woman such as Elizabeth Southwell proved that, like his father, he had, in spite of his uncertain humours, something very lovable in his make-up.

But now he was bereft of her who had given meaning to his struggles. His inner solitude he had to bear alone, but his grief he could at least share with his children, and these had now to become his first care. For a time, the household was presided over by the eldest girl still in Florence, the nineteen-year-old Maddalena. And somehow, the run of family routine went on, despite the lack of her who had been the centre of its unity and mutual affection. But to Dudley, the taste had gone from life.

To distract his mind from his loss, he plunged anew into the writings on maritime matters on which he had been spasmodically engaged for the past decade and longer. It was as well that he had this private preoccupation, for the times were moving, an era was ending, and drastic changes lay close ahead to which he must soon adjust himself.

CHAPTER XX

THE GRAND CHAMBERLAIN

ONE OF THE inexplicable paradoxes that went with Dudley's unique position at the Medici Court during this period was the manner in which he contrived to hold the favour and friendship of the Grand Duke and at the same time earn the interest and beneficence of the Pope. For Ferdinand, in spite of his normal dutiful submission to the See of Rome, to which his deeply held beliefs compelled him, was at serious odds with Urban VIII over one important personal matter.

While Urban was displaying his goodwill to Dudley by recognising the title of Duke of Northumberland, by conferring on him the status of an Italian nobleman, and by supporting his provocative acts against King Charles—and these were certainly marks of favour, for Dudley did not possess the riches to pay for such major preferences—he was treating Ferdinand so outrageously that the young Grand Duke's normally admiring and affectionate subjects were openly critical of him for not taking up arms to resist Papal aggression against Tuscan interests.

This situation had its start in 1624, when Ferdinand's sister, Claudia, lost her husband, heir to the elderly Duke of Urbino, and returned to Florence with their infant girl, now heiress to the Duke. To ensure that this principality, adjacent to Tuscany across the Apennines, should come under Tuscan control, the baby, Vittoria della Rovere, was betrothed to her cousin, the then thirteen-year-old Grand Duke. This union was essential because after Vittoria, Ferdinand was next in succession, his rights coming through his mother, the Duchess Christina, to whom Catherine de' Medici had passed her acknowledged reversion to the Duchy as part of the marriage dowry.

When the two should marry, Urbino would thus be doubly theirs, and become part of Tuscany and the Medici Grand Dukedom. But this logical arrangement was not at all to the liking of Urban, for he was determined to use his Papal authority to win estates and wealth for his family, the rapacious Barberini, among them a son or two, politely designated nephews. One traditional way for the Papacy to acquire landed territory was to lay hands on any "vacant fief", any domain whose ruling family had died out, leaving no direct heir.

Urban knew well how entirely obsequious to the Apostolic Word were the two Duchesses Regent, while as for the Grand Duke, he was still but a boy. The situation was too favourable to be resisted. He made formal claim to Urbino for the Church, which meant for one of his nephews, on the grounds that it would be a vacant fief when the eighty-year-old Duke died. To uphold his claim, he sent troops into Urbino to establish his rights until the old man duly expired. Half-hearted remonstrances by the Duchesses Regent were reproachfully dismissed, and when Ferdinand grew sufficiently old to have stiffer protests made, the only result was to earn the open animosity of the Barberini, and particularly of Urban himself. This antagonism had already been exhibited in the insolence with which Ferdinand was received during his visit to Rome, may well have been at the bottom of the otherwise unaccountable support given to Dudley in his egregious war, so potentially embarrassing to Tuscany, and was to be the motive behind the approaching persecution of Galileo because his teachings rejected the official cosmography of the Church, that the sun revolved around the earth.

As a cardinal, Urban, a Florentine, had been friendly with the Medici, had approved their patronage of Galileo and his scientific works, and was pleased when Galileo dedicated one of these works to him on his election as Pope in 1623. But after the Duchy of Urbino quarrel developed, Urban, seizing on every possible opportunity to harass Ferdinand, had his protégé's latest work on the solar system condemned as heretical. In 1633, although now seventy years of age, Galileo was summoned before the Inquisition in Rome, threatened with torture, forced to recant his teachings on his knees, and sentenced to life imprisonment.

A side issue to this display of bigotry was that the Florentine Inquisitor, Fra Clemente Egidio, another churchman friend of Dudley's, was rebuked by Urban for having given his seal of approval to Galileo's book. Dudley may well have played a part in gaining this approval, for as a man of science, his views might have helped to overcome the animosity normally held by all Jesuits for true philosophy.

The Grand Duke, once more unable to resist the combination of papal and maternal pressures, could not find the resolution to fight

Galileo's case, but did all he could to secure his release. After a few months, the old man was allowed to return to Florence, where he remained for the rest of his life under house arrest. The whole of this mean-spirited affair, evolving mainly out of the Barberini spite for the Medici, was but one angle of the trouble in store for Ferdinand over the Urbino heritage.

In 1625, the widowed Claudia had married again, and when she joined her husband, the Archduke Leopold of the Tyrol, at Innsbruck, had left Vittoria in the care of her sister, Maddalena, a nun in the Convent of the Crocetta, where the child was subsequently brought up. Towards the end of 1631, the little Princess of Urbino was approaching the age when she would be ripe for marriage, and her grandfather had clearly not long to live. It was the urgency of this situation which suddenly inspired the Grand Duchess Maria Maddalena to an unaccustomed spirit of resistance to Rome, for she decided to seek the aid of her brother, the Emperor, against the Pontiff's designs on Urbino. The two sons who were to accompany her, Matthias and Francesco, greatly welcomed her proposal, not because of Urbino, but because they wanted to discover the taste of war, for while this Italian squabble had developed, a more bloody conflict was sweeping southwards across Europe. Gustavus Adolphus, King of Sweden, had intervened on behalf of the Protestant communities whom the Emperor Ferdinand was determined to stamp out in his dominions, and in a sucession of brilliant victories, had brought the fighting to the Emperor's own gates.

But the two youngsters were not destined then to gratify their ambition, for on the journey, passing through Bavaria, their mother fell suddenly ill at Passau, and within a few days was dead. Dazed with grief and disappointment, they brought her body back to Florence. She was buried in San Lorenzo, her funeral ceremonies arousing a great multitude of mourning populace, for she was much loved for her generous heart and attractive person. She was but forty, and everyone knew her, with her red hair and majestic figure, and her flair for rich and regal costume on public occasions.

To Dudley, her death, following so quickly on that of his wife's, fronted him with problems for the future, for there was the risk that in losing these links with the younger generation of the Medici, he might no longer hold his place. Certainly, with the Grand Duchess Christina, his relationship would be closer even than before, for though he was ten years younger than her, he belonged to her era, he had served her and her husband for a quarter of a century. With Ferdinand, too, he was on amicable and harmonious terms. But soon Ferdinand would marry a young girl who knew little or nothing of the ageing Grand Chamberlain, or of his family, or of his past services to the Medici and to Tuscany.

If any such doubts did enter his mind, they were soon dispelled by important events. For Gustavus Adolphus was threatening to cross the Alps and carry the war into Italy. Ferdinand, responding to the danger facing his uncle, the Emperor, despatched Matthias and Francesco, who was soon to die of the plague before Ratibon, with two regiments of Tuscan troops. The tension did not last long, for in November, 1632, Gustavus was killed at Lutzen, in Saxony, and the risk of war entering Tuscany from the north receded.

But the possibility of fighting on another frontier had suddenly intensified, for the Duke of Urbino had at last died, the Pope's troops took full possession of the Duchy, and the Tuscan people clamoured for warlike action. Their ruler vainly tried other ways, for he hated the thought of fighting, but in vain. His formal protests were contemptuously dismissed, appeals for support to the Spanish Court were received coldly, and the Emperor Ferdinand was still too engaged in his war to be able to intervene. The twenty-two-year-old Ferdinand, constrained by his grandmother, as well as by his fear of sacrilege at opposing the will of the Pope, prevaricated. What he would do to help his uncle against the Protestants he would not do to preserve his own and Tuscan rights against the Pontiff. It was when his indignant subjects found that he had no intention of leading or sending troops into Urbino, that, in spite of the popularity he and his brothers had gained during the plague, they abused him heartily for this feeble surrender of his and his future wife's inheritance.

His marriage a couple of years afterwards to the fourteen-year-old Vittoria della Rovere did little to strengthen him, for her convent upbringing had made her even more blindly obedient than himself to the Apostolic See. Their combined appeals to Urban were loftily rebuffed, though he inferentially admitted Vittoria's rights by allowing her to take away removable property from the ducal palace at Urbino, including valuable pictures which eventually found their way to the collection in the Uffizi Gallery.

As a result, the existing bad blood between the Medici and the Barberini became almost a vendetta, in which Pope Urban was to show an active and unrelenting hostility to Ferdinand and his family, and to set himself systematically to injure the State by every means to his hand.

Through all this period of dissension, Dudley seems to have been burdened with no embarrassment whatever. Indeed, despite any apprehension which may have touched him at the prospect of a new Grand Duchess, his position became even stronger, for soon after the wedding ceremonies, in which he, by his appointment, took a key part, she appointed him her Grand Chamberlain. No doubt the influence of her grandmother and her good-natured husband contributed to this decision, but it was not an unreasonable one to take, for by now Dudley had become part of the settled tradition of the Court.

Meanwhile, events in England had also taken a turn in his favour, for to everybody's astonishment, Salvetti had at last succeeded in extracting the Kenilworth debt from King Charles's Exchequer. The reason for this unexpected victory was not clear. Possibly Dudley's "war" had after all drawn the King's attention to his name, or perhaps the Bridling *Proposition*, or even the paper on naval strategy which he had sent to Prince Henry, and which Foulis showed to Charles at this time. Perhaps none of these had counted, but merely that Salvetti had at last found the right ear or palm.

The amount obtained, a mere 8,000 scudi, was pitiful compared with the true worth of what Dudley had renounced, but on the other hand he was lucky, with his record of intransigence, to be granted anything at all. Not that he benefited greatly, for much of the sum was owed to the Grand Duke, as was shown in his letter to Salvetti. "We have heard with pleasure that your negotiations on behalf of the Duke of Northumberland have succeeded, so that you hope soon to consign the money, which will serve to re-imburse ourselves." So was most of even the dregs of his splendid patrimony taken from his hands.

Salvetti was presumably rewarded with the usual "thankful gratuity", though he aimed for something else, for in a letter to Cioli, he said that "if Dudley wishes to recompense me for all I have done, he might do so by using his influence at the Tuscan Court to get me recalled from exile in London, I being now sixty years old, and longing to return to my native land after so long a time abroad". But this ambition Salvetti did not realise for several years.

Less favourable to Dudley in his English background were developments over the manors of Balsall and Long Itchington, whose proper ownership had been in dispute ever since they were seized by Robert Sidney. With the death of the Lady Lettice in 1634, at the ripe age of

ninety-four, the rights in both properties unquestionably reverted to
Dudley, and he at once renewed his suit in Chancery to recover them.
But here possession was nine points of the law, and the young Earl
of Leicester, already wealthy enough to build himself a great mansion
in St. Martin's-in-the-Fields, soon to be called Leicester's Fields,[35] had
no intention of giving up the manors to anyone, especially as he was
in good favour with King Charles, whose ambassador in France he
shortly afterwards became.

Dudley's lawsuit was to drag on for years, until he grew too old to
take any further interest. But on his death, his daughters, Katherine
and Anne, Frances having died, revived the suit. They, through the
able advocacy of Holburne, were able to prove that the entail under
which Sidney claimed the lands was revoked in Leicester's will, and
the lawsuit ended in their favour shortly before the Restoration. As
Anne died during the hearing of the case, Katherine became the sole
beneficiary.

By Leicester's will, Essex House should also have reverted to Dudley
on the death of Lettice, but again some legal flaw precluded his succession, and it came into the full ownership of the Essex family. The
third earl lived there with his new bride, Elizabeth Paulet, for he had
been in no hurry to marry again after his disagreeable experience with
Frances Howard. Unfortunately for him, the second wife was not a
great improvement on the first, so far as morals were concerned, a
situation which was later to lead to Essex House being derisively termed
"Cuckold's Hall".

In fighting his legal battles against the Sidneys, Dudley had the wary
help of the Pembrokes, for Philip, who had succeeded his brother
William as earl, kept alive the friendship of their younger days. This
link was substantiated in 1635, when his sixteen-year-old son, Lord
Charles Herbert of Cardiff, paid a visit to Dudley in Florence, with
whose second daughter, Maddalena, who had recently married Don
Spinetta Malaspina, Marchese d'Olivola, he also stayed.

This wedding, devised like that of Maddalena's elder sister by the
Grand Duchess Christina, was a very august affair, for it took place in
the presence of Queen Christina of Sweden, whose High Steward Don
Spinetta had been for some years. The Malaspina were feudal lords of
Lunigiana under the seal of the Emperor Ferdinand, and Maddalena's
beautiful home was the Castle of Olivola on the slopes of the Carrara
mountains. It was here that young Charles Herbert spent an agreeable
autumn, for there was hawking and hunting in plenty. But when he

returned to Dudley's house in Florence, he fell sick of one of the malignant fevers always hovering over the narrow, insanitary streets, and for once, the Warwick Powder could effect no cure.

"The son of the Earl of Pembroke has died in this city", wrote a member of the Council to Salvetti, "no remedy having availed. The Duke of Northumberland has done everything possible. His Serene Highness the Grand Duke, sent his own physician several times, and has heard with much grief of this sad event, sympathising with the sorrow it will bring the Earl, his father, whom His Highness begs to condole sincerely. The body was sent for burial to Olivola, the place of the Marchese Malaspina, son-in-law of the Duke of Northumberland."

The year following this unfortunate happening came an event which, for Dudley, was the breaking of the last important link with the past. For in December, 1636, the Grand Duchess Christina died at the age of seventy-two. For fifty years, from the moment of her arrival at the Medici Court, to which she brought a new radiance but also a strict probity, she had been the dominating social and moral influence in Florence. A good, even noble, woman, a devoted mother, a serious, well-intentioned ruler, she had nevertheless, more than anybody else, helped to place Tuscany on the downward path. This was much less because she, like her daughter-in-law, lacked the ability to rule, than because, through her excessive reverence for the Church of Rome, she allowed parasital priests to set up corruption in the structure and nature of the State.

"When she died, Tuscany had become almost more under the domination of the ecclesiastics than Rome itself: clerics of every kind and degree swarmed throughout the country, nearly every office was in their power: they treated the Grand Duke's officials with insolence, telling them that they would obey no laws, and pay no taxes but those authorised by the Pope: most of the property of the country was owned by monastic orders and therefore exempt from taxation: there were over four thousand nuns in Florence alone: trade and agriculture were languishing: and licentiousness, crime and ferocity (going unpunished for lack of the strong hand) were rampant. The Inquisition held its gloomy court in the cloisters of Santa Croce, the most dreaded place in Florence, whither all who did not please the Jesuits were eventually summoned. Torture, confiscations, and penalties, under the orders of the Holy Office, became common things to the Florentines: and the dismal pomp of the horrible auto-da-fé threw its lurid glare over the Piazza Santa Croce."[36]

The Duchess could, in the name of religion, tolerate these public burnings of unfortunate heretics, as well as other tyrannical impositions, yet her nature was kindly, and to Dudley, she had been a constant benefactor and gracious friend. For twenty-seven years he had been in almost daily contact with her. He was one of the few members of the Court of her husband's time who was left to her. She had been fond of his wife, had helped her in exile, and after her death, had mothered her children. In him, she had complete confidence, and it was a confidence he never abused. Yet it is unlikely that he had ever exercised even hidden political power, indeed his good relations with the leading Florentine families rested on his forbearance from any but technical or ceremonial matters. For this reason, little or no responsibility can be laid at his door for the decline in Tuscan affairs. Even had he seen what was happening, and tried to advise, directly or indirectly, the adoption of sounder ways, nothing would have been done. No longer was there a strong and energetic Ferdinand I to listen to his ideas and put them into effect.

For Dudley, the Grand Duchess's passing meant not only the end of his longest friendship, but also of the one influence at Court of whom he could be sure for the future. Her successor, an unproved girl of sixteen, could yet be too difficult for him to work with. For Vittoria was, in her release from a convent existence, inclined at first to be vain and frivolous. She was also ignorant of the realities of life, a handicap intensified by the intolerant religious outlook her training had instilled in her. And, conjugally, she and Ferdinand were not well matched, for she was passive and unaware, while he was sophisticated in every kind of sexual licence. It may have been because of this condition that her first two children died soon after birth.

In reaction to the opening aridness of her marital life, she was eager to keep a magnificent Court, and it was here that Dudley found his opportunity to get to know her and to gain her confidence. Certainly, the young Duchess would have been quick to resent any undue assertion of his long-standing authority as Court Chamberlain, and that he won her esteem and liking was testimony to the tact and charm he had by now perfected. It was evidence indeed that over the years as courtier, he had developed much of the adroitness and power to captivate that had characterised his father, and as he had shown over his alignment with the Jesuits, also the paternal ability to trim to the wind.

And so for some time he played his prominent part in the expanding life of the Court in the service of the third successive Grand Duchess. Money was spent extravagantly on splendid entertainments, masques, pageants, the theatre, opera, public fêtes. The Court became much more elgant in attire, and before long, a corps of colourful Swiss Guards replaced the sober Tuscan soldiery. The Palace was extended, and raised at the flanks, inner courts were added, and the terrace and fine Barboli Gardens laid out on the hill behind. The throne room and other principal chambers were decorated with murals, and the whole interior enriched immeasurably.[37]

But Dudley was after all in his sixties, while Vittoria was little more than a child. It was inevitable that she should want eventually to have younger officers around her. And so before long a chief major-domo was appointed, the Marchese Colloredo, who assumed the stewardship of the Royal household, leaving Dudley to deal mainly with matters of Court ceremonial.

It was about this time that he was pensioned from his responsibilities at Pisa and Livorno, though he remained eager to seize on any opportunity to revive his maritime activities, as was shown by a letter written from Castello in September, 1638, to one of Ferdinand's brothers, Prince Giovanni Carlo, on his appointment as High Admiral of the Tuscan Navy. Offering his loyal homage, he declares that "if my nautical experience of many years merits employment in the service of his Highness, I, though old, would be always ready to obey the Admiral's commands".

These changes in his status were among the indications which now appeared that he was at last drawing out of touch with the new generation. Though well treated and much respected by the Grand Ducal couple, he was not so close to Ferdinand, or to his brothers, as he had been to the two previous rulers and their families. Nor could he easily adjust himself to the laxer codes of morals which, soon after the death of the Duchess Christina, began to show in the city.

A further reason for his less active share of Court life was his preoccupation in the task of bringing up and disposing of his children, especially with the ever-present handicap of insufficient money. That the cost of their maintenance and education, especially in Court appointments, was an anxious strain, was indicated in a letter to Cioli, in which he refers to the Grand Duke's uncle Carlo, a Cardinal who after a visit to Florence had returned to Rome, and taken with him as his page, Dudley's twenty-year-old son, Ambrogio.

"Had I known, I would have begged him not to do so", declared

Dudley, "especially as my daughter, Donna Teresa, shows the intention of taking the veil, and I do not know how this can be done with moderate decorum, even with all I possess. Someone must have arranged all this without my knowledge, for I am not accustomed to offer things beyond my power.

"My income, thanks to the grace of his Serene Highness, is about 157 scudi a month. From this I pay more than 50 scudi every month for my son Don Carlo, and give Don Ambrogio 40 scudi a month, besides 17 to his tutor. Think what remains to keep a Duke of Northumberland with three boys besides, and moreover a daughter who wants to take the veil.

"Then there are the expenses of dressing Don Ambrogio for Court, and you know it costs a hundred scudi to buy a new suit of a style worthy the service of so eminent a Prince. Then there is the great expense of a tutor to look after him, otherwise an inexperienced youth would spend his month's allowance in a day.

"Were the case different, I should be ashamed to ask anything of you, but I have no land or private income, and scarcely means enough to put my daughter into a convent, and this I can assure the Reverend Cardinal and Your Excellency. Therefore, I throw myself on the kindness of the Cardinal, assuring him that the goodwill to serve him is not wanting on my part."

The problem of Ambrogio's costly appointment was solved soon afterwards in tragedy, by his death from one of the obscure fevers that stalked the streets of Rome, as of Florence and every other city. Dudley's sorrow at this further blow was lessened a little by the decision of Teresa, the daughter already in the Convent of the Crocetta, close to the family's Villa Castello, not to take the veil after all. Instead, she entered into the life of the Court, and became an intimate of the Duchess Vittoria, who had spent her childhood in the same convent.

On the question of expense, Dudley's other sons gave him no cause for anxiety, for Ferdinand, aged sixteen, whom he mentions in the letter to Cioli as being "in his novitiate and spending almost nothing", was at the monastery of San Domenico at Fiesole, while of the youngest son, Dudley wrote "Don Enrico spends five scudi a month. He is kept at Olivola by his sister, the Marchesa Malaspina." This was the infant born to Elizabeth Southwell shortly before her death, who had been mothered by Maddalena. Later, he was to become a page in the household of Prince Giovanni Carlo, who shortly ceased to be High Admiral and became Cardinal.

Yet another son, and one in whom Dudley took a particular pride, was the eighteen-year-old Antonio, who as a page at the Court had already taken part in the Grand Duchess's pageants. But Dudley wished him to become an officer in the Tuscan Navy, and to help towards this, sought to have him elected into the Knightly Order of San Stefano, to fill a vacancy recently created by the death of a member. Ferdinand was the Grand Master of the Order, and to him in July, 1638, Dudley addressed a request for a recommendation, which was duly granted. But in addition, a legal deed had to be drawn up, proving the boy's noble descent through all four grandparents. This was a task which Dudley welcomed, and he drew up a large illuminated genealogical tree[38] which must have more than satisfied the Court of the Order, for it showed that he himself could claim a lineage from King Henry III of England, and his wife from King Edward II.

After several other formalities and notarial registrations, and a grand initiation ceremony, Antonio was invested with the white robe of knighthood. But the young cavalier was destined not to wear his spurs for long, for three months later he too died of a pestilential fever.

With what intense bitterness must Dudley, under the grief of this latest infliction, have contemplated the inefficacy of his renowned Powder, which had saved the lives of so many strangers, yet been unavailing against the more malign diseases that, in under nine years, had carried off his wife, three sons and a daughter. One of the cruellest ironies of this succession of bereavements was that while the fickle hand of death took away those loved and promising children who had responded rationally and affectionately to their parents' upbringing, it spared always the one who was wayward and even vicious, now heir to the Northumberland title.

Over the past few years, Dudley, to his mixed surprise and dismay, had found Carlo becoming more and more intractable, more ill-dispositioned, more sulkily insolent. He showed none of the readiness of the other sons to enjoy the privileges of his father's background, and openly scorned the formalities and discipline of Court life. When pressed to be as obedient as his brothers, he fled from home. In hiding, he consorted with outlaws and criminals, in whose exploits he took part, and for which he was thrown into prison. On his release, Dudley sent him to stay indefinitely at the Villa Castello.

But Carlo was now actively antagonistic to his father, and cared nothing for the disgrace brought upon his family by his lawless ways. From Castello, a guest, the mother of Dudley's son-in-law, Prince

Appiano, sent her host a warning "that Carlo, since his return from prison, shows extreme ill-will towards you, saying he will not rest until he kills you".

Dudley acted on this threat, and at once had his son taken under escort to the Malaspina's Castle Olivola, but this did not hold him for long, for he joined a gang of thieves, and returned to Florence. In January, 1638, Dudley sadly wrote to Cioli, asking him to report to the Grand Duke that "Don Carlo, with nine men armed with arquebus entered my house while I was at Mass, and carried away all the silver which was not locked up, to the value of 300 ducats. I hope some serious mark of displeasure from the Court will be shown for so great a crime against his father and defiance to the laws of the Prince."

The Grand Duke ordered Carlo to report for punishment at the Bargello prison, but instead he again went into hiding with his reprobate friends. Mortified and baffled, Dudley wrote letter after letter to Ferdinand, explaining that he had done everything in his power to control his son, and prevent him from dishonouring him and his family, but in vain. These letters reveal how deeply Carlo's misconduct had wounded him. In the past, through all his set-backs and humiliations, he had always held his head high, sustained by a stubborn pride in himself and his line. But now, under this baseness out of one of his own flesh, he could do nothing but bend his head in shame, and for the first time admit defeat.

Carlo himself, writing earlier to his brother, Ambrogio, blamed his father for all the trouble, because he had tried to bring up his sons as Englishmen, whereas they were Italians. But Carlo was undoubtedly the victim of his own refractory nature, for he had inherited the worst of his father's faults without any of the redeeming virtues. Dudley had perhaps reached the age when he might reflect on his own earlier character objectively, and see his rashness, arrogance and lack of consideration for others reflected in this unruly son, but unhappily made much the worse by stupidity and dishonesty, together with a streak of real malevolence.

Becoming tired of his fugitive existence, Carlo defiantly took up quarters in the Church of the Santissima Annunziata in Florence, and claimed refuge at the altar. Soon caught, he was sent to the monastery of San Domenico at Fiesole, where his brother Ferdinand was now a monk. Here he misbehaved so badly that he had to be taken forcibly to the Bargello, and in confinement there he had the opportunity for some months to meditate on his misdeeds.

Having to some extent learned his lesson, he condescended to accept the post of gentleman of the chamber to Cardinal Giovanni Carlo, "for which he received as pay 192 ducats a year besides Christmas gifts of wine and meat". After some years he profited from his social background to make a good marriage in France with the wealthy Maria Madeleine Gouffier of Poitou, of the family of the Duke of Rohanet, and widow of the Lord of Marradi in the Romagna.

The cumulative effects of the loss of two cherished sons, and of the humiliations inflicted by the undutiful Carlo, together with the gradual relinquishment of his engineering and Court activities, had driven Dudley more than ever to seek distraction in his writings. Already taking shape was what he intended should be a masterpiece, a compendium of all the knowledge of the time on matters of the sea. In this work he became so absorbed that he paid but little regard to great events taking place beyond the Tuscan frontiers, not only in the rest of Italy, kept in turmoil by Pope Urban's repeated efforts to filch territories for his family, but in central Europe, where after the death of the Emperor Ferdinand in 1637, the Thirty Years War entered into its final phase.

Nor did his interest extend any longer to his native country, where Charles had at last to face the prospect of civil war. Yet one of the minor consequences to issue from the fratricidal conflict soon to burst upon England was to be an act of regal reparation, belated but scrupulous, for the injustices Dudley had suffered some forty years before.

CHAPTER XXI

REDRESS FROM KING CHARLES

AT DUDLEY'S LEGITIMACY Trial in 1605, the course of events had shown that the law was on the side of those to whom the King was patron. Forty years later the same code was again to operate, but on this occasion, remotely and indirectly, in his favour.

It was in August, 1642, that King Charles finally decided that there could be no solution to his problems other than war. Almost since his accession, he had been so greatly at loggerheads with Parliament over his interpretation of his regal rights that, supported by his advisers Strafford and Laud, he had ruled for eleven years without any parliament at all, exerting absolute power through arbitrary courts of the High Commission and Star Chamber. Then forced by the need for money to summon what was to be known as the Long Parliament, he had met with a series of collisions which reached the first climax in Parliament's attainder and execution of Strafford and Laud as traitors.

The second climax of civil war was now about to burst upon a bewildered country. Troops gathered through July and August, and then Charles formally declared war. He resolved to set up his standard at Nottingham, and rode towards that city, escorted by some 800 horse. On the way, learning that Coventry was besieged by a Parliamentary force, he turned aside to intervene, but finding that the so-called besiegers were merely a rabble of demonstrators, with whom he had no wish to become embroiled, he and his cavalry withdrew.

But evening was drawing on, and as the gates of Coventry were now closed against him, he looked about for a lodging for the night. Not far away from where he had halted lay stately Stoneleigh Abbey, and from it rode Sir Thomas Leigh, nephew of Alice Dudley, to place his house at his King's disposal. This was August 19th, and here Charles stayed, an honoured guest, until moving on to Nottingham, where on the 22nd he called his subjects to arms by raising his standard on Castle Hill.

The Civil War began with the Battle of Edgehill in October, which

ended with a slight Royalist advantage. Charles then took possession
of Oxford, which became his headquarters for the rest of the war.
Among the many men of quality who rallied to him here was Robert
Holburne, Dudley's son-in-law. At first, Holburne had been strongly
for the Parliamentarians, which he proved as one of the two counsel
who so ably defended John Hampden in the Ship Money trial of 1637.
But Parliament's contumacious ways, and especially the improper
attainder of Strafford, which he had strenuously resisted, put him out
of sympathy with the anti-royalist party.

King Charles welcomed him, soon made him Solicitor-General to
himself and the Prince of Wales, and in January, 1643, knighted him.
Six months later, Charles remembered the hospitality he had received
at Stoneleigh from Holburne's wife's cousin, and created Sir Thomas
Leigh a baron. Also with the King, sometimes at Oxford, sometimes
with his armies, was Sir Richard Leveson, another of Dudley's sons-in-
law, who was entrusted by Charles with various missions of importance.

Although the King was absorbed in the anxieties of the war, which
had now dragged on indecisively for two years, he was sufficiently
alert to other matters to listen when Holburne and Leveson took
advantage of their closeness to him to pray him rectify a wrong done
in his father's reign. Certainly, they were prompted to it by their
wives and by Alice Dudley, but their motives were much more
honourable than those which had inspired Robert Sidney to exploit
his influence with King James to injure Dudley. No doubt Sir Gilbert
Kniveton would have joined with his brothers-in-law in their petition,
but his wife Frances had recently died,[39] and so far as is known he was
not in touch with them.

To the King was told the story of how Dudley was prevented from
establishing his legitimacy by the intervention of King James in Sidney's
favour, and of the unwarrantable action of the Star Chamber in
smothering the evidence and arbitrarily closing the enquiry. The
documentary records had been locked away all these years in the Star
Chamber archives, and now Charles ordered them to be withdrawn
and examined. Their testimony convinced him that injustice had been
done. He was a man of conscience and good intent, and he decided to
do what he could in reparation.

In May, 1644, he issued Letters Patent in which he testified cate-
gorically, under the Great Seal of England, that wrong had been
inflicted on Dudley nearly forty years before. "Charles, by the Grace

of God, King of England, Scotland, France and Ireland, Defender of the Faith", began this remarkable proclamation, "To all Archbishops, Dukes, Marquesses, Earls, Viscounts, Bishops, Barons, Knights and all other our loving subjects, to whom these Letters shall come, greeting.

"Whereas in or about the beginning of the Reign of our dear father, King James, of famous memory, there was a suit commenced, in our High Court of the Star Chamber, against Sir Robert Dudley, Knight, and others, for pretending himself to be the lawful heir to the honours and lands of the Earldoms of Warwick and Leicester, as son and heir of the body of Robert, late Earl of Leicester, lawfully begotten upon the Lady Douglas his mother, wife to the Earl of Leicester: and all proceedings stayed in the Ecclesiastical Courts, in which the said suit depended for proof of his legitimation: yet nevertheless did the said Court of Star Chamber vouchsafe liberty to Sir Robert to examine witnesses in order to the making good of his legitimacy, and divers witnesses were examined there accordingly.

"Whereupon, by full testimony upon oath, partly made by Lady Douglas herself, and partly by divers other persons of quality and credit who were present at the marriage with the Earl of Leicester, by a lawful minister, according to the form of matrimony then by law established in the Church of England: and Sir Robert and his mother were owned by the said Earl as his lawful wife and son, as by many of the said depositions remaining upon record in our Court still appear, which we have caused to be perused for our better satisfaction herein.

"But a special order being made that the depositions should be sealed up and no copies taken thereof without leave, did cause Sir Robert to leave this our Kingdom; whereof his adversaries taking advantages procured a special Privy Seal to be sent unto him, commanding his return to England; which he not obeying (because his honour and lands were denied unto him) all his lands were therefore seized on to the King our father's use.

"And not long afterwards, Prince Henry (our dear brother, deceased) made overture to Sir Robert, by special instruments, to obtain his title by purchase of Kenilworth Castle, in our county of Warwick, and the manors, parks and chases belonging to the same; which by a great undervalue amounted (as we are credibly informed) to about £50,000, but were bought by the Prince our brother in consideration of £14,500, and upon his faithful engagement and promise of his princely favour unto Sir Robert to restore him both in honours and fortunes.

"And thereupon certain deeds were sealed in the ninth year of the reign of our father, and fines also were then levied, settling the inheritance thereof in the Prince our brother, and his heirs. But the said Prince departing this life, there was not above £3,000 ever paid (if any at all) to Sir Robert's hand; and we ourselves, as heir to the Prince our brother, came to the possession thereof."

The Patent then referred to the Act of Parliament which was passed to enable Lady Alice to alien her estate as a *femme sole* for £4,000 and yearly payments, to be paid out of the Exchequer and the Kenilworth estate, "which have not been accordingly paid unto her by us for many years, to the damage of the Lady Alice and her children to a very great extent.

"Which Sir Robert, settling himself in Italy within the territories of the Great Duke of Tuscany (from whom he had extraordinary esteem), he was so much favoured by the Emperor Ferdinand II, as that being a person not only eminent for his great learning and blood, but by sundry rare endowments (as was best known), he had by letters patent from his Imperial Majesty the title of Duke given unto him; to be used by himself and his heirs for ever, throughout all the dominions of the sacred Empire. Which letters patent have been perused by our late Earl-Marshal and Heralds.

"And whereas our dear father, not knowing the truth of the lawful birth of Sir Robert (as we piously believe) granted away the titles of the said earldoms to others, which we now hold not fit to call in question, nor ravel into our deceased father's actions; especially they having been so long enjoyed by these families to whom the honours were granted (which we do not intend to alter). And yet, we having a very deep sense of the great injuries done to Sir Robert and the Lady Alice and their children, we are of opinion that in justice and equity these possessions so taken from them do rightly belong unto them, or full satisfaction for the same; and holding ourselves in honour and conscience obliged to make them reparation now, as far as our present ability will enable us; and also taking into our consideration the said great estate which Lady Alice had in Kenilworth, and sold at our desire to us at a very great undervalue, and yet not performed or satisfied, to many thousand pounds damage.

"And we also casting our princely eye upon the faithful services done unto us by Sir Richard Leveson, Knight of the Bath, who hath married the Lady Katherine, one of the daughters of the Duke by the Lady Alice; and also the great services which Richard Holburne, Esq., hath done to us, by his learned pen and otherwise (which said Robert

Holburne hath married the Lady Anne, one other of the daughters of
the Duke by the Lady Alice).

"We have conceived ourselves bound in honour and conscience to
give the Lady Alice and her children such honour and precedencies as
are due to them in marriage or blood. And therefore, we do not only
give and grant unto the Lady Alice Dudley the title of Duchess Dudley
for her life in England and our other realms and dominions, with such
precedencies as she might have had if she had lived in the dominion of
the Sacred Empire (as a mark of our favour unto her, and out of our
Prerogative Royal, which we will not have drawn into dispute): but
we do also further grant unto the Lady Katherine and Lady Anne, her
daughters, the places, titles and precedencies of a Duke's daughters, as
from that time of their father's creation, as a testimony of our princely
favour and grace unto them; conceiving ourselves obliged to do much
more for them, if it were in our power in these unhappy times of
distraction."

The Letters go on to require the King's subjects to observe his
commands, under pain of his displeasure, and his Marshals and Heralds
to record and give effect to his dispensations, in neglect of which "they
will answer the contempt at their perils". The Letters conclude, "In
witness whereof we have caused these our Letters to be made Patent.
Witness Ourself at Oxford, the 23rd day of May in the 20th year of our
reign."

It was significant of the sincerity of the King's wish to make such
amends as he could, cooped up as he was in Oxford, with the outcome
of the war still in doubt, that he admitted his father's errors not in
some close and secret commission but in a patent open to all, and
proclaimed to his subjects at large. It was significant too that Charles,
a man of discrimination despite his failings, and in Britain the ultimate
source of authority in such matters, put on record his recognition that
Leicester did legally marry Douglas, and that Dudley was legitimate.
More, that the Dukedom formally confirmed by the Emperor was
valid, not only in the Holy Roman Empire but in England. The
genuineness of the patent is beyond question. It was published in full
by Dugdale[40] who states that he copied it in 1670 from the original in
the possession of Lady Katherine Leveson. And later it was confirmed
by Charles II.

Though the patent was drawn up by Holburne, it seems clear from
the circumspect wording of certain passages, such as those avoiding
any reflection on James other than mistaken judgement, that King

Charles himself approved the letter's phraseology. That with all his heavy preoccupations, not least the backbitings among his closest supporters, and the mistrust which they were trying to instil over his cousin and boldest general, Prince Rupert, Charles could apply himself to a matter so irrelevant to him, was evidence that he did sincerely feel that reparation was due. His promise that when the war was won, he would make even richer amends than merely conferring a title was a firm one.

But it was fortunate for Alice Dudley that the patent was granted in good time, for in July was fought the Battle of Marston Moor, which inflicted a serious reverse on the Royalist fortunes. Whether, after this, Charles would have shown such sympathetic interest in her husband's tribulations is perhaps doubtful.

That Alice should seek and accept this title gives a revealing insight to her character. She and her daughters were not, as might have been expected after their unnatural treatment at Dudley's hands, too bitter to be interested in his Imperial dignities. On the contrary, they were proud of them, and clearly wished to identify themselves with his lately won nobility. This is indicated by the inscriptions set up in the Church of St. Mary's at Stoneleigh-in-Arden and the Beauchamp Chapel in Warwick, which both stress the Emperor's sanction. The inscriptions also show how much prized was the descent from the illustrious Leicester, which is proclaimed as though uncomplicated by any bar sinister.

In the Beauchamp Chapel, the Lady Lettice, lying in effigy in wifely company with Leicester, becomes by inference no lawful wife, but bigamously wed. The tablet in this Chapel was set up to commemorate the benefactions of Katherine Leveson, "which Hon. Lady, taking note of these tombes of her noble ancestors being much blemished by consuming time, but more by the rude hands of impious people, were in danger of utter ruin by the decay of this Chapel, if not timely prevented". She gave fifty pounds for its speedy repair, and later bequeathed "forty pounds per annum for the perpetual support and preservation of these monuments, the surplusage to be for the poor brethren of her grandfather's Hospital in this borough".

Another method of recording noble descent was adopted by the Lady Anne Holburne, this being to dedicate engravings, for which she had paid the cost, in Sir William Dugdale's *Antiquities of Warwickshire*, to Leicester and his brother Ambrose. A third dedication ran "To her ancestors, very honourable by descent, ... especially Richard

Beauchamp, the excellent Earl of Warwick . . . Anne Dudley, one
of the co-heiresses of his noble family, dedicates this engraving of his
tomb". Yet another engraving, that of Kenilworth Castle, was
dedicated to Katherine Leveson by her husband, in token of her
affection for her birthplace.

Such measures were sufficient evidence that the sisters found no
difficulty in reconciling their pride in their father's noble status, and
their wish to share its lustre, with his callous act of trying to bastardise
them. This they did by shutting their eyes to his second marriage, or
rather by looking upon it as a liaison, and the children of it as illegitimate. They simply ignored, and as Protestants, with every justification,
their father's claim that under Roman canonical law, he and their
mother were never legally married.

As the Civil War drew to its close, their position, as of all Royalists,
became precarious. After the surrender of King Charles, Holburne's
estates were sequestered, and action was also taken against those of
Leveson and Kniveton. The Duchess Alice, ensconced in Dudley House
in an aroma of worthy deeds, escaped molestation. The dispossessions
were but temporary, for on the Restoration in 1660, their owners were
reinstated, and as with all who had suffered for their loyalty to the
throne, were also rewarded. But although Charles II formally ratified
his father's Letters Patent and Alice's title, there is no record that he
ever paid her the sums his father admitted he owed her.

As for Kenilworth, it was one of the major casualties of the war.
Besieged by both sides in turn, it became a stronghold of the Parliamentary troops, who blew up parts of the keep and outer walls. After
King Charles's execution, Cromwell handed over the whole estate
to a group of his officers, who demolished the castle, filled up the great
lake, cut down the woods, killed off the deer, and divided the lands
into farms among themselves. So died the splendid house that had
known Elizabeth and her Favourite in their more romantic days, and
that Leicester's son had so heedlessly cast away.

Of the destruction of Kenilworth Dudley would never have known,
for it took place after his death. But there can be no doubt that, though
from the beginning of the Civil War he lacked the normal regular
touch with England, he soon learned of the honour conferred on his
wife and daughters, and by repute or inference, of the recognition of
his legitimacy. This vindication of the rights for which he had stood
so obdurately since the Legitimacy Trial could have evoked only a
bitterness of pride, for here in Italy he had long ago established what

was now so tardily granted in England. Even the acknowledgement that he was Leicester's legitimate son was a barren prize, for although the fiat of Charles ran with no less authority than his father's, Leicester's titles in England, as well as his estates, belonged irrevocably to others.

Whatever Dudley's reaction may have been to this act of reparation, it would not have lasted long, firstly because he was by now too well established in his ducal rank in Italy for the King's action to count for much, and secondly because he was in the last stage of completing his labours on his great work on maritime affairs. Soon after the Patent was granted, the prodigious task was all but over, and the mass of manuscripts and charts and drawings was ready for the printer.

CHAPTER XXII

THE MAGNUM OPUS

THE *Arcano del Mare* was truly a life's labour, for Dudley started the material for it even before he left England, with the treatise on navigation already mentioned. Later, in Tuscany, he completed the three volumes previously described, two in English about 1610, and the third in faulty Italian in 1620.[41] These four works were all in manuscript, and there is no record that they were ever copied. That Dudley very early on had the notion of eventually publishing them as one large book, which he even then proposed to designate *Dell'Arcano del Mare* is shown by the mention of this title in the *Direttorio Marittimo*, the epitome of nautical directions prepared for the Tuscan navy about the middle of 1620.

To this project he kept returning over the years, revising his material and adding to it as his knowledge widened. But as has been seen, not until he retired from his shipbuilding and engineering duties, and later from those of the Court, could he devote himself fully to the task of rewriting the earlier books in good Italian, and drawing the hundreds of maps and charts, diagrams and illustrations which, in the *Arcano*, far outmeasure the text in bulk.

Most of this toilsome undertaking was carried out in the Villa Castello. Some of the earlier charts had been engraved years before, and a few had been published, including a map of Guiana and the Orinoco delta, printed in Florence in 1637. But the great majority had to be engraved from his drawings, and with but few craftsmen available, this was a slow process. When the first two volumes did at last appear, Dudley explained in a preface that the third contained so many charts, most of which he had recently modernised, that the work of engraving could not be completed in time, and the issue of the final volume would therefore be deferred until the following year.

After the text was written and the charts ready, there was still the delay imposed by censorship, for every book, before publication, had to pass the scrutiny of the Inquisition. This was no simple procedure, even for Dudley's almost entirely technical work. First came the Florentine Canon Vincenzio Martelli, who in August, 1645, wrote "I have read with all diligence this truly admirable and most useful work entitled the *Arcano del Mare*, and not having found in the said book anything repugnant to the Catholic Religion or to good customs, I judge it worthy to be printed".

This opinion was confirmed a week later by some unstated authority, who wrote "In accordance with the present report, we judge that the book may be printed, the usual formalities being observed". But this was only the beginning, for the work had now to be re-examined by Padre Alessandro Peri, the Theological Doctor of the Order of San Francisco, who duly gave his approval, and sent the book to Fra Giacomo Cima, now Inquisitor General of Florence, who also passed it without comment. Finally it went to the State Censors, Fra Jacobus, the Grand Duke's Inquisitor General, and Senator Vettori, his Auditor, who added their formal seals to the others.

That the work had so swift a journey through a strict censorship that could normally be a cause of prolonged delay was due in part to Dudley's good relations with the higher functionaries of the Church in Florence, and in part also to some propitiatory opening paragraphs which, with Galileo's past difficulties in mind, he introduced to advertise quite clearly that he, at least, was advancing no heretical notions.

"The omnipotent God", he wrote in an introduction to a passage on the mathematical sciences, "has proportioned the world in regard to magnitude, number and weight, and created things in it which are generally of three kinds, namely, supernatural, natural and a third species which might be called mathematical, and of which we shall principally treat in this discourse". He then points out that "the supernatural are simple, indivisible and incorruptible in an ascending scale; natural objects are complex, divisible and corruptible in a descending scale; but mathematical things are sure and infallible by demonstration; and therefore these things are more excellent than natural things, in which there enters an element of conjecture and probability, and which are inferior to the supernatural, to which human intellect cannot reach".

This sententious exposition satisfied all the examiners, who probably understood little else in so technical a book, and it was allowed to go to press at the end of August, 1645. Not until the following year, however, did the first two volumes reach the public, the third volume appearing, as promised, in 1647.

The title page, announcing "*The Secret of the Sea*, by Sir Robert Dudley, Duke of Northumberland, and Earl of Warwick", declared the work "Dedicated to the Most Serene Ferdinand II, Grand Duke of Tuscany, his lord", and added that it was published in Florence by the Nella Stamperia di Francesco Onofri, with the licence of the S.S. Superiors. Characteristically, Dudley placed immediately after the title page a copy of the Emperor Ferdinand's Patent confirming his right to the title of Duke of Northumberland.

Also on the title page was a list of the six books into which the three thick volumes were divided. The first two volumes contained Books 1 to 4, of which the first dealt with the determination of longitude, the second consisted of maps and charts and portolani, the third covered maritime and military discipline, and the fourth shipbuilding. The third volume, in two books of greatly different size, contained Book 5 on great circle navigation, and Book 6, a collection of original maps.

Dudley begins Book 1 by declaring that the secret of navigation lies in finding the correct longitude. In thirty pages of text, he explains various methods of determining longitude by methods of his own devising. These he illustrated with numerous diagrams of nautical and scientific instruments, some of his own invention.

Book 2 consists of maps and charts of ports and harbours, rectified for longitude and latitude. Included are several portolani, or ruttiers, records of sailing courses and directions, of which the second is Abraham Kendal's log of the West Indian voyage of 1595.[42] There are also chapters on tides and currents, and on prevailing winds and weather conditions in various areas.

The third Book deals with maritime and military organisation and discipline. Developing his earlier writings, Dudley demonstrates that his understanding of the design and functions of fighting ships placed him at least no lower than Raleigh, as among the most discerning naval authorities of the time. His detailed proposals for a navy, to be constructed in five main classes of ships, according to their tactical functions, alone confirms this distinction. The illustrations include a squadron of ships in battle array.

In Book 4, on Naval and Military Architecture, Dudley expounds his extensive knowledge of shipbuilding, especially of war vessels, and gives descriptions of his favourite symmetries, exemplified by out-standing ships of his own construction, among them the famous *San*

Giovanni Battista. This book also contains his ideas on land fortifications, including the plan for fortifying the port and mole of Livorno.

The fifth Book describes what Dudley calls "scientific and perfect navigation, that is by spirals or by great circles". His early experience of great circle sailing in the 1595 voyage was amplified by later studies and developments, through which he had devised easier and more practical methods. In addition to thirty pages of text, this book contains many photographically exact engravings of nautical and astronomical instruments, some again of his own invention.

Book 6 is virtually an atlas of original maps and charts. There are 127 in all, "of the four quarters of the globe, on a large scale: 54 being for Europe, 17 for Africa, 23 for Asia, and 33 for America". With each is an explanatory note or appendix, often lengthy, such as that to Map 4, of the Guiana coast, which contains the report of Captain Thomas Thornton of his 1608-9 voyage for the Grand Duke Ferdinand I. A typical touch is seen in this map covering the Orinoco delta, depicting its maze of large conjectured islands, one of which he has named Dudleana.

Where Dudley obtained all the information needed for such detailed charts and expositions is not stated. His own experience could inform him on only a handful of the coasts and areas pictured and described. He must, over the years, have collected data from every possible source, from maps and charts and records of voyages, such as Hakluyt's *Principal Navigations*, and superimposed on them his own knowledge and theory. He was not very often in error, and those discrepancies that do occur, such as certain faulty magnetic declinations, or the confusing of the Solomon Islands with the Marquesas, some 60° of longitude to the eastwards, were due largely to lack of factual information.

That he collected this material systematically is suggested by his habitual interest in nautical instruments, which he periodically acquired whenever he learned of worthwhile developments. Some of these, and also the two which he had himself invented before he left England,[43] were brought to Tuscany by his merchant friend, Andrew Tracey. Salvetti mentions, in a letter in September, 1624, to the author Targioni, that "he has sent by Tracey, an English friend of Dudley's, a quantity of instruments for perspective, and that he would forward the rest as soon as he finds an opportunity". It was Targioni who declared[44] that Dudley had "rendered himself famous for his mathematical genius".

The cost of production of the *Arcano del Mare*, and especially of engraving the plates, some very large, for the maps, charts and diagrams, threw a heavy charge on Dudley's resources. Some indication is given by Jacopo Lucini, who published a second edition of the book in Florence twelve years after Dudley's death, and who describes how "for twelve years sequestered from all the world in a little Tuscan village, I have consumed no less than 5,000 lbs. of copper in engravings to illustrate the book". To avoid folding the maps and charts, as was necessary in the first edition, Lucini produced the work in very large volumes.[45]

These he dedicated to the Doge and Lords of the Venetian Republic. In his laudatory address to them, he writes of mankind's wonderful achievement in bringing the two great hemispheres, parted by vast oceans, into one single world. "In this worthy emprise, O my Serene Lords", he declares, "if one man is more signally eminent than others, it is the Duke of Northumberland, who, in order to make himself master of marine science, tore himself away from a great House, in which he had princely birth, and sacrificed full forty years of his life in unveiling, for the good of humanity at large, the mighty secrets of the sea."

Though not entirely valid, this testimony serves to show the high repute that the book won for Dudley. This masterly achievement, the collection of all the most advanced technical knowledge of the ramifications of the sea, as well as numerous subjects, such as fortifications, outside this scope, was striking evidence that the range of his learning extended vastly beyond the standards of the age. To be competent to present and illustrate the manifold specialised and abstruse subjects covered in the six linked books, he had to be expert in hydrography, cartography, oceanography, chorography, meteorology, astronomy, navigation, ship design, shipbuilding, military architecture and engineering, marine strategy, naval tactics, and other related sciences, as well as possess a high degree of skill as an artist and draughtsman.

But the Arcano del Mare is not only a record of what was known and established. Despite his advancing years, his brain still surged with innumerable projects, as in his earlier days. The book contains scores of imaginative schemes and proposals for the further development of navigation, shipbuilding, sea commerce, maritime power, whose subsequent recognition and fulfilment is testimony to his far-ranging vision.

It is to be expected that his writings and some of his diagrams, are too technical for the unqualified reader to understand, for as Dr.

Kippis commented in his *Biographia Britannica*, his projects "are delivered in a manner not very intelligible to vulgar understandings". To expound and assess the *Arcano del Mare* to the degree that it invites would not only need as wide a knowledge as Dudley's own, but the space of a large volume.

So far as one aspect of his achievement is concerned, a modern observer may be quoted who is well qualified to comment, a former Superintendent of the Map Room of the British Museum.[46] "By far the greatest of the early English chart-makers", he states, "was Robert Dudley. His *Arcano del Mare*, a maritime atlas of the whole world . . . in many ways a century before its time. It was the first sea atlas in which every chart was on Mercator's projection, the first to give the magnetic declination of a large number of places, and the first to show the prevailing winds and currents at all important harbours and anchorages."

"The engraving is superb", he continues. "Handsome compass roses, ships and little anchors are abundant, soundings are marked, and the coasts are shaded inwards, an improvement, at least for charts, on the usual custom of hatching outwards. Large engravings of the surveying and navigational instruments—the best of their day—used or designed by Dudley, are included, giving the work an additional value."

The *Arcano del Mare* was received with immense acclaim, and established Dudley as the leading authority on nautical matters. That a second edition of so large and expensive a production was undertaken was evidence of the interest it created, and of its wide circulation. Copies found their way all over Europe—one was taken to England in 1661 by Dudley's nephew, Lord Leigh of Stoneleigh, then on a visit to Florence—and the book was clearly regarded as a phenomenal achievement.[47]

Its chief handicap was perhaps that it was written in Italian. Had it been in English, although its circulation might not have been large at the time, it could eventually have become, despite its vast range and technical erudition, as much of an English classic as Raleigh's comparable writings. Instead, its brilliant progress was that of a comet across the sky. After a few decades of renown, it was, along with many other great achievements, overtaken by violent political changes in Tuscany, and subsided into obscurity, lucky indeed to survive in the museums of the Medici.

Nevertheless, the *Arcano del Mare* is Dudley's most notable memorial, the one that best revealed his especial genius, and the one which brought him a European fame such as his other achievements had not gained, a fame which led him to be regarded by contemporaries as among the most eminent mathematicians and geographers of his time.

CHAPTER XXIII

THE END OF A WRONG TURNING

LOOKING BACK OVER the achievements of his life in Tuscany, culminating in the publication of his *magnum opus*, Dudley must sometimes have reflected on the perversity of fate by which the rare gifts he possessed had been denied to his own country and devoted to the benefit of a foreign state. And that it was an unlucky day for England when, through what is now well enough established as a perversion of justice,[48] she was deprived of the services of this brilliant son, is a view on which most historical writers have since been generally agreed.

Among those who do not accept this opinion entirely is Horace Walpole. In his Catalogue of Royal and Noble Authors, though he praises Dudley as "too great an honour to his country to be omitted" from the list, despite his being "never acknowledged as a peer of England", he says "considering how enterprising and dangerous a minister he might have made, and what variety of talents were called forth by his misfortunes, it would seem to have been happy both for the duke and his country that he was unjustly deprived of the honours to which his birth gave him pretensions".

In putting forward this view, Walpole was influenced chiefly by the *Bridling of Parliament* treatise, yet Dudley was no ardent protagonist of a military dictatorship, but merely an exile trying to conciliate his king by recommending the familiar Tuscan polity. Even had he been as potentially dangerous as Walpole feared, he could hardly have exerted a worse influence on English affairs than men such as Somerset, Buckingham and other sycophants around James and Charles, who helped to bring about the Civil War.

Compared with the largely sterile performances of most of these time servers, Dudley accomplished much, even in exile. There were at that time few other Englishmen of comparable birth who could have matched his record in Tuscany, where he arrived as an outcast, without wealth or influence, and by his knowledge and industry won extraordinary repute throughout Italy. As he had shown in his earlier days, responsibility brought out his powers of initiative and decision, while his impatience and intolerance, mellowing with increasing years, except for the occasional reaction to rebuffs from home, were replaced by an unusual discretion and diplomacy. Equipped with no more than an agreeable but convincing personality, he secured a prominent place at the Medici Court, and earned the patronage of three generations of the Grand Ducal family.

What he was able to do in Tuscany in initially unfavourable circumstances, he could surely have bettered had he been allowed to take his due place in the ruling hierarchy of England. Secure in the possession of rank, wealth and pragmatic office, his intelligence and resolute character should have carried him to the summits of statesmanship, with the power and opportunity to earn for himself a niche in British history no less notable than that held by his father.

Instead, in exile, though exceptionally esteemed by the Tuscan rulers, he had to be content with employing his faculties at a much less elevated level. And although his work gave him occupation and income, as well as self-respect, for it distinguished him from other English Catholic exiles in Europe, mostly living on the bounty of the King of Spain, he was denied a lofty all-embracing objective to which he could dedicate himself entirely. His inspiration and energy were thus to some degree dissipated. His fertile mind, in no way extended by his inventiveness in shipbuilding and engineering, turned into strange byways, such as silk-making and the medical compound, which ranked for little except as evidence of his versatility.

But in the long run, all these activities, and later his duties as Lord Chamberlain, built up into a career that he found rewarding enough, as well as satisfying to his *amour-propre*. And this last was a material factor. Lord Henry Howard had once written to Queen Elizabeth, with whom he was then much out of favour, "I would rather shorten my days than live beneath the compass of my birth". To live beneath the compass of his birth was something Dudley learned to do, and very creditably. The callings of shipwright and engineer were not for men of noble blood, yet he was able to take a genuine pride and pleasure in his work while holding always to the status and dignity of his high descent.

That he was able to do this was a testimony to his moral courage and determination, but the task consumed much effort, for the rank he would have carried in England without being conscious of it, had, in Italy, to be asserted at every opportunity, and supported by the orders and escutcheons of his several degrees. To other people, these may have seemed vain and empty things, with an element of self-deception, but to him they reflected the distinguished line from which he sprang, and in Italy they gained for him a uniform respect as an Italian nobleman with English titles.

As he grew older, the impulse to magnify his prestige clearly grew upon him, as was seen in some exaggerations of his exploits as a sea-captain, which appear in later nautical writings, including the *Arcano del Mare*. Even this admirable work, although chiefly an expression of his creative urge, had also behind it the impulse of self-assertion. He did not undertake the labour of compiling this encyclopaedia of a book out of pure altruism, which was not in his character, nor to win advancement, for which he was now too old, nor for financial profit, for there could be little with so well embellished a production. He wrote it from pride, to show that he was a man of many parts and multifarious learning, a not unworthy motive that has inspired many another notable literary work.

This humour was in keeping with his attitude to his private background in Tuscany. He was resolved to live up to his rank and his honorific posts at Court, with the consequence that his exile was one long struggle to find the income to match his pretensions, and especially to live in a fashion appropriate to the intimate favour that he and his family enjoyed with successive members of the Medici.

The same spirit was displayed in his determination to see his sons educated as cadets of a great house, and his daughters married into noble families. Even if he received aid from the Grand Duchesses towards the provision of dowries, his essential share imposed heavy financial burdens on him. In recent years, since the Malaspina wedding, he found the money to marry off one daughter to the Marchese di Clivola, another to the Duca di Castillon del Lago, and in 1645, a third, the twenty-two-year-old Teresa, to the Duca della Cornia, of the influential Perugian family. Because of her friendship with the Grand Duchess, she was married in the regal presence in the Palace, the Grand Duke being one of the witnesses. In the evening, Vittoria gave a splendid fête at the Palace in honour of the bride, so crowning the most impressive of all the Dudley weddings. His gratification at these marks of exalted favour was possibly tempered by the thought that the dowry needed for so brilliant a match had all but ruined him.

But this auspicious union was quickly terminated, for Teresa's husband was dead within a couple of years, and soon afterwards his posthumous boy. Once more the Church pounced on a vacant fief, and the ill-starred Teresa was left almost penniless. After a while, she attended Court again as Lady-in-Waiting, where she was described as "the beautiful and interesting young widow, the Lady Teresa Dudley, Duchess Cornia".

Although after the publication of the *Arcano del Mare*, Dudley was free to ensure her security, it was not until 1649 that he could arrange a suitable marriage. But this was not nearly so sumptuous an affair as the first, for he could no longer afford a large dowry. Teresa had now to wed a man much older than herself, Count Mario Carpegna di Montefeltro, High Steward to the Cardinal Carlo de' Medici.

Dudley's dowry took the form of a deed giving Teresa and her husband the use for five years, of his house in the Via della Vigna Nuova, which was conveniently situated for their Court duties. To make room for them, he went to live in his Palazzo at Castello. He also bestowed on them a property of a very different nature, which he valued greatly, his cherished cerusicheria, or medicine chest, "an ebony cabinet, with its silver boxes and everything that is contained in it, reserving to himself the use of it during his lifetime".

He did not seem to be much concerned over the future of his youngest son, Enrico, also employed in the household of the Cardinal, and even less so over the unfilial Carlo, whose wants were well satisfied by his wealthy wife. But Dudley wanted to be fair, even to Carlo, and in his will was to bequeath him an equal share, with Enrico and Teresa, in the house in Florence, which was all that he had to leave.[49] He may well have reflected ruefully on this penurious background to the closing days of his colourful course in Tuscany, by which he had little left but his dignity and his titles, and the knowledge that the intractable Carlo would inherit them.

Yet of all his children, the only one who was to have any contact with the land of his birth was Carlo. When he came to succeed to his father's titles, he found favour for a time with the Grand Duke, but before long his truculent ways led to a decree of exile. He lived for many years in Rome, from where in 1670 he tried to establish his ducal rights in England by writing an appeal to King Charles II, which was ignored. Seven years later he visited England to present his claims to the House of Lords, where he was laughed at as an eccentric. Allowed by the Grand Duke Cosimo III to return to Florence, he lived again at the house in the Via della Vigna Nuova, but once more fell into trouble through his violent and cantankerous actions, and was finally immured by the Grand Duke in the Bargello prison, where he died a year or so later.

His daughter, Christina, had previously married the Marchese Andrea Paleotti of Bologna, where her beauty, fascination and profligacy won her a wide if scandalous renown as the "Illustre Avventuriera, Cristina di Nortumbria". One of her daughters, Adelaide, visiting Teresa di Carpegna in Florence, met Charles Talbot, Duke of Shrewsbury, who married her and took her to England. She became a Lady-in-Waiting to the Princess of Wales, and a leader of London Society, for whom "she held receptions every Sunday and Thursday".

Unfortunately, her brother Ferdinand, who possessed as wild a temper as grandfather Carlo, followed her to London, where he gave her and her husband much embarrassment, culminating in his fatally stabbing his Italian manservant. He was hanged at Tyburn in March, 1718, the execution being formally attended by the London envoy of the Grand Duke. In the manner of his end on the scaffold, he showed something of the arrogant spirit of his Dudley forbears. "He made a special request to the hangman that he might be hanged apart from the other prisoners, who were to be executed at the same time (on Black Monday) so that he might not be defiled by being touched by them in their death struggles." So did the blue blood of the magnificent Leicester and his "base sonne" return to the homeland and expire there in defiant ignominy.

It was good for Dudley's peace of mind, this shameful episode was to take place long after his time. He was to be spared too the mortification of knowing that in spite of the large family he and Elizabeth had established, the line male was not to persist, and the name of Dudley was to die out in Italy after the third generation. And though his blood was to descend through his daughters into many eminent families, it was soon submerged in the ramifications of the Italian nobility.

Perhaps, as he passed the quiet days of what was to be his last summer in the peace of Castello, he thought sometimes of the father whose passion for Lettice Knollys had been the real cause of his spending half his existence in exile. This was something he never held against Leicester, of whom he was always excessively proud. He would certainly have delighted in the similarities between himself and his illustrious parent, in their physical resemblances, in their ability to captivate others, in the passage of their adult years against the refulgence of a throne, even in the pattern of their several marriages.

One of the chief differences between them had been his own deep enthusiasm for the sea and all that pertained to it, something that Leicester only touched at second-hand. But for many years now, the sea had been lost to him, except in his writings, so recently brought to their climax in the *Arcano del Mare*. The sands of time were running out, and with the publication of his master work, the zest for achievement had become exhausted. His lifelong optimism was fading, the disillusions of age were at last gathering over him. All around, life was thrusting on, leaving him alone among a generation he did not understand.

For the world he had known had become a vastly different place. In England, the victory of Cromwell and his Ironsides had finally closed the era of dashing adventure which he had shared at its peak under Elizabeth. The country now lay in the grip of a military dictatorship no whit easier than the Tuscan brand he had proposed to James. When the news came of the execution of King Charles, Dudley realised that his England had vanished, along with the generations of his early days.

All save one, the wife he had abandoned nearly half-a-century ago, for Alice, Duchess Dudley, at least was still alive and flourishing. Wed at seventeen, abandoned at twenty-six, she had absorbed the rest of her long life in benevolence, in granting benefactions to indigent clergy at Kenilworth and other Warwickshire villages, as well as sums for communion silver for their churches, in paying for the repair of Lichfield Cathedral, and patronising her favourite St. Giles-in-the-Fields. She was to outlive Dudley by twenty years, and die at Dudley House at the age of ninety. She was buried in the little church at Stoneleigh-in-Arden, which she had attended as a child. Not without some justification was she to be described in her funeral sermon at St. Giles as "A Mirror of Christianity and a Miracle of Charity".

The changes that had come about in England were too remote for Dudley to be affected by their impact, but there were changes too in Tuscany, which though not so violent as civil war, did touch him deeply. Gone was the strict morality of the Court, and the happy intimacy of the Medici families. Ferdinand and his wife now lived separate lives, following on her finding him in immodest dalliance with a young page, for the Grand Duke, like his Cardinal brother, Giovanni Carlo, did not confine his libertinisms to the opposite sex.

And his easy-going rule, though acceptable to the people, was allowing Tuscany to descend deeper into a slough of apathy, that improved only slightly when Pope Urban died in 1644, and the ecclesiastical grip on the State was loosened by his successor, Pope Innocent. The relief came too late, and already Tuscany's former influence in European affairs was passing, and her economic prosperity dwindling beyond redemption.

The decline was to be made absolute by Vittoria della Rovere, who in her outraged pride, became a cold and bitter woman, seeking consolation in the Church, and allowing her children to be brought up under almost as close a priestly domination as she herself had been. Through her bigoted influence, her eldest son, one day to succeed his father as Cosimo III, was in half a century of intolerant and doltish misrule to bring the Medici to the last chapter of their extinction, and to consign Tuscany to the role of appanage to the House of Austria.

All this lay in the future, and Dudley was to witness only the beginnings of the decay of the State to which he had devoted so much of his life and being. For his end was near. In September, 1649, he died quietly at the Villa Castello, at the age of seventy-five. He was not buried at the side of his wife in St. Pancranzia. The body was taken to the monastery at nearby Boldrone, where it was still entombed a quarter of a century later.[50]

No private monument was erected to his memory. His heir still held a grudge against him, and probably neither he nor Dudley's other progeny could meet the cost of a sepulchre to match the splendour of the one built for their mother. Neither was there any public memorial, nor even any gesture comparable with the immense portrait which an earlier Florence had placed in the Duomo to honour Sir John Hawkwood, fourteenth-century *condottiere* and guardian of the city.

Dudley had outlived Tuscan gratitude. By now, very few remembered or even knew of his engineering and shipbuilding achievements, especially as the benefits they conferred were already being dissipated. He had become just a venerated pensioner of the Court. It is indeed ironical that today, after all he once did for Tuscany, there should be no permanent record of him other than a plaque on the front of the Villa Castello, and that raised in recent times by an Englishman.[51]

Yet perhaps it is more fitting that Dudley's memorial should be not some neglected stone but the more lasting record of his eventful life. From his youth he seemed, despite his bastardy, to be marked for greatness. The intelligence, the courage, the enterprise, the incredible self-confidence, which he showed on his West Indies voyage, and later at Cadiz, all pointed to one who, as Captain Wyatt wrote, "hereafter will prove to be the world's wonder".

But this expectation was defeated by a denial of justice which drove his brave and reckless spirit to revolt. In exile, he displayed all the resolution and initiative, and even more the intellect, of his earlier days. By persistent achievement, he strove to recover the place he had lost, but this he could never do, though the privileged position he made for himself in a foreign state was something he could be proud of. The extraordinary way in which, for over forty years, he held the esteem and regard, not of one regal woman as his father had done, but of three men and three women of varying ages, was testimony to a powerful as well as persuasive personality.

Though his domestic background was marred by the abandonment of his family in England, it is right to set against this still inexplicable blemish, the passionate and lasting love which he shared with Elizabeth Southwell until her death.

Dudley's life was shaped by caprices of destiny which he could not control, but which he faced always with unyielding courage. In England, he won his proud place among the stalwarts of Elizabeth's reign. In Tuscany, there were few actions of his that did not bring credit to him and to the race of Englishmen. By his character, his genius and his achievements, he proved himself worthy to stand alongside the most illustrious of the Howards and Dudleys whose blood flowed in his veins.

APPENDICES

WAS DUDLEY LEGITIMATE?

THE STAR CHAMBER TRIAL (1605) AND THE LISLE BARONY CLAIM (1824)

THE ISSUE OF Sir Robert Dudley's legitimacy was never judicially decided, either in the Star Chamber enquiry, or in another held later by the House of Lords. Historically considered, Lady Douglas Sheffield's version of her marriage, by which her son was heir to the earldoms of Leicester and Warwick, has never been disproved.

Most historical writers, from Sir William Dugdale (who found copies of the suppressed depositions in the library of Sir Richard Cotton) and Horace Walpole onwards, have concluded that the Esher ceremony—and that some kind of ceremony was held there was not denied even in the Star Chamber—ranked as a valid marriage. But in addition, Leicester and Douglas were already in a state of wedlock by private contract, a process known and recognised as Spousals. Although the presence of priest and witnesses was desirable, their absence did not invalidate the marriage.

Even more decisive was the fact that during their long cohabitation, the two had "consummated the contract" with a child, which was sufficient under custom and under canon law to confirm a state of marriage.

Much play was made in the Star Chamber hearing of Leicester, in his will, referring always to his "base sonne". Yet as Dugdale rightly says, "nor could he have done otherwise, having openly married Lettice". He burnt his boats at Wanstead: he tried to make restitution by leaving his son the bulk of his estate: had he truly regarded him as a bastard, a thousand pounds a year would have been an ample legacy.

Dugdale, whose account of Dudley's early background is entirely reliable as far as it goes, after writing of Leicester revealing to a lackey that Robert was his true son, added "likewise what Ambrose, Earl of Warwick, had uttered, which for brevity's sake I omit". This tantalising remissness has not been made good by later research.

It is a significant angle on the contemporary view of Leicester's two marriages that the author of *Leycester's Commonwealth* should point out the conflict that would arise if the legitimacy of the Lady Lettice's son, Lord Denbigh, were challenged by the then next heir, Sir Philip Sidney. When both died, the same conflict, but in reverse, arose between Dudley and Sir Robert Sidney.

One of the writers who do not consider Dudley legally born is Sir George Warner, who in his introduction to *The Voyage of Sir Robert Dudley to the West In-*

dies, gives his opinion after examining the Star Chamber and other documents contained in the Dudley papers at Penshurst and Longleat. But even these records do not supply the definitive answer, for they are not only incomplete but mostly copies or in summarised form. Warner selects quotations to support his point of view, and in establishing several queries on detail, tends not to see the wood for the trees. For even if some of his minor arguments have weight, the major premises remain, first that a ceremony did take place at Esher which was not proved invalid, second that Leicester's cohabitation and paternity constituted a contract, and third, that the Star Chamber's avoidance of a ruling on legitimacy by the subterfuge of suppressing the evidence and neutralising the witnesses, was in itself an admission that a ruling could only have been in Dudley's favour. This conclusion was substantiated by King Charles in 1644, and later by Charles II.

Nearly two centuries later, this same issue played a cardinal part in the disposal of the claim to the barony of Lisle and Dudley then in abeyance, by Sir John Shelley-Sidney, Baronet, of Penshurst. The Committee of Privileges of the House of Lords, after hearing Sidney's case, agreed that he had established his pedigree back to Ambrose, Earl of Warwick, except for the vital uncertainty over Leicester's son. If Dudley were legitimate, then there might be descendants with a better claim than the plaintiff. And King Charles had recorded his belief in the legality of Leicester's marriage.

Sir John's counsel, trying to "extinguish the line of issue from the Earl of Leicester", argued so unconvincingly from the Star Chamber evidence about a "conspiracy of nefarious perjurers" as to be deemed "amusing" by Sir N. H. Nicholas, who recorded the case.

The members of the Committee, though side-stepping a formal decision on the validity of Dudley's birth, "resolved that there was not sufficient ground to advise King George IV to allow the petitioner's claim". As the Committee had accepted Sir John's descent from Ambrose, their finding was tantamount to a recognition that there was more than an even chance that Dudley was legitimate.

As for Sir John, his plea was resolved by his son, who married a daughter of the Duke of Clarence by Mrs. Dorothea Jordan, the actress. When the Duke succeeded his brother, and became King William IV, he created his son-in-law Baron of Lisle and Dudley.

BIBLIOGRAPHY

The following are the four principal sources of collected information on Sir Robert Dudley, each dealing mainly with one or two particular phases of his life.

ADLARD, G. *Memoirs and Correspondence of Sir Robert Dudley* (in *Amye Robsart and the Earl of Leicester*). 1870.

LEADER, J. TEMPLE. *The Life of Sir Robert Dudley, Earl of Warwick and Duke of Northumberland.* pub. Florence, 1895.

THOMAS, THE REV. VAUGHAN (Vicar of Stoneleigh, 1775–1853). *The Italian Biography of Sir Robert Dudley.* Originally printed privately. pub. 1856.

WARNER, SIR GEORGE (ed. by). *The Voyage of Sir Robert Dudley to the West Indies.* Hakluyt Society, 1909.

Other books and authorities to which reference has been made include the following:

AUBREY, J. *Brief Lives.* ed. O. L. Dick, 2 v. 1949.

BARGRAVE, J. (Canon of Westminster, 1662–1680). *Pope Alexander VII and the College of Cardinals.* ed. by Canon J. C. Robertson. Camden Society, 1867.

BIRCH, THOMAS. *Life of Henry, Prince of Wales.* 1760.

BRENAN, G. and STATHAM, E. P. *The House of Howard,* 2 v. 1907.

Calendar of State Papers Domestic (James I), ed. M. A. Everett Green, 1857.

CAMDEN, WILLIAM. *Britannia.* 1586.

——. *Annals.* 1615.

Chamberlain, John, Letters of, ed. N. E. McClure, 2 v. 1939.

CHAMBERS, SIR E. K. *Sir Henry Lee.* 1936.

Cherbury, The Autobiography of Lord Herbert of, intr. by C. H. Herford. 1928.

Complete Peerage, The. ed. by Hon. Vicary Gibbs, Lord Howard de Walden, H. A. Doubleday, and others.

CORBETT, SIR JULIAN. *The Successors of Drake.* 1900.

CRAIK, G. L. *Romance of the Peerage,* 1848–50, v. ii, iii.

Devereux, Lives and Letters of the, Earls of Essex 1540–1646. W. B. Devereux, 2 v. 1853.

DEVLIN, C. *Robert Southwell.* 1956.

Dictionary of National Biography.

Dodd's Church History of England. 1840. ed. Rev. M. A. Tierney. v. iii.

DUGDALE, SIR WILLIAM. *Antiquities of Warwickshire.* v. i. 1656.

——. *Baronage.* v. ii. 1675.

GARDINER, S. R. *History of England 1603–42.* v. ii, iii. pub. 1883–84.

HARRISON, G. B. *Life and Death of Robert Devereux, Earl of Essex.* 1937.

HAWARDE, WILLIAM. *Les Reports del Cases in Camera Stellata, 1593–1609.* ed. W. P. Baildon. 1894.

HOLLES, GERVASE. *Memorials of the Holles Family, 1493–1656.* ed. A. C. Wood. Camden Soc., 1937.

JENKINS, ELIZABETH. *Elizabeth and Leicester.* 1961.

KIPPIS, DR. ANDREW. *Biographia Britannica.* 1778–93.

LEADER, J. D. *Mary, Queen of Scots in Captivity.* 1880.

Leycester's Commonwealth. 1641. ed. F. J. Burgoyne. 1904.

LODGE, EDMUND. *Portraits and Illustrations.* 1838.

LYNAM, EDWARD. *British Maps and Mapmakers.* 1904.

MACKIE, J. D. *Negotiations Between James VI & I and Ferdinand I, Grand Duke of Tuscany.* 1927.

MATTINGLY, GARRETT. *The Defeat of the Spanish Armada.* 1959.

NICHOLS, JOHN. *History and Antiquities of Leicestershire.* 1815.

———. *Progresses and Public Processions of Queen Elizabeth.* 1823.

NAUNTON, SIR ROBERT. *Fragmenta Regalia 1641.* 1824 edn.

NICHOLAS, SIR N. H. *Report of Proceedings in the Claim to the Barony of L'Isle.* 1829.

RALEIGH, SIR WALTER. *Discoverie of Guiana.* 1596.

READ, CONYERS. *Mr. Secretary Cecil and Queen Elizabeth.* 1955.

ROWSE, A. L. *The Expansion of Elizabethan England.* 1955.

STOYE, J. W. *English Travellers Abroad, 1664–67.* 1952.

WALDMAN, MILTON. *Elizabeth and Leicester.* 1944.

WALPOLE, HORACE, EARL OF ORFORD. *A Catalogue of the Royal and Noble Authors of England.* vol. v. 1806.

WILLIAMS, E. C. *Bess of Hardwick.* 1959.

WILLIAMSON, J. A. *The Age of Drake,* 4th edn. 1960.

WOOD, ANTHONY à. *Athenae Oxonienses,* 2nd edn. 1721, v. iii.

Wotton, Life and Letters of Sir Henry. ed. L. P. Smith. 1907.

———. *Reliquiae Wottonianae.*

YOUNG, COLONEL G. P. *The Medici,* v. 2. 1909.

NOTES AND REFERENCES

Note
No.   Page

1   19   As established by the late Dr. Conyers Read. See *A Letter from Robert, Earl of Leicester to a Lady*, Huntington Library Quarterly, April, 1936.

2   26   Which are, with Leicester's Barn (the old stables) the best preserved of the ruins that remain today.

3   27   In *Kenilworth*, Sir Walter Scott does not display this situation, for he takes free licence with facts, introducing, for example, Amy Robsart, fifteen years dead.

4   28   The interesting possibility that Robert Devereux, Earl of Essex, could have been Leicester's son and Robert Dudley's half-brother, depends on the date of his birth being November, 1566. This date is accepted by Sir Sidney Lee in his article on Essex in the *Dictionary of National Biography* (1908 issue), on the authority of *Sloane MSS*, 1697 f. 54b. Earlier writers such as Camden and Fuller, followed later by Devereux, accept November, 1567, on the authority of Thomas Milles' Catalogue of Honour, 1610. *See* G. B. Harrison's *Robert Devereux, Earl of Essex*. The "cold conceit" quotation is from *Reliquiae Wottonianae*, by Sir Henry Wotton, Essex's secretary and friend for several years.

5   31   Not until the Marriage Act of 1754.

6   35   The Beauchamp Chapel of St. Mary's Church at Warwick, where the Noble Impe lies in the company of his father and mother and uncle. His tiny page's suit of armour is still to be seen nearby, in the Great Hall of Ambrose's Warwick Castle.

7   48   The Leycester's Hospital of today.

8   64   Six days before Raleigh left England.

9   74   *See* Note 7.

10   78   " 'Twas his first Lady", according to John Aubrey in *Brief Lives*.

11   87   Stoneleigh Abbey is still in the possession of the Leigh family.

12   89   Subsequently, after experiencing better luck in later, very profitable voyages, Lancaster was knighted and appointed a director of the infant East India Company.

13   89   A. L. Rowse, in his *Expansion of Elizabethan England*.

14   90   The first fleet of five ships sent to India by the East India Company on its formation in 1599 cost £68,000.

15   93   Some previous writers, unaware that Sir Robert's father, Thomas Southwell of Woodrising, in Norfolk, married twice, and that the

frail Elizabeth was the child of the second union, have assumed that Essex's flame was either the matronly Lady Southwell, Sir Robert's wife, or their daughter, a child who had not yet come to Court.

16   95   By D. W. Ferguson in his introduction to *The Travels of Pedro Teixeira* (Hakluyt Society, 1902), and his letter to the *Geographical Journal* of March, 1903.

17   99   Quoted in full in Temple-Leader's book on Dudley. *See* Bibliography.

18   106   Ecclesiastical Court of Appeal.

19   117   According to a petition afterwards laid by Sir Thomas Leigh, Alice had seven children, of whom two died in infancy. Of the five surviving when Dudley left England, four—Alice, Frances, Anne and Katherine—reached womanhood, but of the fifth, not even the name is recorded.

20   125   Much later on, and today, called the Pitti Palace, because of the traditional jealousy of the principal Florentine families, who would not allow the name of the Medici to be perpetuated. The Pitti family originally owned a small part of the land on which successive Grand Dukes created their vast palace and its splendid gardens.

21   129   This eye-witness account exists in manuscript at Stoneyhurst College, endorsed in Robert Parsons's hand as being "the relation of the Lady Southwell, *primo Aprilis*, 1607". It is published in full in Tierney's edition of Dodd's Church History of England, Vol. III.

22   158   A powerful combination of short and long range weapons.

23   158   The Galley Royal was practically a small galleass, firing broadsides.

24   165   The house still stands at the junction of the Via della Vigna Nuova and the Via della Spada. At this corner, facing the Via Tornabuoni, is a tabernacle carrying the crest of the Rucellai family.

25   169   Various authorities, including Sir Sidney Lee in the *Dictionary of National Biography*, following Adlard, quoting Craik, have dated this treatise as 1612, when Prince Henry was alive. But it is addressed to the King, and Sir George Warner shows plainly that the paper was produced in 1614.

26   175   His effigy, and that of his wife, lie on an alabaster monument in Chiswick Parish Church, a few yards from the Thames.

27   177   *See* Note 19.

28   178   Quoted in full by Temple Leader.

29   179   Quoted from Vaughan Thomas.

30   183   The Villa Castello, also called the Villa Rinieri, belonged in later generations to the Corsini family, since when it has had a chequered history as a hostel, and in other proletarian roles.

31   186   Her effigy lies with that of her mother in St. Mary's Church, Stoneleigh-in-Arden.

32   188   An ancestor of the Duke of Sutherland.

INDEX

THE SON OF LEICESTER

Robert Dudley: from the miniature by Nicholas Hilliard